D1614295

The City at Stake

The City at Stake

SECESSION, REFORM, AND THE BATTLE FOR LOS ANGELES

Raphael J. Sonenshein

PRINCETON UNIVERSITY PRESS

PRINCETON AND OXFORD

Copyright © 2004 by Princeton University Press
Published by Princeton University Press, 41 William Street, Princeton, New Jersey 08540
In the United Kingdom: Princeton University Press, 3 Market Place, Woodstock,
Oxfordshire OX20 1SY
All Rights Reserved

Library of Congress Cataloging-in-Publication Data

Sonenshein, Raphael.
    The city at stake : secession, reform, and the battle for Los Angeles /
Raphael J. Sonenshein.
        p. cm.
    Includes bibliographical references and index.
    ISBN 0-691-11590-7 (cloth : alk. paper)
    1. Los Angeles (Calif.)—Politics and government. 2. Los Angeles County (Calif.)—
Politics and government. 3. Los Angeles (Calif.)—Charters. 4. Secession—California—
Los Angeles County. 5. Secession—California—Los Angeles. 6. Los Angeles
(Calif.)—Race relations.   I. Title.

JS1003.A2S66 2004
320.9794'94—dc22   2004044253

British Library Cataloging-in-Publication Data is available

This book has been composed in Galliard

Printed on acid-free paper. ∞

pup.princeton.edu

Printed in the United States of America

10 9 8 7 6 5 4 3 2 1

To Phyllis, Julia, and Anna

Contents

Maps

Tables

Preface

REFORM UNDER THE GUN

> Depend upon it, sir, when a man knows he is to be hanged in a fortnight,
> it concentrates his mind wonderfully.
> —Samuel Johnson

ON DECEMBER 6, 1998, residents of the San Fernando Valley submitted more than 200,000 signatures on a petition to require a study of the feasibility of seceding from the City of Los Angeles (Sullivan 1998). Four years later, the County of Los Angeles placed separate measures for Valley and Hollywood secession on the November 2002 ballot. By the turn of the twenty-first century, Los Angeles was closer than any modern American city to actual breakup by democratic vote.

On June 8, 1999, the voters of Los Angeles chose by a 60 percent majority to adopt a new city charter, the city's first comprehensive charter revision in seventy-five years. Secession generated a reform that had eluded Los Angeles civic activists for generations. The charter's most visible feature was the creation of a new system of neighborhood councils, a major departure for a city with low levels of citizen participation. With its informal election procedures, the neighborhood council system was designed to be at least theoretically open to the large noncitizen population of Los Angeles.

Under the threat of a municipal breakup with major implications for equity among racial, ethnic, and socioeconomic groups, Los Angeles had accomplished a major governmental reform. Many hoped that the new charter would help reduce sentiment for secession by creating a more democratic and responsive city government.

City leaders drew on the participatory reforms in the new charter to wage a powerful battle against secession. By Labor Day 2002, polls showed that a citywide majority had coalesced against municipal breakup. On November 5, 2002, Los Angeles voters turned down Valley secession by a two-to-one majority, although the measure narrowly passed in the Valley. Hollywood secession failed by a larger margin, not only citywide but within Hollywood itself.

The creation of a new Los Angeles city charter was a case of reform under the gun, with political pressures and strategies that went to the root of the city's political existence. Reform was a muscular *political* enterprise, not an abstract exercise in good government. Los Angeles civic leaders had to conceive and implement a dramatic reform program, get it on the ballot, and win at the polls. Then they had to gear up again to win the secession election three years later.

City leaders had to construct powerful coalitions around communal goals and with everything on the line, make the case to two distinct voter majorities. They had to win elections under two different mayors, who were political rivals with different political constituencies. These coalitions had to be constructed in a city that had changed profoundly in its demographics, its politics, and its economic structure. In Los Angeles charter reform, the "new institutionalism" met the "new diversity."

In 1999, while Los Angeles was in the process of generating this remarkable reform project in the face of civic danger, a forty-community study of social capital concluded that in ethnically diverse cities like Los Angeles, residents were less likely to trust other people, to participate in politics, to connect with other people, and to forge linkages across class lines (Saguaro Seminar 2001). Los Angeles was found to be weak on civic organizations, and on the connective tissue that was assumed to underlie the capacity to undertake civic enterprises. How could the extraordinary civic project of charter reform have been completed in Los Angeles, a city that by measures of social capital had little potential for it?

Those who study the institutional structure of cities would be equally unlikely to consider Los Angeles to be the site for such a civic effort. Los Angeles has been described as "fragmented" (Fogelson 1967); "reluctant" (Fulton 1997); "decentralized" and "attentuated" (Carney 1964); and "horizontally organized" (Jones-Correa 2001). A new wave of writing about Los Angeles in comparison to New York City argues that Los Angeles lacks sufficient governmental coherence to integrate immigrants (Mollenkopf, Olson, and Ross 2001), to respond to civil violence (Jones-Correa 2001), or to manage intergroup conflict peacefully (Joyce 2003).

As often happens with Los Angeles, and indeed California, great attention during the secession struggle was focused on the apparently dysfunctional nature of the system, reminiscent of media coverage of the 1992 riot, and later in the California power crisis of 2002 and the 2003 recall campaign against Governor Gray Davis. In the eyes of many observers, therefore, the secession movement became inextricably tied to the nature of Los Angeles. Correspondingly, there was not much exploration of the reformist solutions that Los Angeles discovered for the threat of secession.

One might have imagined that Los Angeles would break apart simply from indifference and civic anomie. But Los Angeles held together.

Charter reform is not the first surprise that has issued from modern Los Angeles politics and government. Despite its reputation for weak minority politics and its penchant in the 1950s and 1960s for urban conservatism while many cities were labor-dominated Democratic strongholds with minority officeholders, Los Angeles became the home of a historic biracial coalition behind Mayor Tom Bradley. The Bradley alliance of African Americans and liberal Jews dominated Los Angeles city hall for twenty years, between 1973 and 1993 (Sonenshein 1993).

The Bradley coalition challenged urban scholars to look differently at the prospects for dramatic racial change in the western cities whose reform-style politics had often left them ignored, and to consider the broader possibility that biracial politics were not dead (Sonenshein 1993). After all, Los Angeles had neither the sophisticated partisan structures that brought some mobility to minorities, nor the heavy dose of civic participation of traditional cities. Yet not only did these factors not prevent the rise of the Bradley coalition; they even assisted it.

The story of the Los Angeles biracial coalition was about more than Los Angeles; it was about whether our habit of treating more traditional cities in the East and Midwest as the sum total of urban politics was leading us to miss larger things about such issues as *race*. In this book, I suggest that our focus on the politics of traditional cities may be causing us to miss important things about *reform*. Furthermore, we need to more fully understand the relationship between race and reform.

Urban scholars have tended to marginalize reform politics as the struggle of white elites to disenfranchise minority and working-class voters. But in this study I suggest that reform is a much more vital and diverse phenomenon that can be conservative in one setting and progressive in another. Reform is a contested symbol that is critical to the politics and governance of diverse American cities. The results of this case study suggest that progressives need to reexamine the potential of institutional reform as an important part of an overall program of equity and justice (Purcell 2002).

The contested nature of reform was demonstrated in Los Angeles as liberals and conservatives, whites and minorities sought the high ground of reform. In Los Angeles, the process of building a coalition for charter reform was played out on two levels: an outside game and an inside game. While participatory structures were the outcome of a battle over how to open up city hall (the outside game), their creation was the result of a series of battles and compromises over power at city hall (the inside game). Political actors sought to build coalitions around their positions in both the outside and inside games.

Reform is a process of coalition building (Stone 1998). Race, ideology, and geography structure the search for enduring reform coalitions. Among the key factors in coalitions are ideology, interest, and leadership (Sonenshein 1993). Trusting relationships among leaders are particularly important in the formation of coalitions (Hinckley 1981). In short, the analysis of coalitions requires close attention to human decisions, beliefs, and ideals in the context of racial conflict and ideological disagreement.

This is a story of reform coalitions in an age of racial and ethnic diversity. Coalition lines in American cities were fairly predictable in the last third of the twentieth century, with African Americans and their white liberal allies often joined by Latinos, arrayed against white conservatives (Browning, Marshall, and Tabb 1984; Sonenshein 1993). But with the rise of immigration and the increasing role of ethnic diversity in urban politics, the nature of coalition building has become more complex.

While there was broad support for governmental reform in Los Angeles, there was considerable dispute over how to get there. The charter reform struggle generated at least two broad visions of reform government: a progovernment camp that drew on older traditions of clean government and an antigovernment camp that sought to upend existing arrangements of power to improve efficiency and responsiveness.

The progovernment camp drew in African Americans, organized labor, the city council, and the city bureaucracy. It was heavily Democratic, and in some cases liberal as well. Ironically, that coalition had arisen decades earlier as an insurgency against an even older, more conservative vision of reform government. But by the end of the century, the former rebels had become the status quo. Through the charter reform process, the progovernment coalition was slowly able to develop a vision of reform beyond simply defending the existing order. Still, the progovernment side was divided between those who would defend current arrangements to the bitter end and those who favored reform of the government structure.

The antigovernment camp drew on the appeal of smaller government, as well as a consistent critique of government inefficiencies. It drew its greatest support from white Republicans, but appealed to other groups as well. They were themselves divided between secessionists dedicated to the formal breakup of the city and reformers like Mayor Richard Riordan, who opposed secession but favored radical government reform.

Newly energized Latino and Asian American voters were not locked into either camp, and were the subject of competing efforts to win their support. And once the charter struggle got under way, the ideological lines became blurred as the camps managed to win support from key activists across the political divide.

These competing visions of reform took on an organizational life, through the remarkable phenomenon of two separate and competing charter reform commissions, one elected and one appointed. Behind the formation of the two commissions lay the vitriolic dislike and philosophical antipathy between Riordan and most of the members of the Los Angeles City Council. Few believed that charter reform would overcome the deeply entrenched animosity among the city's leaders.

In the face of the political gulf between the mayor and the council and between the two charter commissions, the leaders of the two commissions forged a unified charter, won backing from their commissions, key elected officials (especially the mayor), and major interest groups. The mayor and other key political leaders then guided a citywide coalition to victory at the polls.

For better and for worse, the central actor in Los Angeles charter reform was Mayor Richard Riordan. A Republican in formally nonpartisan but heavily Democratic Los Angeles, Riordan drove and energized the charter process and also nearly derailed it. Charter reform was the most enduring accomplishment of the eight-year Riordan mayoralty, and nearly its greatest failure. Ironically, Los Angeles opened up broad new lines for citizen participation through a process that was largely driven by a mayor whose own vision of reform centered on increasing executive authority at city hall.

With a reform charter in hand, Riordan's successor as mayor, labor-supported Democrat James K. Hahn, was able to make the case that secession would not be in the best interests of a reforming city. He then led a victorious alliance against secession, built around the progovernment coalition of organized labor, African Americans, and liberal whites.

This book tells the story of how the charter reform coalition was built, how it was carried to victory, and how it influenced the battle over secession. It is a portrait of reform in action. It is a narrative about leaders and voters, under great pressure, deciding what Los Angeles democracy in an age of diversity will look like.

The creation of a new charter forced residents of Los Angeles to reconsider the type of government they had. The charter reform debate activated the positive and negative ways in which Los Angeles residents viewed New York City's political structure. New York City became a character in the local drama of reform. Could Los Angeles gain some of the participatory strength of New York City without the accompanying negatives associated with hierarchical mayoral authority and perceived corruption?

What should be the balance between professional government and leadership by politicians? How could the city government be responsive and inclusive of the city's growing diversity? Most of all, what should be the balance between centralized government and decentralized neighborhoods?

These choices were not abstract versions of reform dreamed up by scholars. With secession looming, wrong choices could have resulted not only in bad government but in the dissolution of the city itself. And such a breakup would have had important, perhaps severe, consequences for minority and low-income residents of the city of Los Angeles. The structure of political institutions is rarely seen as relevant to the struggle of disadvantaged groups, but in the context of Los Angeles, nothing could have been more vital.

The study is based on interviews with key participants, analysis of voting in city elections, examination of newspaper articles, and review of the files of the two charter commissions. Because of the central role of "place" in the battle over secession and reform, I have extensively utilized mapping technology, in association with geographer Mark Drayse.

The book also draws on participant observation. I had the privilege of a front-row seat in charter reform. I was named Executive Director of the Appointed Charter Reform Commission in 1997, and during my two years of full-time service participated both in the development of the appointed commission's draft charter and in the negotiations with the elected commission over the creation of a unified charter.

Los Angeles charter reform represents a great experiment in whether large reform government can become responsive government for diverse communities. Innovations in the new charter, such as neighborhood councils, represent a fresh turn toward grass-roots democracy that has long been underdeveloped in Los Angeles.

While Los Angeles has created a strong beachhead for a new generation of municipal reform, it is not certain that it will be able to create and sustain a true "reform regime," able to do more than block secession. The outcome is uncertain, and whether Los Angeles will find its way to the democracy its residents envision will be a question for the twenty-first century.

Reform of government is a very difficult undertaking. Pressure to make institutional change must be intense, either from popular movements, court decisions, secession efforts, powerful political alliances, or other forces. Even with these pressures, reform efforts may fail. Yet as difficult as reform can be, it is worth the effort. Reform has too often been seen as the province of upper-class conservatives seeking to disenfranchise the working classes. Rather, reform is a valuable and contested symbol of governmental flexibility that can belong to whichever group manages to build the strongest reform coalition and can, in the right context, be a force for equity and progressive change.

With governance in flux throughout the democratic world, with the nation-state being redefined on a daily basis, with secession movements showing vitality in the aftermath of the breakup of the Soviet Union, the questions of what defines a democratic community and what holds it together have never been more acute. Can reform prevent, or should it prevent, the breakup of governments? The travails and triumphs of Los Angeles's democracy over the past decade may have insights to offer as these phenomena unfold.

Acknowledgments

THE PROCESS OF writing this book crossed boundaries between the theoretical and the practical, between the academy and everyday politics and government. I came to the charter reform process because Anton Calleia, a member of the appointed commission, encouraged me to apply for the position of executive director. My charter reform experience would never have happened without Anton's persistence.

When I became a Los Angeles charter reformer, I knew that others had shaped the terrain on which the charter reform battle would be fought. Dr. John Randolph Haynes and Dora Haynes were pioneers in the search for a Los Angeles government that would be both clean and just. Marvin Braude and Joy Picus, former city councilmembers and leading municipal reformers, pursued reform effectively and with integrity. The League of Women Voters of Los Angeles, founded by Dora Haynes, had long toiled to keep the idea of governmental reform alive. Xandra Kayden, Doris Nelson, Sharon Schuster, and Cindy O'Connor of the League fought to enact a new charter and to create neighborhood councils.

As a charter reformer, I had the great honor of working in the trenches with the chair and members of the appointed charter commission. George Kieffer was the ideal leader of the commission and a true partner for me and the staff. George never wavered in his belief that a unified effort would be needed to overcome political conflicts.

The elected commission, led by the indefatigable Erwin Chemerinsky and backed by staff director Geoffrey Garfield and research director H. Eric Schockman, began as rivals and ended as allies. In retrospect, it is hard to imagine how charter reform could have succeeded without both commissions. Like George, Erwin believed above all in a unified charter.

I am grateful to those in and out of government who consented to be interviewed for this study. Naturally, I take full responsibility for any conclusions that appear in this work.

My staff was willing to work long hours under difficult conditions. I especially thank Mary Strobel, Julie Benson, George Wolfberg, and Karen Kelly-Tobin. Assisted by her legal team, Mary was the true author of the words of the new charter. Karen and Sandra Baldenegro prepared a collection of news articles that became essential to my research, and Sandra prepared the records of both commissions for the city archives.

I came to admire and respect the ability, dedication, and care of the people within and around the government of the City of Los Angeles. I particularly thank those who helped me in my charter work and in my research, including CAO Keith Comrie, city clerk Mike Carey, and assistant city clerk Kris Heffron, Mike Barclay in the chief legislative analyst's office, Theresa Patzakis of the mayor's office, Hynda Rudd, Todd Gaydowski, and Jay Jones of the city archives, election consultant Dave Ely, and Susan Pinkus and her staff at the *Los Angeles Times* Poll.

The trustees and staff of the John Randolph Haynes and Dora Haynes Foundation have been pillars of my research for as long as I have been writing about Los Angeles. The Foundation generously gave me two research grants to gather material and write the book. In addition, they selected me as the 2001–2 Haynes Fellow, during which time I could further explore Los Angeles governance. Diane Cornwell, the administrative director, and the trustees believed in me and my work and made sure the wind was always at my back.

I had the chance in this book to explore mapping technologies for displaying demographic and voting data. John Robillard introduced me to mapping technology and helped whip the initial data into shape. Mark Drayse became the indispensable mapmaker, statistician, and table developer and an invaluable and productive colleague in the process.

All or parts of the manuscript have been read by Mark Drayse, Alan Saltzstein, Jane Pisano, George Kieffer, and Tom Hogen-Esch. Princeton University Press showed its interest from the very start, when Chuck Myers responded very positively to my initial proposal. Anonymous reviewers at Princeton University Press made enormously helpful comments that I hope have been successfully addressed in this book. Kevin McInturff guided the book manuscript toward production until his tragic and untimely passing. Jill Harris took over as production editor, with skill and a firm hand. Cindy Crumrine copyedited the manuscript with great care. Dimitri Karetnikov helped make the maps book-ready.

Portions of this book have appeared in other publications. The voting analysis of the 2001 mayoral election, coauthored with Susan Pinkus, appeared in *PS: Political Science and Politics*. The comparison between New York City and Los Angeles government was explored in David Halle, ed., *New York and Los Angeles: Politics, Society and Culture, A Comparative View* (Chicago: University of Chicago Press). The discussion of boroughs appeared in revised form in *Building a Civil Society*, published by the Edmund G. "Pat" Brown Institute of Public Affairs at California State University, Los Angeles. All are reproduced with permission.

Appendix 1 is taken word-for-word from the ballot summary prepared under the direction of Ronald Deaton, the chief legislative analyst.

I had the opportunity to present much of the material in this book at the University of Southern California political science department, at the USC School of Policy, Planning, and Development, in the Dunning Lecture of the Los Angeles Historical Society, with Mark Drayse at the annual meeting of the Western Political Science Association (Sonenshein and Drayse 2003), and with Tom Hogen-Esch at the annual meeting of the American Political Science Association (Sonenshein and Hogen-Esch 2003). I thank the many students who have heard the charter story in my Fullerton class on the politics of Los Angeles, and in UCLA classes on Los Angeles politics and charter reform.

The faculty and the staff at the Cal State Fullerton Political Science Department have been, as always, great friends and wonderful colleagues. Alan Saltzstein, in particular, has critiqued my writing and studied Los Angeles with me for nearly twenty years. My dean, Tom Klammer, and my departmental colleagues gave me the freedom to leave campus for two years to serve the City of Los Angeles, and to return in good standing.

My family has borne with me throughout the charter years, both during the long nights of charter commission meetings and through the hard process of translating that experience into this book. While Julia and Anna became charter fans with me, and were caught up in the excitement of creating change, their best contribution was simply to be themselves growing up.

Phyllis was a fountain of support, a thoughtful and wise critic and indispensable adviser, and most of all a warm, loving, and kind companion.

PART ONE

The Dynamics of Urban Reform

CHAPTER ONE

The Politics of Reform

THE NEW INSTITUTIONALISM MEETS
THE NEW DIVERSITY

> Those who make peaceful revolution impossible will make violent
> revolution inevitable.
> —John F. Kennedy, 1962

IN THE FACE OF global disorder, the fall of empires, the movement of peoples across national boundaries, and agitation for secession, can government adapt? Can government at all levels reform itself, or be reformed? Can it be flexible and improve its performance and responsiveness? Can government cope with diversity of race, ethnicity, class, religion, and place, and can it respond to the needs of disadvantaged and disenfranchised groups? Can government change its own institutional patterns in order to be more nimble and creative? What are the prospects for the reform of government in an age of diversity?

It is not just America's cities that wrestle with these questions. But it is in America's cities that some of the answers may be found. There is probably no level of government in the United States or perhaps worldwide that compares to the American city as a site for experimentation in the reform of political institutions and, at the same time, as a place of diversity. The American city has been the main outlet for the ideas and programs of institutional reform.

But where political scientists once marveled at the potential of Progressive reform, the study of urban reform has fallen on many decades of hard times.

The belief that institutional structure matters played a central role in the titanic urban struggles of a century ago. The politics of American cities were once dominated by the conflict over the structure of local government, and the impact that structure would have on who would rule cities. Then, as now, the diversity shaped by immigration served as a backdrop for the struggle.

In city after city, reformers fought the political machines to restructure the organization of city government. The stakes were enormous, and included both the material resources of city government and the political symbols of leadership. It was a struggle over power, a battle of philosophies and visions, and a conflict among social classes and ethnic groups. The battle was over urban democracy itself.

The visions of the two sides in the reform struggle could not have been more different or more sincerely opposed. The machine politicians disdained the reformers as "morning glories," and accused them of being elitists who wanted to disenfranchise the immigrant working classes. The reformers believed that corruption hurt workers, who would benefit less from a turkey at Christmas than from a well-operated city government.

Political scientists were entranced by the debate, and even personally active in it. Issues of the *American Political Science Review* contained updates of the latest reform battles. Most scholars were on the side of the reformers, although sociologists saw in the political machine certain qualities that made it valuable (Merton 1968). Unlike the sober and serious-minded reformers, machine politicians were endlessly colorful and fascinating (Gosnell 1937; Riordan 1963).

Political scientists, however, by and large lost interest in the urban reform movement. The urban Progressives of the last century had an often well-deserved reputation for cloaking class warfare in good-government rhetoric. The charge that reformers were seeking to disempower immigrants and working-class voters was often on the mark. Hostility to immigrants and minorities motivated many reformers, and many sought to devise "neutral" structures that would enhance their own influence in the city (Salisbury 1961).

The history of nonpartisanship and at-large elections lends support to this view. Minority political power was severely limited by at-large elections, which made it extremely difficult for minority candidates to win seats on city councils. Nonpartisanship reduced levels of participation among working class and minority voters, and advantaged the white middle class (Welch and Bledsoe 1988).

The study of urban reform also suffered from methodological changes in political science. The behavioral movement focused close attention not on the structure of urban institutions, but on the informal pathways of power. The central debate in urban politics became: Who holds the actual power in the city? Structuralists saw private centers of power that could manipulate city politics to their economic advantage. Pluralists saw a city of diverse interests in which political leaders could make decisions with some autonomy from private power brokers.

An updated structuralist argument saw power in the city resting in the hands of a "growth machine" dedicated to controlling land use (Logan and Molotch 1987). Clarence Stone (1989) reframed the debate on urban power with his regime theory, which suggested that cities are governed by coalitions of public and private power. In these discussions of power, the design and reform of political institutions were distant concerns.

According to Gittell (1994, 136), the failure to take seriously the reform of urban democratic institutions has consequences for how we view cities:

> There has been a visible lack of interest in structural and process reform of cities. The vitality of the grassroots reform efforts of the 1970's, which looked to expansion of citizen participation and the role of neighborhood and community organizations, was depreciated by the pessimism of growth politics. This change in the emphasis of urban scholarship took its toll on the political and intellectual status of the city in American political life.

REEXAMINING URBAN REFORM

It is time to reexamine the potential of urban reform. The demands on government to become more effective and responsive make it necessary. Changing intellectual cross-currents and analytical tools make it possible. This is not just a theoretical issue. For those who are involved in practical politics, a greater understanding of political reform is essential. Those who control the high ground of reform have a pronounced edge in urban politics and government. For progressive and minority communities in particular, the potential of reform coalitions has been insufficiently appreciated.

Berry, Portney, and Thomson (1993) argue in *The Rebirth of Urban Democracy* that there has been significant movement in the direction of citizen participation and greater governmental responsiveness in a number of American cities. The authors see in the movement for neighborhood participation signs of an enhanced urban democracy.

These steps have been bolstered by theorists who contend that cities are showing the potential for greater autonomy in economic development (Clarke and Gaile 2000). Scholars in Europe have been drawing attention to the reform and decentralization of local government (Amnå and Montin 2000). There is reason to question the highly pessimistic and limited view of urban autonomy expressed in Peterson's *City Limits* (1981).

The field of globalization studies has been moving steadily toward a greater recognition of the importance of local politics in the global city. New attention has been paid to the claims made by "new social movements" for representation and power within the city. These tentative explorations of the political and electoral spheres are important steps for a field that has previously devalued local political processes (Clarke and Gaile 1997; Sassen 2000; Purcell 2002).

A number of cities have reformed their charters as a method to reexamine the effectiveness and responsiveness of governing institutions. Within the last fifteen years alone, major charter reforms have been conducted in New York City, San Francisco, and Los Angeles.

Can there be a new Progressive era at the municipal level that revives democracy and enhances government (Levine 2000)? Will there be a re-birth of urban democracy? What will be the consequences of urban reform movements for minority incorporation? Will urban reform be dominated by white constituencies, with minority groups on the outside? Will contemporary urban reform be liberal, conservative, or ideologically undefined?

Benjamin and Mauro (1989, 11–12) highlight the differences between contemporary and "classical" urban reform. They argue that there are two critical differences. "Democracy is now the primary goal; achieving efficiency is secondary." Secondly, the new reformers seek to embrace and expand the political system instead of disdaining politics. I would add a third difference: the reformers of today must respond to demographic diversity not as a force to be feared, but as a key reason to reform and expand the reach of political institutions.

There are, however, vast differences among reformers about how to achieve those worthy goals, and those differences tap into a range of political constituencies. It is certainly no longer a simple matter of upper-status people calling for reform and working-class people opposing it.

The battle today is really not between the reformers and the party regulars. It is between competing visions of urban reform: for example, businesslike efficiency weighed against greater representation for minorities. And that is why the study of reform in western cities where reform has been the dominant ideal can be most revealing.

The reexamination of urban reform is facilitated by a renewed interest in urban institutions. A new institutionalism has emerged in political science that incorporates behavioral models, but assumes that just as behavior shapes institutions, institutions shape behavior (March and Olsen 1984).

New institutionalists have reopened the question of the impact of institutions on political behavior. In so doing, they have indirectly brought the question of reform back to the table. As March and Olsen argue, "Political democracy depends not only on economic and social conditions but also on the design of political institutions" (1984, 738).

What we are only beginning to learn is the *chemistry* by which institutional change, or reform, occurs. Institutions shape behavior, but people make choices with imperfect information and uncertainty about whom to trust. Reforms are not abstract ideas. They are competing proposals that require elite and mass constituencies, and which may in the hands of different leaders activate different constituencies. Successful reform is a mixture of lofty ideals and effective politics.

Much of traditional institutional analysis elaborates the inertial forces that prevent change; more research is needed to identify the dynamics by which institutional reform actually occurs. As Pierson (2000, 476) has noted, "Political scientists have had much more to say about institutional effects than about institutional origins and change."

Institutionalists have tended to emphasize the limitations that institutions place on political choices. Pierson (2000) refers to the "lock-in" effects by which institutional actors constrain the behavior of future actors. He explores a series of prior commitments by which political leaders seek to limit themselves and their successors, thereby "locking in" the status quo. Others discuss the "stickiness" of institutions, or the decision costs involved in institutional change (Jones, Sulkin, and Larsen, 2003). Ferman (1997) shows how the dominance of different arenas of power in a community shapes the possibility of participatory reforms.

The reform of governmental institutions is an extraordinarily difficult task. As Pierson indicates (2000, 490–91), "formal political institutions are usually change-resistant. . . . Efforts to change rules higher in the hierarchy (e.g., constitutions) require even greater levels of consensus."

Demands that government officials reform themselves and alter the structure of their world are likely to be met with defensiveness and self-justifications. Buffeted by charges that the government is poorly organized or badly run, they draw inside their comfortable world of city hall, away from the noise of the invading hordes.

It is critical to understand the obstacles to the reform of political institutions, if only to reduce the disappointment that reform is not more frequent or easy, and to appreciate the significance of reform when it does happen. But we are still left with the question of how reform happens at all. And how does reform interact with the social, racial, ethnic, and economic forces within the community?

To understand how reform can be accomplished, the new institutionalism can best be utilized in combination with behavioral approaches. Institutional analysis is now beginning to help elaborate the dynamics of reform. Jones, Sulkin, and Larsen (2003) have presented an ambitious analysis of how "policy punctuations" occur in American political institutions. Noting that institutions have "friction" that resists change, they contend that major changes occur in sudden bursts after long periods of relative stability.

In their study of the adoption of direct democracy reforms, Bowler, Donovan, and Carp (2002) argue that reform efforts are the result of two sets of forces: exogenous and endogenous. Exogenous forces are external to the institutional structure and create strong pressures to reform. But endogenous forces within the institution may be equally important. Despite the view that institutional actors are entirely resistant to reform, Bowler and his colleagues show that if people within an institution favor change, they can join with exogenous forces to bring it about.

Given the tendency of institutions to be stable, to be responsive to exogenous forces and to the beliefs of leaders about the appropriate form of institutions, how can coalitions be built to create reform? And can the new institutionalism be extended into the areas of racial and ethnic diversity?

Reformers must create an effective coalition to prevail over the forces of "lock-in" and "stickiness," to overcome the tendency toward institutional inertia and incremental change. The study of institutional reform has focused its attention on elite actors. Yet for reform to succeed, it must also gain a constituency in the electorate. After all, popular response to proposed reforms is likely to play an important role in the prospects for reform.

Until recent years, urban politics and government have not been major sites for the application of the new institutionalism. That has begun to change (e.g., Ferman 1997; Steinacker 2001). In the condition of racial and ethnic diversity that characterizes America's twenty-first-century urban scene, how can institutions change? What is the connection between the new institutionalism and the new diversity?

REFORM AND THE POLITICS OF DIVERSITY

In his study of school reform, Clarence Stone (1998) applied regime theory to the question of reform. Stone argued that reform is not just a set of ideas or, in the case of schools, a new superintendent. Reform is a process of coalition creation and maintenance. Reform can be implemented and institutionalized only if a long-term coalition is built. These coalition battles will be fought on terrain that involves interests and ideologies maintained by diverse racial, class, and ethnic groups (Henig, Hula, Orr, and Pedescleaux 1999; Portz, Stein, and Jones 1999; Stone, Henig, Jones, and Pierannunzi 2001).

Can cross-racial coalitions be built to pursue reform ideals? Can the mixture of self-interest and belief that helps define coalition development be activated in the interests of improving government? Is reform relevant to minority and disadvantaged communities? Is there any role for beliefs or ideologies in the politics of reform coalitions?

As race and ethnicity are integral parts of urban politics, the process of reform is likely to activate racial divisions and coalitions. Some believe that such coalitions are built on self-interest alone. Rational actors will find partners to maximize mutual advantage (Riker 1961). In matters of race, some find that only self-interest can overcome racial animosity (Carmichael and Hamilton 1967). Others see beliefs and shared ideologies as fundamental (Browning, Marshall, and Tabb 1984).

I have developed a model of interracial coalitions that suggests that interest, ideology and leadership are of fundamental importance in coalitions. Interests are real and can influence the outcome of coalitions, but interests themselves are shaped by the actions of leaders. In other words, interest conflicts may be real or they may be perceived; much depends on how key political leaders shape the debate (Sonenshein 1993). Ideological agreement helps to build leadership trust. Leadership connections are essential to coalitions because they build the trust that is needed to overcome mutual suspicion (Hinckley 1981). Voluntary choices by people are critical to coalitions.

The dynamics of coalition building—ideology, interest, and leadership—will play a key role in whether coalitions can be built, and whether they can endure. Coalition patterns may be structured and stable, as in the urban racial politics of the 1970s and 1980s. Alternatively, coalition patterns may be complex and multidimensional. It is no longer certain that the African American position will be the white liberal position, or that Latinos will join with African Americans. In a big city, reform coalitions may or may not be progressive multiracial coalitions, and in a diverse setting with a rising role for Latinos, they may not always include African Americans.

With urban politics shaped by dividing lines of race, ethnicity, ideology, and geography, some groups will have greater stakes in the status quo than will others. They may perceive that their interests will be affected favorably or unfavorably by proposed reforms.

As in the formation of coalitions for racial equality, alliances for reform will not be solely determined by self-interest narrowly defined. In a study of the failure of a proposed reform to adopt regional governance in Miami, Steinacker (2001) shows that the effects of self-interest are balanced by the role of a leading policy entrepreneur, how the proposed reform is framed to the public, and the timing that opens and closes a window of opportunity. These factors emerge strongly in the Los Angeles charter reform story.

The notion that urban reform is intricately involved in the minority search for equality has received little attention. Yet the story of the rise and fall of minority coalitions in American cities is also the story of reform. Beginning in the 1960s, minorities and white liberals wrote a new chapter in the governance of cities (Browning, Marshall, and Tabb 1984). A central feature of progressive minority coalitions was the connection between minority communities and liberal whites (Browning, Marshall, and Tabb 1984). In city after city, the ability of minority candidates to win the support of a share of white liberals made up for the loss of those whites who were reluctant to support a minority candidate. The triumph of minority incorporation was simultaneously the triumph of urban liberalism, white and nonwhite (Sonenshein 1993).

While there is widespread recognition that *ideology* played a central role in the surge of urban minority power, there is less understanding that *urban reform* played an important role in that development. The rise of African American mayoral candidates in most cities happened outside of, and often in opposition to, regular Democratic party forces. Harold Washington was elected in Chicago as the city's first African American mayor, but also as a reformer who pledged to clean up party corruption. He was opposed by the great majority of party organization leaders.

Kenneth Gibson in Newark in 1970 challenged both the Democratic party and the forces of organized crime that had corrupted city government (Sonenshein 1971). John V. Lindsay, the minority-supported mayor of New York City, was well-known as a "silk-stocking" urban reformer who was outside the party machine.

In Los Angeles, Tom Bradley rose up within the Democratic party by leading the Los Angeles wing of the reform Democratic movement. He was bitterly opposed to the statewide Democratic party organization headed by Jesse Unruh and Mervyn Dymally. Bradley's organization was not only liberal and biracial; it was also an alliance of reformers. They were perfectly suited to win power in a city structured by nonpartisan elections and with a widely held belief in political reform (Sonenshein 1993).

Thus, reform in the 1960s and 1970s was essential to the rise of minority politics. This connection had occurred earlier, during the era of immigrants searching for representation. In his study of progressive coalitions in the first part of the twentieth century, Finegold (1995a, b) showed that in those cities where immigrant and working-class communities formed alliances with reformers, their chances of political success were greater than in cities where they lacked a reform agenda. In other words, urban reform often had a *progressive* role in urban coalitions.

In retrospect, the connection between black politics and white liberal reform politics seems natural. But for many years, it was an uphill battle to forge those alliances. It was a political process of coalition building. In those cities with strong and powerful party organizations, reformers had a difficult time persuading minority activists that the rewards of reform politics outweighed the concrete benefits offered by the machine.

Even in Los Angeles, where party organizations were weak or nonexistent, the barriers to linkage between black activists and white reformers were formidable. In his study of reform Democrats in New York City, Los Angeles, and Chicago, James Q. Wilson (1962) noted the negative attitudes that black politicians and white liberal reformers had toward each other (1962, 80). Conversely, many African American politicians felt that the liberal reformers were blind to the interests of the black community, and had little to offer in the way of political benefits (Sonenshein 1993, 49).

In western cities, where party organizations were overshadowed by the nonpartisan model of urban government, minority activists had to develop their own progressive model of reform. The status quo regimes, built around nonpartisan and at-large elections, were themselves reform-based (Browning, Marshall, and Tabb 1984). The only way to beat an earlier regime of conservative reformers was to become *progressive* reformers (Sonenshein 1993). At the same time, the lack of traditional party inducements for partial minority incorporation made it easier to build outsider unity around challenges to the system.

Because this movement for minority incorporation was not only built around shared liberal ideology, but also around the doctrines of urban reform, it had a greater community appeal than simply minority identification and liberal ideology. Its opponents fell back on racist attacks, or on dirty tricks, or on fear, but could not articulate a thoughtful reform agenda of their own. Mayor Hugh Addonizio of Newark was in federal court after his indictment on corruption charges when he ran against African American city engineer Kenneth Gibson (Sonenshein 1971). Sam Yorty could defeat Tom Bradley in 1969 only with an openly racist campaign. The only vision of governance these opponents shared was the fear of change and a rejection of a role for minorities in city leadership. Black mayors and their supporters held the high ground of reform.

In the late 1980s and early 1990s, African American mayors in New York City, Los Angeles, Chicago, and Philadelphia, then the four largest cities, were succeeded by white mayors (Sonenshein, Schockman, and DeLeon 1996). In Cleveland and Detroit, African American candidates drawing support more from whites than from blacks defeated African American candidates whose base of support rested among blacks. Not only did white mayoral candidates and moderate black candidates drawing support from white voters win mayoral victories; even Republicans enjoyed success. In the two largest American cities, New York City and Los Angeles, Republican mayoral candidates swept to victory in 1993.

The new mayors were an eclectic lot. There were strong Democrats like Richard M. Daley, Jr., in Chicago and Edward Rendell in Philadelphia (Bissinger 1997), and of course Republicans Richard Riordan and Rudolph Giuliani. What they seemed to have in common was an emphasis on reforming government operations and, if necessary, government structures, and in the three largest cities, opposition from African American voters. They appealed to white middle-class voters, but also won significant support from Latinos and Asian Americans (Sleeper 1993). While cities continued to elect black mayors (Alozic 2000), the mantle of reform had subtly shifted.

The alienation of white middle-class voters led to a new kind of urban reform. In the era when minority complaints drove the reform agenda, the threat of civil disorder drove municipal reform. Today, it is the threat of exit, tax revolt, or secession.

Mayor Ed Koch of New York City (1977–89) was a precursor of these developments. A former liberal turned conservative, Koch built a center-right coalition that drew support from middle-class whites, Jews, and Latinos. As John Mollenkopf demonstrates in his study of the Koch coalition, Koch managed to appeal to many of the liberal reformers who had worked for Mayor John Lindsay and also to good government groups (Mollenkopf 1992, 191).

Just as the connection between the African American movement and urban reform is often overlooked, so has the connection between these "new mayors" and the energy of reform. It became harder for minority and liberal coalitions to develop and communicate a reform vision that could match the white-led coalition view of urban leadership, beyond the defense of institutional protections hard-won through the struggle for minority incorporation. The loss of connection between minority and liberal reform politics contributed to the difficulty of creating new progressive multiracial coalitions.

In this sense, the new mayors were quite different from the white reactionary mayors of the 1960s and 1970s, even though their electoral coalitions bore much similarity. The decline of minority coalitions came with the decline of liberal urban reform, and its replacement with less liberal versions of reform.

The significance of the "new mayors" as reformers should not be underestimated. But neither should it be considered an inherent feature of *conservatism*. Urban reform does not have to be conservative.

Reform can be a vehicle for a liberal mayor of Oakland (Jerry Brown) to expand his authority over the schools, but it can also be a means by which a Republican mayor of Los Angeles (Richard Riordan) gets the authority to increase the number of city jobs exempt from civil service. There are progressive reforms, such as the shift from at-large to district elections and police reform. As reform moves from being perceived as an ideological tool of the upper class to a contested symbol, the prospects for wider participation in urban politics increase.

The contemporary setting for reform coalitions has also been influenced by the major changes caused by immigration. Massive levels of immigration to American cities moved a dialogue about black and white (that tended to fit rather neatly into a conservative-liberal dichotomy) into a broader setting of diversity.

Immigration changed the roles of key urban players. African Americans, once the exemplar of the minority struggle, now competed for physical space, jobs, and political power with Latinos and Asian Americans. To some degree, African Americans felt pressure as an established urban group facing the challenge of an up-and-coming bloc. In this setting, African Americans might resist institutional reforms that could further jeopardize their already precarious standing. But to new immigrants, some reform proposals might seem to offer a welcome reshuffling of the deck.

As a result, the possibilities for shaking up the stable alliances of recent decades have become greater than before.

This study examines the formation of elite and mass constituencies for major governmental reform in one major city characterized by demographic diversity. How were the interests and ideologies of key groups in Los Angeles shaped by leaders into a winning coalition? How durable is this coalition for reform? What does this reform battle tell us about how reform happens in the twenty-first-century city? And what will the "new" groups of immigrants choose among the options placed before them?

CHAPTER TWO

Studying Los Angeles Politics

> Los Angeles has a low quotient of civic feeling. As a political community, it is highly attenuated. As a body politic, it is gangling and loose, and the nervous system which co-ordinates that sprawling body is haphazard and feeble. . . . One feels that the Angelenos are drawn together more on one of those sorrowing nights when the Giants bomb Koufax early in the game than they are on a day of a municipal election. . . . It is not that politics seems futile or ugly or threatening to the Angelenos. To most of them, politics seems unnecessary.
>
> —Francis M. Carney, "The Decentralized Politics
>   of Los Angeles," 1964

> Nearly everyone in the city takes part in the city's political and governmental system. Taking part in "politics"—that is, engaging in deliberative efforts to determine who gets public office (whether elective or appointed) and to influence what public officials and employees do—is an almost universal avocation among New Yorkers.
>
> —Walter S. Sayre and Herbert Kaufman,
>   *Governing New York City,* 1960

THE STUDY OF urban politics has been dominated by the great partisan cities, especially New York City and Chicago. The history of the politics of the big cities of the East and Midwest is dominated by party machines and organizations. Reform there has often been the province of "silk stocking," upper-status citizens.

But the study of urban *reform* inevitably draws us westward. Reform has been far more influential in the West and Southwest than in the East and Midwest (Shefter 1983). By expanding our urban focus from traditional eastern and midwestern cities, we can explore settings in which reform is clearly a contested symbol.

In her book *Morning Glories,* Amy Bridges (1997) recasts the history of urban reform by placing her focus not on the part of the country where reform is weak, but in the Southwest and West, where reform has been central to urban government. To study government west of the Mississippi River is not to study the fine points of the party; it is to explore the nature of reform:

Although the municipal reform movement eventually had profound effects on city politics everywhere, in the large cities of the Northeast and Midwest, municipal reformers celebrated few victories at the polls, and when they did win, their time in office was most fleeting. . . . In the Southwest municipal reformers enjoyed a different history. . . . Just as the big cities of the Northeast and Midwest were commonly governed by political machines, and the cities of the South by Bourbon coalitions, so the cities of the Southwest have in the twentieth century been governed by municipal reformers (1997, 3).

Western cities are likely to have a different structure from the eastern and midwestern cities that have shaped discussions of urban politics. The forms of democracy their residents admire will look different. The salience of politics and voter participation will be lower. By including the West and Southwest in the discussion, we can develop a broader theoretical view of how cities work. A similar approach has widened our view of urban biracial coalitions by incorporating the experience of the West (Sonenshein 1993).

Certainly the flaws of reform are just as visible in the West and Southwest as they were in the East and Midwest—and are in some ways even more glaring. Bridges and Kronick (1999) found that southwestern cities used charter reform to change the electoral rules to advantage middle-class voters, and for that reason, these reforms were met by widespread working-class opposition. In cities where the reform agenda triumphed, working-class political participation declined over the long haul.

The western metropolis provides an invaluable research setting for the close study of reform in an environment far different from New York City. Observing the reform process in a city where reform institutions and values are preeminent, we have the opportunity to view reform not just as the province of the "good government" crowd, but as the game itself. It is illuminating to explore the process of reform in a city where there are no party bosses and machines, where reform *is* politics.

Where reform is king, all potential kings are reformers, even if their reform visions vary wildly. The actual shape of reform emerges from the competitive struggle of local politics. Seen up close in the reform metropolis of Los Angeles, reform becomes a less consistent but much more interesting creature than the "morning glories" and "silk stockings" of traditional analysis. Rather than a single vision of reform imposed by elites, reform appears more to be the resultant of divergent vectors of reform visions.

Furthermore, if reform regimes have less citizen participation than traditional political systems, and if interest groups are less energetic and organized, then strong coalitions can be built among those who are deeply, passionately committed to a civic vision as long as they are united. In the kingdom of the blind, the one-eyed are kings.

At the level of the biggest cities, the comparison between East and West, traditional politics and reform, can be seen in New York City and Los Angeles. Qualities in the political cultures of these two great cities endure over decades; descriptions of their political nature seem quite up-to-date even when written decades ago. The contrast between New York City and Los Angeles has attracted increasing attention among those who study urban political institutions (see Mollenkopf, Olson, and Ross 2001; Kaufmann 1998; Jones-Correa 2001; Joyce 2003; Sonenshein 1993, 2003).

Mollenkopf, Olson, and Ross (2001) examined the absorption of immigrants and found considerably more opportunity for political participation in traditional New York City than in Los Angeles. Jones-Correa (2001) observed that government responses to rioting and other civil disorders were more coherent in New York City than in Los Angeles. Joyce (2003) concluded that different institutional structures channeled black-Korean conflict in New York City into peaceful protest but into violence in Los Angeles.

My own research on interracial coalitions explored structural differences between the two cities, and found that the prospects of biracial coalitions were significantly better in Los Angeles than in New York City. Party organization and strong government in New York City created numerous disincentives to coalition building. The more exclusionary Los Angeles created the conditions for an alliance of outsider progressive groups. Partial incorporation was not a possibility in the absence of party organizations; it was win citywide power or be excluded (Sonenshein 1993).

In a recent study of riots in the two cities, Halle and Rafter (2003) note that despite the great attention devoted to the 1992 Los Angeles riot, the nature and scope of racial violence in New York City has been equal or greater. They argue that both cities have been highly susceptible to racial violence, and that the assumption that Los Angeles is a unique hotbed of historic levels of such intergroup warfare is unsupported by the evidence.

The emerging debate over political institutions in New York City and Los Angeles involves different styles of political life, one more traditional and political, the other more reformist and less political. What can Americans learn about governance from its most traditional cities? What can we learn from our newer, reform-oriented cities? What can older and newer cities teach each other?

The battle over charter reform in Los Angeles illuminates the surprising extent to which *images* of New York City governance affected arguments about how Los Angeles should design or redesign its government. This tendency to design western urban government as in part a reaction to older models of urban governance is consistent with Los Angeles history.

New York City government has been extensively studied, and has had a major impact on all American cities. For some, it has represented the best of urban government; for others, it has been the model to avoid. As Mollenkopf notes,

New York has had a disproportionate influence on national political development, despite its dwindling fraction of the national vote. Among its innovations have been machine politics as practiced by William Marcy Tweed, Richard Croker, and Charles Murphy; the attack on machine politics launched by Progressive opponents like Theodore Roosevelt and Seth Low. (1992, 11)

Projections from the New York City political experience have been extraordinarily powerful. The stogie-chomping boss and the silk-stocking reformer are both images that are deeply rooted in New York City. The main viewpoints on black-Jewish relations were developed regarding New York City. Thus, when blacks and Jews fought with each other in the late 1960s in New York, it was assumed that this relationship was dead. It took the study of the black-Jewish coalition in Los Angeles to challenge generalizations based on the New York City experience (Sonenshein 1993).

The differences in political institutions are not as simple as the common images of Los Angeles as the "reform metropolis" and New York City as the city of party organizations. If New York City nurtured America's most fascinating and colorful political machines and bosses, it has also been the cradle of the urban reform movement (Mollenkopf 1992; Viteritti 1989).

On the other hand, Los Angeles is not a pure reform metropolis. Los Angeles has many of the standard features of unreformed big city government: the mayor-council system with no city manager, and district elections for city council (McCarthy, Erie, and Reichardt 1998, 84–96).

Both cities faced significant secession movements in the 1990s. Los Angeles survived only by winning a citywide election. The borough of Staten Island took its case all the way to the state legislature after a referendum for secession passed on the Island. The governor was ready to sign a secession bill, but the state assembly leader ruled that the secession could not go forward without the concurrence of the City of New York.

Staten Islanders often felt as derided by the rest of New York City as Valleyites did by Los Angeles. As Robert Straniere, a candidate for Staten Island borough president commented:

You know, when you tell people you're from Staten Island, their reaction is usually a smile. You have that garbage dump, you have that quaint little ferry boat, it's the backdrop for the Godfather, or they could have filmed the Sopranos just as well on Staten Island as New Jersey, or Working Girl, kind of personifies working women on Staten Island. (Kroessler 2001)

Valley Girl or Working Girl: The same feeling of stereotyping, of unsophistication, of outsidership in a cosmopolitan diverse metropolis helped drive the goal of separation.

There are, however, very real institutional differences between the two cities. In their comparative study of the political incorporation of immigrants in New York City and Los Angeles, Mollenkopf, Olson, and Ross

(2001) listed some of these contrasts. New York City has one contiguous political jurisdiction, while Los Angeles's boundaries cross independent jurisdictions; New York City is highly partisan and organized, while Los Angeles is nonpartisan and weakly organized; New York City is much more densely populated than Los Angeles; New York City has a far larger number of elected offices, and greater media attention to them than Los Angeles; and New York City has a much larger public sector and many more public employees (37–40).

In his study of Mayor Edward Koch's political coalition, Mollenkopf (1992) noted that a massive array of public and private interests contend in New York City politics, and that the mayor must adeptly gain their support or defeat their opposition.

New York City's elected officials (particularly mayors) are central actors, and they dominate the government. New York City's mayor stands very high in the traditional hierarchy of mayoral power. Theories of "executive centered leadership" come naturally to the student of New York City government.

The strong mayor is a long-ingrained feature of New York City government. According to Viteritti (1989, 20),

> The government that came into existence in 1898 gave its chief executive more institutional power than the mayor in any other major American city ever had and perhaps ever will. . . . Given the magnitude of the mayor's power, it could hardly be claimed that New York City had an effective system of checks and balances.

The mayor utterly controlled the citywide Board of Estimate, and it took five-sixths of the votes of both houses of the local legislature to override the mayor's veto. In addition, the great size of the council was established early on, and the connection between size and weakness was evident: "The geometrical growth in the size of New York's Municipal Assembly was inversely related to the level of its prestige" (21).

In 1961, Mayor Robert Wagner appointed the Cahill Commission to redraw the city charter. Most significantly, the new charter gave the mayor the "residual powers" of the city, namely, those powers not specified in the charter. According to the Los Angeles appointed commission's research (Appointed Commission 1998f), New York is the only city that grants to the mayor all residual powers of the city (those powers not explicitly given to other bodies). In most cities, such powers rest with the city council.

In 1972, Governor Nelson Rockefeller appointed a state charter commission that radically altered the role of community boards in local governance. The Goodman Commission report in 1975 sought to provide direct citizen participation as an alternative to the control exercised by elected officials. The plan involved a two-tiered system of community boards and borough boards.

In the 1980s, a decision by a federal judge that the Board of Estimate violated the one-person, one-vote principle set off a major constitutional revision. Two successive commissions developed a new charter that was passed by the voters in 1989. This charter abolished the Board of Estimate, enhanced the city council, and generally maintained the power of the mayor. Borough presidents were considerably weaker under the new charter (see table 1).

Los Angeles

Los Angeles, the nation's second largest city, is the prototypical western metropolis. It has burst into world consciousness with startling suddenness. It is hard to mark a single point where attention to Los Angeles emerged, but the riot of 1992, with its massive violence and geographic spread, was a key moment. Where once it was ignored, now Los Angeles is labeled a global city comparable to New York, London, and Paris (Abu-Lughod 1999). Where once Los Angeles was only disdained, now it is admired, examined, and explored (though often still disdained).

There has been a veritable explosion of research and writing on Los Angeles. Los Angeles is being examined from every conceivable angle. Its architecture, cultural artifacts, growth patterns, history, ethnic and race relations, and patterns of economic development and immigration have all generated creative and exciting research.

Los Angeles has been projected as a model and trend-setter for the twenty-first century. The sprawl of Southern California has been seen to prefigure the future of metropolitan America unless there is planning for land use (Southern California Studies Center 2001). Numerous studies have been published about the impact of immigration on the Los Angeles community (e.g., Waldinger and Bozorgmehr 1996; Scott and Soja 1996).

Urban scholars have begun to question whether the "Chicago School," with its emphasis on the great downtown and satellite neighborhoods, should be replaced by a "Los Angeles School" built around multicentered metropolitan areas (Dear 2001).

A knowledge base is being gathered that will greatly expand our understanding of Greater Los Angeles. In the area of the contemporary urban politics of Los Angeles, however, the field is thinner. The strength of the research is historical. There are some fine studies of the early era of Los Angeles democracy that have traced the rise and evolution of the Progressive system of local government in the first part of the century (Sitton 1999; Fogelson 1967; Erie 1992). Specific minority groups and racial and ethnic relations have drawn considerable research.

The City of Los Angeles has yet to take its place as a site for modern urban *politics* in the minds of those who study cities. The nature of the

TABLE 1
Los Angeles and New York Charters Compared

	New York City		Los Angeles	
	Old Charter	New Charter (1989–)	Old Charter (1925–2000)	New Charter (2000–)
Council Size	35	51	15	15
Council Election	District	District	District	District
Partisanship	Partisan	Partisan	Nonpartisan	Nonpartisan
Governing Body	Mayor	Mayor	Council	No governing body
Budget	Mayor & council	Mayor & council	CAO advises mayor & council	CAO advises mayor & council
Government	Boroughs/community boards[a]	Boroughs/community boards	None	Neighborhood Neighborhood councils/Area Planning Commissions[b]
School Board	Appointed, with mayor making two appointments and each borough president making one	No change[b]	Elected by district	Elected by district

TABLE 1 (continued)

Department Heads	Called "Commissioners"; serve at pleasure of mayor; no civil service protection	No change	Called "General Managers," mayor appoints & removes with council majority; no civil service protection for department heads[c]	Mayor appoints with council majority; mayor removes with right to appeal to council and 2/3 council vote to override; no civil service protection for department heads
Council Authority	Extremely weak due to role of Board of Estimate	Council legislative & oversight roles strengthened	Great administrative authority	Reduced administrative authority; greater focus on oversight & legislative roles
Board of Estimate[d]	Immense power	Abolished	None	None

Notes:[a] New York City's Community Boards are basically advisory only, although their views are often taken quite seriously. By contrast, the new Area Planning Commissions in Los Angeles make decisions on certain land use matters.

[b] As of 2002, the mayor appoints the school chancellor directly and eight members of a thirteen-member board.

[c] In 1995 a charter amendment took department heads out of civil service.

[d] The Board of Estimate had to approve every contract signed with the city, which gave it enormous power. It was composed of the five borough presidents, plus the mayor (who had two votes), the city comptroller, and the city council president.

Source: Sonenshein 2003

national and international attention now being paid to Los Angeles magnifies Los Angeles, but also diminishes it as a self-governing community that has been struggling for decades to emerge as a full democracy.

Attention to modern Los Angeles politics has come in fits and spurts, usually spurred by dramatic events. For example, the Los Angeles riots of 1965 and 1992 garnered great attention (Governor's Commission 1965; Sears and McConahay 1973; Baldassare 1994). The historic electoral battles between Tom Bradley and Sam Yorty in 1969 and 1973 generated valuable voting studies (Jeffries and Ransford 1972; Maullin 1971; Hahn and Almy 1971; McPhail 1971; Pettigrew 1971; Sears and Kinder 1971; Halley 1974; Hahn, Klingman, and Pachon 1976; Halley, Acock, and Greene 1976; O'Laughlin and Berg 1977).

The thoroughgoing nonpartisanship of Los Angeles elections (Adrian 1959) and the low level of political organization have further discouraged scholarly research. Pessimism about the structure of Los Angeles democracy has long characterized the urban literature. Writing in 1963, Banfield and Wilson found a highly decentralized political system with few active political organizations. Carney, in 1964, found little coherent power structure. Mayo, also in 1964, traced the lack of impact of partisan organizations. In such a place, is there any sort of local political system worth studying?

The 2001 mayoral campaign that featured a competitive Latino candidate, Antonio Villaraigosa, brought Los Angeles politics national and even international attention. But the sound trucks, cameras and laptops disappeared when Villaraigosa lost the election, only to reappear during the secession campaign of 2002. What has been missing is the *consistent* attention that reflects a belief that politics and government in the nation's second largest city matter.

My book on the Tom Bradley coalition (Sonenshein 1993) appears to be the only full-length study of Los Angeles politics covering the second half of the twentieth century (Ethington 2000). Keil's study of Los Angeles in a global environment stands out for its mixture of globalization theory and political analysis of Los Angeles (1998). Like Abu-Lughod, Keil argues that there is nothing inevitable about the impact of globalization on local politics, and that local political forces can shape the impact global forces make.

The battles over secession and charter reform have revived interest in Los Angeles politics. Hogen-Esch (2001) and Purcell (1997, 2001) have explored the coalition behind secession, and its implications for the urban power structure. Purcell (2002) has analyzed the charter reform of 1999 in light of debates over the political role of new social movements in the global city. Purcell argues that both formal political structures and electoral politics are significant features of urban politics and that new social movements must engage formal politics in order to transform cities.

The contemporary field of Los Angeles studies has been influenced not only by the neglect of politics but by dystopian views. Los Angeles has provided a field of nightmares for urban analysts. It has been seen as a den of iniquity and inequity, with the rich and poor living in Calcutta-like distance from each other. Los Angeles has been portrayed as violent, polluted and anomic, like the *Bladerunner* scenario. Mike Davis (1991), whose vivid writing has portrayed a divided, unequal city on the precipice of destruction, has been the most influential example of this point of view.

Despite the ambivalence toward the study of Los Angeles politics and government, Los Angeles is a major city well worth studying. Its city budget of more than $4.8 billion in 2002–3 was matched by an additional $4.6 billion budget for its three proprietary departments (Water and Power, Airport, and Harbor). By any measure, Los Angeles City is a governmental colossus, the most important city government west of the Mississippi River.

It is easy for even practical politicians to underestimate Los Angeles politics. Los Angeles election history is strewn with the defeats of state politicians who returned from the partisan State Capitol to seek easy victories for city council or citywide offices in what they considered a city of political rubes and yahoos. Their discovery that Los Angeles politics is not so easily dominated, and that its twists and turns are quite difficult to navigate, has usually come too late in the game. In 2001, for one example, all six state elected officials who ran for city offices were defeated.

To study Los Angeles politics is first to look at it as a physical entity (map 1). The geography of Los Angeles makes its governing challenges nearly unique. There is the long "shoestring" that connects the city to its harbor, down the Harbor Freeway. There is the mountain range that separates the San Fernando Valley from the rest of Los Angeles.

The dispersal of governmental authority among the City of Los Angeles (which handles police, fire, sanitation, water, electric power, and other basic services), the County of Los Angeles (which handles welfare and other social services), another 87 local governments within Los Angeles County, and even numerous special districts makes it difficult to place accountability.

There are independent cities within the physical boundaries of Los Angeles. Travel west from downtown and you will enter Beverly Hills. Travel farther west and you are back in Los Angeles, in the sections known as Beverlywood and then Westwood. But keep going west or south and you will find yourself in either Culver City or Santa Monica, each independent cities. Go a bit south of Santa Monica, and you will enter Venice, a community within the city of Los Angeles.

One of the spurs to secession is that from almost any point in the City of Los Angeles, one can quickly travel to an independent, affluent city that

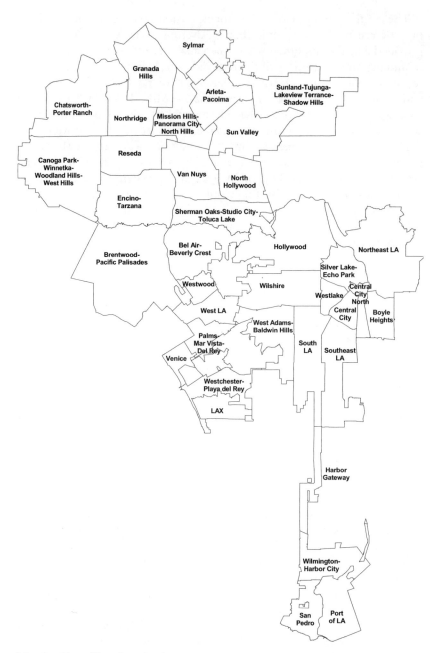

Map 1. City of Los Angeles Areas

seems cleaner and better run than the big metropolis. New York City and Chicago do not have to compete with their own suburbs within their own borders.

Is it any wonder that around election day many Los Angeles residents are not quite certain whether they vote in the City of Los Angeles or in one of the 87 other cities in Los Angeles County? Or that local television stations find it uneconomical to cover Los Angeles City Hall when there are so many viewers who are not Los Angeles city residents? How can we be surprised at low voter turnout in city elections when the dispersal of governmental authorities makes it difficult to know who does what?

The study of New York City politics is a natural task for political scientists. It is a rich environment filled with politics. The study of Los Angeles politics requires more digging, more excavation. The politics are not so visible, the alliances and mechanisms of power harder to define. Yet with its mix of weak political culture and politics beyond parties, Los Angeles politics may yet yield important insights into twenty-first-century American politics and government.

PART TWO

The Roots of Los Angeles Charter Reform

CHAPTER THREE

Reform, Los Angeles Style

A CITY WHOSE early-twentieth-century leaders sought to create an oasis of clean government with an active citizenry became a city of detached residents with little connection to their city government. A city whose modern government was built on a landmark set of governmental reforms itself became highly resistant to reforms that would reduce that detachment. A city built on principles of good government generated a governance structure that later government reformers could not easily alter.

The political history of modern Los Angeles has been marked by an enduring struggle to design a local democracy without political parties. The city's government has been shaped by strong doctrines of political reform, along a path different from that of the great cities of the East and the Midwest. Yet when those Progressive structures themselves became an obstacle to democratic governance, they proved stubbornly resistant to improvement.

Founded in 1781 by Mexican explorers under the rule of Spain, Los Angeles became an American city in 1850 with California's entry into the Union. Nineteenth-century Los Angeles was a small town with a frontier atmosphere and a diverse population. There was no organized police department in early Los Angeles, and the usual method of fighting crime was to organize a posse of leading citizens and string up the apprehended miscreant (Woods 1973). Local politics were organized on a partisan basis and elections were vigorously contested. The majority of residents were of Hispanic origin. A lively, thriving Jewish community played an active role in the city's politics (Vorspan and Gartner 1970).

A massive in-migration of tens of thousands of white midwesterners beginning in the last quarter of the nineteenth century reshaped Los Angeles. The economy was transformed as the large Spanish landholdings, the *ranchos,* were sold and subdivided, and as land use became intense and profitable. The community shifted from agriculture under Spanish dominance to manufacturing and land speculation under the control of white Americans. In the wide open spaces of Los Angeles, *rancheros* had seen fields for plowing and grazing. Americans saw subdivisions and manufacturing plants. Those who purchased land made fortunes as property values soared.

Economic transformation had large social consequences, as the American landowners married into *ranchero* families, inherited the land, and turned it to industrial and commercial uses. The easy multiethnic community of early Los Angeles was altered irrevocably by the massive in-migration promoted by business-oriented local boosters.

Among the leaders of the booster era was the *Los Angeles Times,* which welcomed each new migrant in the pages of the newspaper. Boosterism helped create the idea of Los Angeles, with its glorious weather and seemingly limitless economic opportunities, as a place to seek the "good life." A self-conscious local business class, led by the Merchants and Manufacturers Association, saw itself as "city builders." They competed mightily and successfully to obtain federal support for a Los Angeles harbor and to have a cross-country railroad connection to Los Angeles instead of to San Diego. Under the leadership of these local capitalists, water was brought from Northern California, numerous communities were annexed to Los Angeles, and a major metropolis was created.

Over time, this new Los Angeles community leadership shaped the politics of the city as well. As early as the 1880s, Los Angeles began to take on the character of a white-dominated, business-led, growth oriented Protestant community of midwestern migrants with rigidly conservative views. It became the prototype of the reformist, entrepreneurial city (Elkin 1987):

> All entrepreneurial cities have in common a relatively unimpeded alliance at work composed of public officials and local businessmen, an alliance that is able to shape the working of city political institutions so as to foster economic growth. In each, moreover, electoral politics is organized so that businessmen play an important role, and urban bureaucracies are adept at organizing their domains so that they are neither dominated by elected officials nor in the service of local businessmen. (61)

While New York City and Chicago were incorporating immigrant groups through the Democratic party, the leadership of Los Angeles was hostile to immigrants and the political organizations that would advance their influence. Soon the government structure itself reflected the Progressivism of its leading constituency: white midwesterners. Bolstered by a unified white conservative, often religious base of voters, these migrants held most of the public offices and dominated official power (Singleton 1979). No African American, Latino, or Jewish person held elected office in the city of Los Angeles between 1900 and 1949, when Edward Roybal was elected to the city council.

The ability of this dominant group to shape local democracy was enhanced by legal changes in the status of cities. In the late 1880s, many American cities began to enjoy the benefits of home rule for the first time. Before then, Dillon's Rule—the judicial theory that cities were mere legal creatures of state governments—had restricted the legal autonomy of cities. As states began to authorize greater leeway for urban governance, city charters emerged to codify the empowerment of cities.

The 1879 California state constitution allowed large cities to write charters. In 1887, state voters amended the constitution to extend home rule

(Erie and Ingram 1998). In 1888, Los Angeles voters adopted the city's first home rule charter, to take effect in 1889. Most top officials were elected, for a term of two years (Hunter 1933, 71–73).

The 1889 charter established for the first time Los Angeles's remarkable system of citizen commissions to manage city departments (Erie and Ingram 1998, 60). It also guaranteed municipal control of the water supply. The strong city council completely overshadowed the mayor, outraging local reformers (61).

In 1902, reformers won at the polls with a major series of charter amendments. They created a civil service system, strengthened the mayor, and became the first city in the country to institute direct democracy through the recall, referendum, and initiative (Erie and Ingram 1998, 63). In 1909, voters replaced the ward system that had led to councilmanic corruption and replaced it with an at-large structure. They also instituted nonpartisan elections, two years before the state constitution was amended to make all local elections nonpartisan (65). A half-century of lively party competition ended in Los Angeles.

Los Angeles voters continued to innovate in 1911. Voters approved the creation of a fire and police pension system; extended the recall from elected officials to include appointed officials as well; and approved campaign finance legislation (Erie and Ingram 1998, 66).

The founders of modern Los Angeles had their own version of the Progressive philosophy of political reform that was sweeping the nation, especially in the western and southwestern states. Los Angeles was constructed in its modern form as a paradise of reform, to avoid all the pitfalls of big-city machine politics: to have the virtues of the small midwestern town and to dress in the clothes of a great metropolis. "The people of Los Angeles desired the size but not the character of a modern metropolis . . . to combine the spirit of the good community with the substance of the great metropolis" (Fogelson 1967, 191).

The midwestern migrants to Los Angeles carried with them a vision of a homogeneous community, free of corruption but uninviting to immigrants and other groups who had to struggle mightily to gain acceptance in the growing metropolis (Sonenshein 1993). They would consciously build a metropolis to be unlike New York City or Chicago.

The 1925 Charter

The framework for twentieth-century Los Angeles government in the Progressive era was the 1925 charter. The charter was developed by a Board of Freeholders elected by the voters in June 1923. It was placed on the ballot in 1924, passed overwhelmingly, and took effect in 1925.

Los Angeles's distinct governing character could be discerned in the 1925 charter, from the mixture of separated governmental structures, near socialism in the area of utilities, and provisions for citizen involvement. The 1925 charter distilled the Los Angeles political culture, its fear of corruption by elected officials, and its provisions to keep the "best people" involved in government. The basis was laid for the vast power of civil servants, and for limitations on the actions of elected officials.

The 1925 charter strengthened the mayor and forebade the city council from interfering in administrative matters. The charter established citizen commissions appointed by the mayor to run city departments.

The 1925 charter was very modern for its time. The mayor's authority was expanded over what it had been in earlier charters (Hunter 1933; Erie and Ingram 1998). The city leaders did not get all they had hoped for. They lost a battle to impose at-large elections on the council. The main charter proposal, which passed overwhelmingly, contained at-large elections. A second proposal on the same ballot called for council elections by individual district, and also won, by a lesser amount. The State Supreme Court ruled that the voters had shown their preference for district elections (Hunter 1933, 178).

As Los Angeles was developing its reform government, it was also expanding geographically. Led by a dominant growth machine and entrenched bureaucracy, modern Los Angeles grew by annexation. The basis for the annexation movement in Los Angeles was the control by the City of Los Angeles of such resources as water, electric power, and the harbor.

Crouch and Dinerman (1963) provide a detailed analysis of the annexation movement that created modern Los Angeles. A number of smaller cities were not amenable to annexation and continued to exist as viable entities. Thus, Santa Monica and Beverly Hills, two affluent communities, sit right in the middle of Los Angeles City, but remain legally separate. But there was considerable demand among other cities to join Los Angeles. In fact, the incorporation movement was so successful that Los Angeles became reluctant to accept new additions.

While the leadership of a transformed Los Angeles rested in the hands of conservative, growth-oriented leaders, their dominance was by no means absolute. Even with a system hostile to unions and to what city leaders considered "radicalism," discontent boiled beneath the surface. In 1911, city voters nearly elected a socialist mayor, and were stopped from doing so only by the public reaction to the deadly bombing of the *Los Angeles Times* in the midst of a labor dispute. On the other hand, there is plenty of evidence that the combination of cowboy capitalism and good-government reform was popular with the voters. Bond issues passed with wide margins for William Mulholland's water projects, and the 1925 charter received massive voter support (Erie 1992).

Neither were the city's leaders uniformly conservative. One of the principal organizers of Los Angeles reform movements and a pillar of the local establishment was Dr. John Randolph Haynes, an avowed socialist. Haynes's ideas were influential in the development of Los Angeles government during the Progressive era, and he led the successful battle for public control of local utilities, embodied in the Department of Water and Power (Sitton 1999).

The voters turned down several measures that would have strengthened the hand of conservative reformers. One was the plan to have at-large council elections in the 1925 charter, defeated twice by the voters. When the voters rejected the *Times*'s advice to pass at-large elections in 1924, one reformer suggested that the voters had simply made a mistake in expressing their intentions (Dykstra 1925). Another rejected plan was to have a city manager system, akin to smaller cities in the West and Southwest (Erie and Ingram 1998).

Other big cities in the first half of the century might have featured the clash of interest groups and political organizations that the pluralist model of power describes. Los Angeles did not. The electoral system provided only raw support for the actions of a tightly knit, economically powerful leadership joined to a semiautonomous and entrepreneurial bureaucracy that dominated the city's life.

Bureaucrats and private interests were astonishingly powerful compared to elected officials. As Erie (1992) has indicated, important city-building measures in Los Angeles were opposed even by local business elites and were rammed through by powerful bureaucrats. A particular example is the Owens Valley water project.

COMPLAINING ABOUT THE CITY CHARTER

Long before the rise of the secession movement, there had been complaints and problems with the structure of Los Angeles government—often focusing on the city charter. The reform movements that grew out of these complaints were, however, unable to comprehensively reform the charter. They had to surmount the problem that the charter itself was a pillar of local reform. Instead of taking on a corrupt party machine, good-government forces in Los Angeles were taking on earlier reformers.

The charter could not prevent the corrupt regime of Mayor Frank Shaw (1933–38), but reformers managed to fight back. The charter did provide the ultimate solution, which was the voters' recall of Shaw in 1938.

The Shaw regime stands as the great moral lesson of Los Angeles reform. Those active in the Los Angeles charter debate of 1996–99 often made reference to the most corrupt regime in local political history. Shaw operated under the 1925 charter, but before it had been amended to provide civil service protection to general managers of departments. But even existing civil service positions were not safe from Shaw, who manipulated his appointed civil service commission.

In the context of local reform philosophy, the Shaw regime reinforced the belief that with too much power, elected officials would become corrupt. It led to a series of charter amendments that granted civil service protection to the general managers of departments, a provision not altered until a vote of the people in 1995.

The first of a series of charter commissions issued a report in 1934, criticizing the charter for its ambiguity and lack of accountability. Citizen commission after citizen commission complained that the mayor's authority was too constrained by the powerful city council (Appointed Commission 1997a). By the 1950s, the charter was being called hopelessly outdated, filled with detail and confusion (Bollens 1963).

Mayor Fletcher Bowron, elected in 1938 to replace Shaw, made an effort to strengthen the office of the mayor and to exercise authority over departments. Complaining that department heads bypassed the mayor to go to the city council, he sought to create a City Administrative Officer in 1945. The council refused to support his proposal. In the same year, he instructed department heads to report to the council only through the mayor.

Finally, Bowron succeeded in getting a measure placed on the 1951 ballot to create a City Administrative Officer to bring executive direction to the budget. The CAO plan won a narrow victory, with less than 52 percent of the vote. Bowron appointed Sam Leask, Jr., as the first CAO (Rigby 1974).

The new CAO reported both to the mayor and the council, but for the first time made it possible for the mayor to set priorities for departments. When Bowron was defeated in 1953 by Norris Poulson, Leask continued as CAO. Leask soon found himself joining with the mayor to try to rein in the extraordinarily powerful chief of police, William Parker.

Within the charter lay one of the city's greatest democratic problems: the difficulty of developing civilian oversight over the police department. The LAPD joined the ranks of the great semiautonomous local bureaucracies (along with the already established Department of Water and Power) in 1950, with the appointment of the new chief, William Parker. The role Parker attained fit well within the entreprenurial model of bureaucratic autonomy.

A divided Police Commission appointed Parker after the sudden death of a police commissioner (Cannon 1997). Parker took over a department that had an early, often overlooked history of innovative professionalism (Woods 1973; Cannon 1997) but had deteriorated into an undisciplined and corrupt organization.

Building on his experience as military police director in postwar Germany, Parker instituted a rigidly hierarchical command operation. He intended to instill pride and discipline into the Los Angeles Police Department (LAPD) while tapping the latest scientific technology. He worked to improve the department's image as a Los Angeles version of the FBI, building close ties to J. Edgar Hoover and Hollywood and particularly to actor Jack Webb of the *Dragnet* series.

As Cannon summarized it (1997), "Parker wanted a department that answered to no one but its chief. He achieved this goal and in the process became a chief who answered to no one." The charter assisted Parker's plan, since it guaranteed him civil service protection. His ability to develop political power through intelligence gathering and intimidation made him nearly untouchable at city hall. Thus it was no small thing for Poulson and Leask to take on Parker in budget discussions. Poulson recalled that in his 1953 campaign he was approached by a plainclothes officer seeking to learn his views of the department and of the chief (Poulson 1966). When Poulson questioned Parker's budget, the chief replied in no uncertain terms that it was none of the mayor's business (Rigby 1974).

Between the Shaw regime and the election of Sam Yorty in 1961, elected officials were not the centerpieces of the power structure of Los Angeles. The downtown business community and the *Times* were very powerful. Government bureaucracies had great autonomy. Neither power relations nor nonpartisanship nor the charter encouraged elected officials to play the role they had developed in New York City and Chicago, with the aid of party machines or strong-mayor charters. Minorities had little representation. The LAPD was undoubtedly the most popular and powerful agency of city government. There were few democratic institutions to play the functional role of party organizations to inform the public and mobilize the voters.

Banfield's field examination of Los Angeles for the study *City Politics* (1963) found weak minority participation and few political organizations to channel the public will. Los Angeles was a great reformed city, but not a particularly democratic one. Its version of conservative reform was deeply constricting.

These institutional structures overlapped with the social culture of individualism that marked Los Angeles. People came to Los Angeles to make a new start, to buy a plot of land, and to own a house. With spectacular weather and constant economic growth, politics could seem irrelevant.

SAM YORTY AND TOM BRADLEY

Two major politicians, Sam Yorty and Tom Bradley, pioneered new roles for elected officials in Los Angeles government. Yet neither could change the formal institutional structures of the city charter.

Yorty was a maverick, former leftist, and one of the city's first *electoral* entrepreneurs. In his 1961 mayoral race, he was opposed by the downtown business establishment, by the state Democratic party he had bolted in anger in the 1950s, and by the Republican party organization (Mayo 1964). The downtown crowd pulled together behind the ailing Poulson and persuaded the reluctant mayor to run for a third term with guarantees that they would take care of the campaign (Mayo 1964).

In the absence of grass-roots political institutions or activist networks beyond the downtown establishment, Yorty pieced together his own electoral organization. Yorty built support from two outsider groups: San Fernando Valley home owners and minority groups in the inner city. He attacked the downtown establishment and the major political parties, both of whom opposed him. He emerged from a crowded field in the nonpartisan primary to face Poulson in the runoff.

For the Valley, Yorty challenged a city recycling plan that required people to separate their trash. For the inner city, he promised to "school" Chief Parker on police misconduct, and he attacked Poulson for not protecting inner city residents from police abuse. When police used excessive force against a group of young minority men in Griffith Park not long before the election, Yorty blasted the LAPD and Poulson (Poulson 1966).

Yorty was devastatingly effective against Poulson. Yorty used the support of a well-known radio personality to reach the voters. When Poulson lost his voice to illness, Yorty frequently challenged the mayor to debate in order to highlight the incumbent's infirmity.

In the runoff election, Yorty shocked the establishment by defeating Poulson. Other than the Shaw regime, modern Los Angeles had never had such a "political" force at city hall, a politician who had faced down the business community and had even challenged Chief Parker. The Yorty-Poulson race marked a transition from an era when business leaders could simply pick the mayor to a new period when effective politicians could chart their own course.

Not long after his inauguration, Yorty's promise to school Parker went by the wayside, when Parker showed up at Yorty's office with a bulging briefcase, presumably containing damaging material about the mayor (Bradley interview). As his support for minority interests evaporated, Yorty turned increasingly to a new type of conservative electoral constituency. Built around white non-Jews, especially in the Valley and on the Eastside, and conservative Latinos, Yorty established a hard-edged conservative base that became an enduring part of the Los Angeles political scene (Allen 2000). Yorty had greatly increased the role of the *electoral constituency* as a key player in Los Angeles politics, installing some elements of pluralism in local politics.

As race became a growing issue in Los Angeles in the 1960s, Yorty placed himself firmly on the reactionary side. Race was shaking the comfortable quietudes of Los Angeles government to its very roots. Race led to questions about the accountability of the police and the weakness of elected officials.

THE REINING COMMISSION

Inevitably, Yorty had great trouble with the powerful Los Angeles city council. In the aftermath of the Watts riot, Yorty testified before a skeptical, indeed derisive, U.S. Senate committee about his woeful lack of charter authority. Soon he began to explore charter reform.

In 1966, Yorty appointed a charter reform commission under the leadership of Henry Reining, a dean at the University of Southern California. The Reining Commission worked for two years, and produced the draft of a new city charter.

The Reining Commission's proposals were far-reaching and controversial. They abandoned the existing charter and wrote a new one. They granted much greater authority to the mayor than did the existing charter; instituted a system of elected neighborhood councils with advisory powers; and largely removed citizen commissions as managers of city departments. Under the Reining Commission's charter, the City Administrative Officer would report only to the mayor, not to the mayor and the council.

While Yorty was delighted with the commission's recommendations, the city council was not. Under the leadership of Councilman Ed Edelman, chairman of the Charter and Administrative Code Committee, the council rewrote the Reining draft charter. The CAO's dual reporting role was restored and neighborhood councils were deleted. A section regarding boroughs (community service areas) in the original charter, however, was redrafted by Edelman. The council's revised charter did improve and simplify the charter, removing much unnecessary detail (Herbert 1971).

While the council's charter won widespread elite support, Yorty was tepid at best, and rumored to be opposed (Herbert 1971). The council activated a hornet's nest by adding a provision making it easier for the city government to obtain revenue from the semiautonomous Department of Water and Power (Erie and Ingram 1998). The DWP mobilized its forces and ran a campaign against the new charter. Voters defeated the new charter twice, in 1970 and in a revised version without the DWP provision, in 1971. Thus, the main attempt to comprehensively revise the 1925 charter ended in failure.

The Reining Commission story prefigured much of what was to occur in the later charter battle. The mayor had a new charter in mind; the council did not agree. The Reining draft altered the CAO to report only to the mayor, not to the mayor and council.

Former CAO Sam Leask offered powerful testimony to the council about the importance of the dual reporting relationship, in words that were very similar to those used by CAO Keith Comrie thirty years later to argue against Riordan's similar proposal (Rigby 1974). Some of the players returned for the later engagement. Ed Edelman became a member of the appointed charter commission in 1996, and fellow council committee member John Ferraro played a significant role as president of the city council.

Despite the failure of charter reform in the Yorty years, the Reining experience created a set of lessons for the charter reformers of 1996–99. Those lessons were the need to generate public involvement in the process, to avoid "poison pill" provisions like the DWP funds transfer, and to find a way to get the council to accede to reform or to get around the council's opposition (Los Angeles City Charter Commission 1970). It also hurt that Mayor Yorty provided only desultory support for the revised charter. The mayor would have to be a pillar of any charter reform campaign.

Clearly, any charter reform in Los Angeles would have to find a way around the resistance of the city council to any change in its powers. The council had been the graveyard for most charter reform proposals (Bollens 1963). Without the mayor taking a leadership role, however, there would be little credibility surrounding a governmental reform effort. If a new charter were to recalibrate the balance of power between mayor and council, winning the support of both mayor and council would be a huge political task.

Yorty had considered creating an elected Board of Freeholders to draft a charter that would not have to pass through the council, but the cost of mobilizing a signature campaign was prohibitive (Herbert 1971). The expense was not to deter Richard Riordan from doing just that thirty years later.

With the failure of comprehensive charter reform, Los Angeles adopted a series of piecemeal amendments over the next thirty years. These amendments followed a pattern, which was increasing the authority of elected officials over previously inaccessible bureaucracies and steadily reducing the power of citizen commissions over city departments. Taken a step at a time, the changes did not much arouse the electorate or vested interests. But as a whole, they had a considerable impact in weakening the citizen commission system and undercutting the autonomy of proprietary departments. They also continued the process of expanding the slim 1925 charter into a bulky, confusing mess.

REFORM IN THE BRADLEY YEARS

Although charter reform was stymied again and again in Los Angeles, another route to reform opened with the rise of the Tom Bradley coalition. In 1969, city councilman Tom Bradley challenged Yorty for the mayoralty. Backed by the LAPD, which openly worked for Yorty's reelection, Yorty defeated Bradley with a racist campaign. By 1973, Bradley had returned for a rematch, backed by a highly effective electoral coalition of African Americans and Jews.

The 1969 and 1973 campaigns showed that in the absence of political parties, there was something that could get people out to vote: bitter racial antagonism. The turnout in 1969 was 76 percent of registered voters; in 1973, it was 64 percent.

Bradley's coalition brought a new electoral player to the table. In the absence of stable political institutions, Bradley built his alliances around the Democratic party reform movement and civil rights organizations (Sonenshein 1993). Like Yorty, Bradley brought new political resources and organizations to the electoral arena.

Bradley's coalition of African Americans, liberal Jews, and to a lesser degree Latinos and Asian Americans marked a profound change at city hall, and represented a case of strong minority incorporation. Upon his election, Bradley pursued an agenda that included bringing the LAPD under civilian authority and increasing minority hiring at city hall. He formed an alliance with the powerful growth machine around downtown redevelopment. Bradley had the enthusiastic support both of public employee unions and the private-sector unions (Regalado 1991).

With the backing of this urban regime, Bradley was able to increase the power of elected officials in a manner that had not happened in decades in Los Angeles. He did it without much charter change. In some ways, as a black mayor of a white city, he had to tread cautiously in increasing his formal authority. On police matters it was hard enough to pursue civilian oversight of police shootings, let alone try to end the police chief's civil service protection.

Bradley's ability to increase the authority of elected officials over the government came from the adept use of his political resources, particularly his ability to attract large amounts of federal funds that were passing through the mayor's office (Saltzstein, Sonenshein, and Ostrow 1986), and most of all by his ability to forge an enduring coalition with the members of the city council. Bradley concentrated more on his informal sources of power than his formal levers.

Still, there were continuing issues about how well the charter structured governmental authority. In a departing memorandum, C. Erwin Piper, the CAO under Sam Yorty and for part of Bradley's term, responded to a request by a city councilmember to give his views on Los Angeles government.

In his memo (Piper 1979), the CAO recommended that:

- The Mayor should be designated as the Chief Executive Officer of the City with responsibility for administering its affairs.
- The Mayor shall be the City's chief spokesman and shall designate the City's representatives in all dealings with other governmental agencies, subject to Council approval.
- The Controller should be appointed, not elected.
- The mayor should have appointment power over general managers and commissioners, subject to Council confirmation.
- All commissions, with certain exceptions, will be advisory in nature.

Bradley made several attempts at charter reform, with mixed results. For example, he successfully took on the charter-based pension system in a rough battle with the police and fire unions in the early 1980s (Sonenshein 1993).

In the 1980s Bradley took on the issue of civil service reform. The effort to create an Executive Service for top managers of city departments illustrates how reform can be viewed very differently when it comes from an African American Democratic mayor than when it is later proposed by a white Republican mayor.

In 1978, the city appointed Jack Driscoll as general manager of the personnel department. Driscoll, who moved from the Seattle city government, was the first outsider ever to hold this sensitive position. Driscoll believed that greater flexibility was required in city management. He found that even the best managers in one department had virtually no opportunity to transfer to another department; as a result, they became demoralized at their lack of upward (or, more precisely, horizontal) mobility. He proposed to Bradley that the city establish an Executive Service for top managers.

Driscoll (interview) found that "Tom had to be talked into it":

Tom had an honest distrust of the departments because his experience was that if they had additional flexibility, they might not select a qualified woman or minority for a position. Tom loved the civil service system. He believed it was fair, honorable, and allowed people to work their way up from the bottom of the system. I argued that the changes I proposed would actually broaden opportunities for those people who wanted to work their way up through the system.

Bradley eventually agreed to pursue the Executive Service proposal, and the measure was taken to the city council, which placed it on the ballot for the 1980 election. Driscoll recalled that the "affirmative action community" supported it. Joy Picus, then a member of the city council, spearheaded the political effort. A year before, she had led the successful push to place a measure on the ballot to limit the veterans' bonus in civil service—a change that would obviously benefit women in city employment.

Picus recalled (interview) that the main opposition came from the Department of Water and Power retired executives: "They were the absolute worst; they said it was Chicago style politics, and Mayor Daley. And they had plenty of money." The DWP group had demonstrated its ability to block charter reform with their campaign against the Reining Commission's charter a decade before. Their argument prevailed again, and the measure failed.

The Executive Service plan was placed on the ballot again in 1984, and this time only narrowly lost. Indicating the ideological and racial lines of the measure, the ballot argument for passage was signed by Tom Bradley and the opposition argument by his main adversary in city politics, Police Chief Daryl Gates. The measure passed in the white liberal fifth district, and in the three African American districts, but was heavily opposed in the San Fernando Valley. Reform of the top managerial positions was not to pass until the 1990s, when the measure was championed by Richard Riordan, whose antipathy to city government and conservative philosophy managed to overcome conservative opposition.

By the late 1980s and early 1990s, the dominant political coalition constructed and maintained by Bradley was in serious trouble. Increasing divisions between Jews and African Americans, a financial scandal involving Bradley personally, conflicts over growth, and the impact of immigration were creating severe tensions that the Bradley regime could not easily accommodate.

The decline of the entrepreneurial/progressive growth machine under Tom Bradley was to play an important role in the debate over democratic reform in Los Angeles. In an earlier time, the parameters of a debate over civic democracy might have been set by the *Los Angeles Times,* the Bradley electoral coalition's leaders, the downtown business community, the League of Women Voters, the Chamber of Commerce, major developers, and whatever other groups (such as labor) could form alliances with the growth machine. But in the post-Bradley era, there was less unity among the local leadership.

These divisions made it hard to form a civic coalition. The rise of Latinos and Asian Americans further altered the debate from the two-sided biracialism of Tom Bradley to a far more complex multipolar debate.

Politics in black and white had defined Los Angeles during the Bradley era, and had set the parameters for ideological debate; that was changing.

In 1991, a restive city council passed an ordinance to place a charter amendment on the ballot to allow the council to overturn and redo decisions by city commissions. Aimed at the Harbor Commission, known for its imperious ways with the council, the measure was anathema to Bradley and represented an unusual challenge to his authority. He intended to veto it, but accidentally signed it. A court refused Bradley's challenge to the measure, and it went on the ballot and passed overwhelmingly. Once in the charter, it became known by its ballot designation: Prop. 5 (as in, "The council Prop. 5'ed that decision.")

The battle over Proposition 5 revealed that a pillar of the Bradley governing regime—his close alliance with the powerful city council—was eroding. A serious financial scandal involving Bradley in 1988 and his close reelection in 1989 made Bradley vulnerable. Further battles took place over term limits, with Bradley using unaccustomedly strong language against the council (see next chapter).

The civil disorder of 1992 marked the end of the Bradley era. Rioters burned the offices of the Watts Labor Community Action Center, which Bradley had helped create. His ability to hold the city together was in doubt. The changing demographics of South Central Los Angeles had created not a melting pot, but a tinder box.

As Bradley's overall program began to erode, the consensus solution to Los Angeles's governing problems that he had provided gave way to a more free-form, less structured situation of competition among the city's forces. It also provided greater energy for the belief in *structural* solutions than had been the view during the years of Bradley's smoothly informal leadership.

In 1989, a citizens' commission chaired by Geoffrey Cowan developed a set of recommendations for an ethics commission in city government. The Cowan Commission issued its report in November 1989 and voters passed a ballot measure on ethics in 1990. The executive director of the commission, Xandra Kayden, wrote a report, "Ethics Commission Call for Charter Reform," that was issued separately by the commission some months later.

Kayden had arrived in Los Angeles not long before from the East Coast, and concluded (interview) that "more than ethics reform, the city needed a better governing structure to respond to a more diverse population than the homogenous white community of the 1925 charter." Kayden's report (Commission to Draft Code of Ethics 1990) set out the main charter issues as the balance of power between mayor and council: the role of citizen commissions, nonpartisan elections, salaries of elected officials, and term limits.

Mayor Bradley and council president John Ferraro expressed strong support for a process of charter reform. Kayden (interview) argued to the mayor's staff that "a reform charter could be his legacy." Councilmember Ruth Galanter joined the discussions and introduced a council motion to create a Charter Study Group. This group in turn recommended the appointment of a twenty-one member citizens' commission on charter reform with a significant budget. However, budget constraints and the pressure of the city's response to the 1992 riots eventually took charter reform off the front burner at the end of the Bradley era.

But a different type of charter reform was still to come in the Bradley period. Bradley had one big task left to achieve, and that was reform of the unaccountable police bureaucracy. And in this endeavor, Bradley took on the unaccustomed role of charter reformer.

On March 4, 1991, a videotape was seen worldwide, showing the police beating of black motorist Rodney King. The King beating finished what Bradley had started decades before—the move to break the stranglehold of the LAPD on the local political system. Bradley and Police Chief Daryl Gates entered into their final battle. Bradley won on the reform issue. And the police reform issue proved that reform could be a mobilizing issue for liberal and minority forces.

After the King beating, Gates asked some associates to form a commission to examine police practices. Bradley immediately overshadowed Gates by selecting Warren Christopher, the city's leading private citizen, to head a commission. Christopher effected a merger between the two commissions and the historic Christopher Commission was under way. After dramatic hearings and extensive research, the Christopher Commission issued its report with an array of recommendations for charter and policy changes. In contentious meetings of the city council, most of the Commission's recommendations were placed on the ballot as Proposition F.

Prop. F made crucial changes in the charter, removing civil service protection for the chief and strengthening the civilian leadership of the police commission. These measures were by far the strongest charter changes in the direction of civilian authority over the LAPD. Prop. F passed in June 1992, powered by the remaining pieces of the tattered Bradley coalition. It was perhaps the single most important charter change since the 1925 charter. By removing the civil service protection of the most visible general manager, the chief of police, it also laid the groundwork for the larger civil service reforms that were passed in 1995 and 1996 under Bradley's successor, Richard Riordan.

PROBLEMS OF LOS ANGELES GOVERNMENT

The enduring challenges of Los Angeles government have been the fragmented power of elected officials, the incentives to informal elite rule, and the lack of institutions to link the public to the government. Political interest has been low, except in rare cases, and the city has had few avenues for public participation.

Nonpartisanship has been firmly rooted in Los Angeles. When Charles Adrian developed a typology of nonpartisan elections in 1957 (Adrian 1959) he found that Los Angeles was in the category of cities that were nonpartisan in reality as well as in form, but had some informal slating organizations.

Yet, Los Angeles government has also been a magnificent spectacle, building a water system from nothing, growing while other cities were declining, and generating historic electoral coalitions. The unfinished work of Los Angeles was to strengthen the leadership role of the mayor, rationalize and streamline government lines of authority, and forge institutional links between the public and the government.

The flaws in Los Angeles government, especially its dispersal of political authority and its lack of participatory structures, had long agitated good-government reformers. The dream of a revamped city charter with new structures of authority and new lines of participation had died from city hall resistance and the lack of a majority coalition in the electorate in favor of massive change. The good-government argument for reform sat off the coast, awaiting a political storm to carry it to shore. It was not until the 1990s, with the rise of secession and a reform-oriented mayor, that the winds blew so strongly that good government reform could at last succeed.

There was certainly a body of ideas about how to reform Los Angeles government. While there was disagreement on the details, the broad outlines of reform were apparent: an enhanced role for the mayor in managing the government, greater control by elected officials over departments and citizen commissions, and provisions for democratic participation.

Los Angeles also had an identifiable reform constituency, even if it seemed insufficient to overcome the institutional inertia and resistance to change. An educated, generally liberal, disproportionately Jewish bloc of voters and activists located on the Westside of Los Angeles supported reform in various permutations. With no obvious connection to their self-interest, these well-informed, empowered residents of Los Angeles were drawn to the substance and symbolism of governmental reform. Reform had been a factor in their attachment to Tom Bradley. They voted for various measures to increase mayoral authority over department general managers. They strongly backed police reform.

Table 2 below summarizes support in selected city council districts for key structural reforms on the Los Angeles ballot between 1980 and 1992. Reform's base was strongest in the liberal fifth district, and weakest in the white conservative twelfth district.

A symbol of this liberal reform constituency was city councilmember Marvin Braude. Elected to represent the affluent Westside eleventh district

TABLE 2
Vote on Key Reform Measures by Council District, 1980–1996

	Council District			
	5 *White Liberal*	8 *African American*	11 *White Liberal*	12 *White Conservative*
1980 Executive Service	67.8	30.8	59.8	47.5
1984 Executive Service	55.6	67.5	48.9	36.1
1990 Ethics Commission	62.7	52.7	60.4	49.9
1992 Police Reform	71.1	74.2	66.3	46.3
1995 General Manager	69.0	54.5	72.2	58.6

in 1965, the independently wealthy Braude became a pillar of the reform community. Known as a strong advocate of ethics laws, Braude also pursued and supported charter reform.

Voters in the fifth and eleventh council districts, located principally on the Westside (map 2), were particularly valuable to reform efforts because of their high civic involvement. City commissioners came in unusual proportions from these two districts. There were active attorneys with ties to city hall. Most of all, the voting registration and turnout levels in these two districts made them blue-chip allies for any reform effort. In a normal city election, the fifth district would cast five times as many votes as the Latino first district on the Eastside. The eleventh was rarely far behind.

The Los Angeles reform constituency bore a resemblance to similar blocs in New York City and Chicago. The "Manhattan" crowd in New York City, particularly in the upper eastside "Silk Stocking" district, was a leading base for reform. In Chicago, former Mayor Richard J. Daley used to refer to such areas as "the newspaper wards," meaning the areas around the Lake Shore where newspaper endorsements would be influential. But in Los Angeles, this block was both relatively larger and more central to the city's politics than in New York City and Chicago.

Whoever won this reform constituency—whether Richard Riordan, the secessionists, or liberal forces in the city council—would have an immense advantage in battles over governmental reform. Yet by itself this reform base would never be enough to make reform happen.

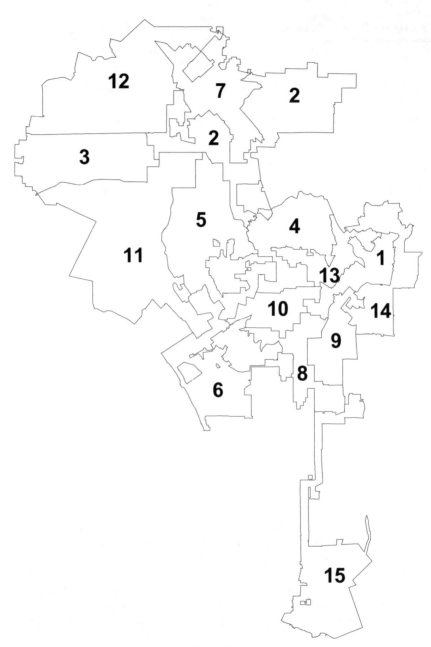

Map 2. City Council Districts, 1992–2002

THE NEW IMMIGRATION AND THE ETHNIC TRANSFORMATION
  OF LOS ANGELES, 1960–2000

Reform would take place in an atmosphere shaped by immigration and diversity. The renewed debate over charter reform took place in a city that received hundreds of thousands of immigrants after the 1960s, mostly from Mexico, Central America, and East Asia, but also including large groups from countries as diverse as Russia, Ethiopia, and Iran. The new diversity in Los Angeles is part of a broader urban restructuring that has transformed the region's economy and created a sprawling global city-region (Soja 2000). It has also shaken up existing political alliances and provided the basis for new reform coalitions to confront urgent social and economic problems.

In 1960, Los Angeles was still an Anglo city. The 1960 Census recorded a population that was 73 percent white, 14 percent black, 11 percent Latino, and 3 percent Asian. By 2000, a remarkable ethnic transformation had taken place. The city's population was now 47 percent Latino. The Asian population had increased to 369,000, representing 10 percent of the city's population (table 3).

On the other hand, the traditional white and black communities were in decline. Migration to peripheral suburbs and out of the region altogether resulted in a sharp decline of the city's white population from 1.8 million in 1960 to 1.1 million in 2000. The black population, which grew to a peak of 17 percent of the city's population in 1980 represented only 11 percent of the city's population in 2000 (map 3).

Eastside neighborhoods such as Boyle Heights and Lincoln Heights were the traditional hearts of the city's Latino population. After the 1960s, Latinos moved into neighborhoods south and west of downtown. Immediately west of downtown, Latinos settled in rental apartments in the Pico-Union and Westlake areas, neighborhoods with some of the highest population densities in the city. South of downtown, they moved into neighborhoods once dominated by African Americans, especially east of the Harbor Freeway. The Latino community in the harbor area has also grown considerably.

Latinos have greatly increased their presence in the San Fernando Valley, where they are the majority population in much of the eastern half of the valley. The East Valley was the fastest growing portion of Los Angeles in the 1990s; the traditional Latino Eastside was the slowest.

As a result of the new migration, the Asian American community in the City of Los Angeles increased by a factor of five between 1960 and 2000. Most new Asian immigrants are Korean, Chinese (mainly from Taiwan and Hong Kong), and Southeast Asian. While the largest Asian communities in the region are outside of the City of Los Angeles (e.g., the Chinese

TABLE 3
Demographic Shifts in Los Angeles, 1960–2000

Ethnicity*	1960 Population	1960 Percentage	1980 Population	1980 Percentage	2000 Population	2000 Percentage
Latino	260,389	10.5	816,076	27.5	1,719,073	46.5
White	1,801,419	72.7	1,419,413	47.8	1,099,188	29.7
Black	334,916	13.5	505,210	17.0	415,195	11.2
Asian	75,980	3.1	196,017	6.6	369,254	10.0
Total Population	2,479,015		2,966,850		3,694,820	

Source: US Census Bureau, Census of Population and Housing, selected years.

*The Latino population was based on the Spanish Surname population (1960), Spanish Origin population (1980), and Latino population (2000). The white population in 1960 and 1980 was calculated by subtracting the Spanish Surname and Spanish Origin populations, respectively, from the White population. The white population in 2000 was based on the census for Non-Hispanic Whites. The Asian American population was based on Persons of Asian Ancestry in 1960.

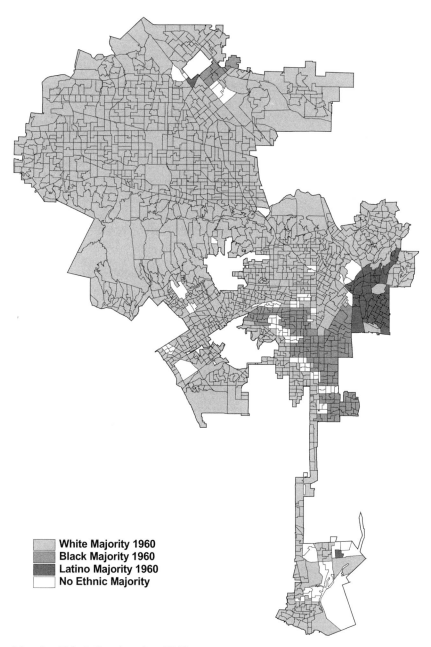

White Majority 1960
Black Majority 1960
Latino Majority 1960
No Ethnic Majority

Map 3a. Ethnic Los Angeles, 1960

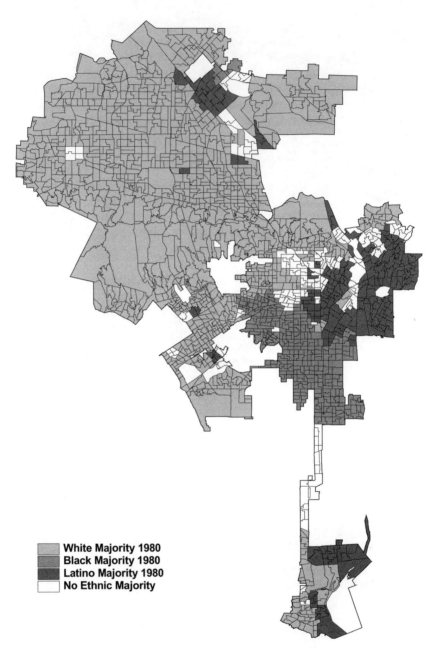

White Majority 1980
Black Majority 1980
Latino Majority 1980
No Ethnic Majority

Map 3b. Ethnic Los Angeles, 1980

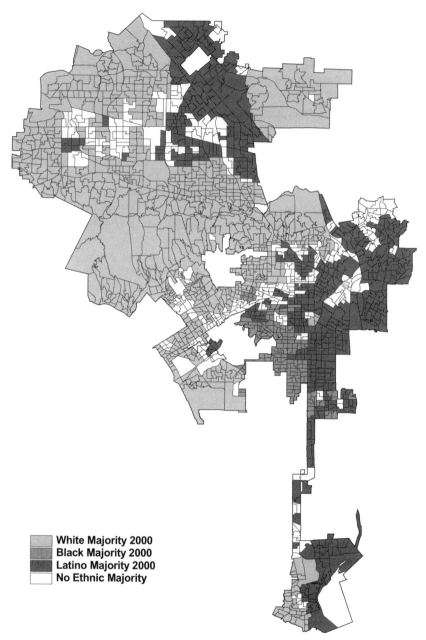

White Majority 2000
Black Majority 2000
Latino Majority 2000
No Ethnic Majority

Map 3c. Ethnic Los Angeles, 2000

ethnoburbs of the San Gabriel Valley or Little Saigon in Orange County),
many Asians—especially Koreans and Filipinos—have moved into neighborhoods west of downtown and in the San Fernando Valley (Cheng and
Yang 1996; Li 1998).

By 2000, whites had vacated much of the central core and eastern San
Fernando Valley. Spatially, whites now dominate the western half of the
city, in four distinct areas: the western San Fernando Valley, the Santa
Monica Mountains, West Los Angeles (including communities such as
Palms, Mar Vista, and Rancho Park), and Westchester. In the central core,
the remaining white majority communities are found in the Hollywood
Hills, the Hancock Park–Fairfax areas, and Silver Lake.

The new diversity and changing ethnic geography of Los Angeles have
reconfigured the map of urban politics. Three characteristics of the city's
political demography stand out: (1) the decline of a black population
struggling to hold on to political gains made during the civil rights era and
the Bradley administration; (2) a Hispanic community whose political
clout is catching up to its rapidly growing population; and (3) the consolidation of a diverse white electorate in the western half of the city (map 4).
Map 4 presents precincts with concentrations of Jewish (20 percent or
more), white Republican (35 percent or more Republican, 70 percent or
more white), and Latino (50 percent or more) registered voters.

The westward shift of the black community has created black majorities
in unincorporated county districts such as View Park–Windsor Hills and
West Compton, but weakened their political power in the City of Los Angeles. At the same time, African Americans remain an important constituency in building political coalitions in the city.

Recent immigrants are less likely to register to vote and participate in
elections than are other residents. As a result, the number of precincts in
which Latinos are a majority of registered voters is significantly smaller
than the Latino majority precincts based on total population. The electoral
strength of Latinos is lagging behind their demographic presence, a situation that will change in the near future with continuing mobilization of
the Hispanic community. In the 2001 Los Angeles mayoral election,
Latinos cast 22 percent of all votes compared to only 10 percent in 1993
(*Los Angeles Times* Poll 2001).

There is considerable ethnic and ideological diversity within the white
population. For example, the western San Fernando Valley is predomi-
nantly conservative white Republican territory, as are portions of Westchester. In between, the Santa Monica Mountains and West Los Angeles
areas are home to a high concentration of politically mobilized, liberal
whites, many of whom are Jewish. In 1993, Jews in Los Angeles were
nearly twice as likely as non-Jewish whites to call themselves Democrats
and to hold racially liberal views (Sonenshein and Valentino 2000).

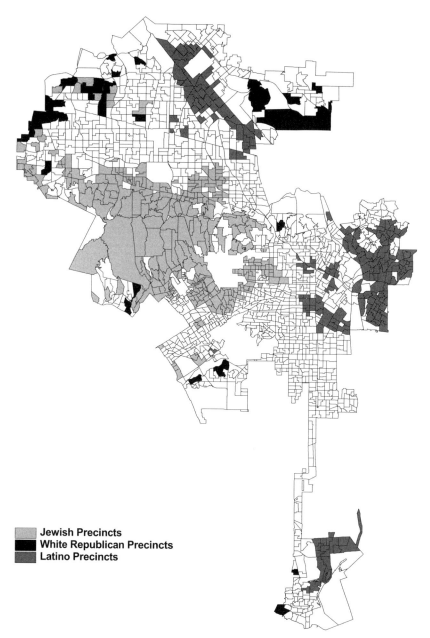

Map 4. Political Demographics, City of Los Angeles, 2000

The economic and ethnic restructuring of Los Angeles has created major challenges for urban governance, while at the same time undermining and reconfiguring political constituencies and ethnic coalitions. Rocco (1996) identifies three political challenges facing a diverse metropolis: (1) coping with economic inequality and the growth of an increasingly Latino working poor population; (2) confronting racial and ethnic hostility; and (3) creating a new sense of community linking the city's diverse ethnic groups for a common purpose. While these challenges are daunting, Scott (1998) argues that the current era "offers many new and potentially progressive opportunities for political devolution to the regions, and to many new kinds of political engagement" (155).

The challenges of urban governance will be confronted (or avoided) through the process of urban politics, which will shape the future development of the city. How could a reform coalition be built uniting segments of the city's diverse population around these social and economic challenges?

How Diversity Affected Reform

The diversity that resulted from immigration to Los Angeles had several powerful effects on the social and political context of institutional reform. Long before immigrants became a political force in Los Angeles, they were a social force that was reshaping communities and constituencies. In South Central Los Angeles, they changed what had been a largely African American area into a diverse community of Latinos and African Americans. In the East Valley, they changed a previously white area into a largely Latino community.

The first political effects of immigration on Los Angeles came through the political *reaction* to immigration. In 1993, immigration played a subtle role in the election of Richard Riordan. Karen Kaufmann (1998) found that among white liberal voters, those who expressed concern about immigration were more likely to support Riordan than those who were not concerned. In 1994, Proposition 187 was placed on the ballot, with the goal of denying public services to undocumented residents. The measure became a litmus test of attitudes toward immigration.

In Los Angeles, the base of support for Proposition 187 was the white Republican region of the San Fernando Valley. The highest vote for Proposition 187 came in the twelfth district in the northwest Valley, where 65 percent of the voters favored it. It won 63 percent in the neighboring third district. The two most liberal white districts, the Westside fifth and Hollywood's thirteenth, each cast 57 percent of their votes against the measure. Latinos were the most opposed. In the first district, 67 percent voted no, in the fourteenth, 65 percent.

So far, the traditional pattern of Los Angeles coalition politics—whites split ideologically and minorities in the liberal camp—was holding up. But the surprise was that in heavily African American districts, the vote on Prop. 187 was split. In the eighth, 51 percent favored the measure; in the ninth, 51 percent and in the tenth, 46 percent. The vote on Proposition 187 raised questions about the future of multiracial liberal coalitions in Los Angeles.

Proposition 187, however, had a second effect. It led to a massive mobilization of Latino residents to become citizens and to register to vote. In so doing, Latinos went from being a cause of political reaction to a potentially valuable coalition partner. As the city's dialogue about race turned increasingly from a black-white focus to the discussion of diversity, immigration became an argument for institutional reform. One of the most widely used statements in the charter reform struggle was a variant of the theme that the 1925 charter was written when Los Angeles was a white, middle-class community, and was therefore in need of updating for a diverse, modern metropolis.

Where would Latinos fit into the emerging debate on municipal reform? Which version of reform (the progovernment or the antigovernment, the liberal or the conservative) would win their support? What would be the connection between the good-government forces and the emerging Latino bloc?

Neither central players in the liberal biracial coalition nor at the head table in white-led alliances, Latinos can be pivotal in the politics of reform. They will be the recruitment targets for coalition builders from the left and from the right. They can potentially tip the scales toward one vision of reform or the other. In Los Angeles, Latinos provided some support for the generally unpopular position of reforming government by expanding the size of the city council. Neither African Americans, who wanted to keep their share of council seats, nor white conservatives, who did not want to pay for more politicians, shared that position. As the Latino voice continues to emerge, new coalition patterns are likely to emerge with them.

With the emergence of Latinos, the types of available coalitions become more complex. Reform coalitions could be built on the liberal model of African Americans, white liberals, and Latinos. Conservative coalitions that begin with conservative and moderate whites might garner support from Latinos. An example is the coalition around a Republican Latino candidate for mayor of Houston in 2001.

But since immigration provides a cross-cutting social challenge that makes Latinos more than simply an additive entrant in existing coalitions, we should consider two other possibilities. Latinos may find themselves opposed to African Americans but allied with liberal whites, as in the coalition against Proposition 187 in 1994 and in Antonio Villaraigosa's campaign for mayor in 2001. African Americans may occasionally find themselves in the same camp as conservative whites, as in the election of James K. Hahn in 2001.

In any case, the struggle for reform in the late 1990s would be a different enterprise in a diverse city shaped by demographic diversity and uncertain coalition lines.

CHAPTER FOUR

Richard Riordan and Conservative Reform

> Los Angeles will never elect an old, rich, white Republican as Mayor.
> —Adviser to mayoral candidate Michael Woo, 1993

WHEN CHARTER reform reappeared in Los Angeles, it came as the city's answer to the calls for secession from the San Fernando Valley, advocated by a Republican, reform-minded businessman-turned-Mayor, Richard Riordan. The calls for structural reform were coming from a conservative leader in response to the alienation of the most conservative part of town.

The movement for secession and Riordan's desire for more formal mayoral authority generated the energy and political strength to revive the long-standing effort at charter reform. There had been increasing talk of charter reform sparked by Bradley and Galanter's Charter Reform Study Group and by a public call issued by the commission that presented a set of ethics reforms in 1990. But none of these efforts could move beyond the good-government world; it was secession, when melded with Riordan's strong desire for more formal authority, that provided the political energy for change.

The rise of Riordan to city hall leadership was part of a broad movement toward moderate or conservative white mayors in the nation's largest cities. New York City was moving in a parallel direction to Los Angeles. In 1993, a white Republican, Rudolph Giuliani, was elected mayor over incumbent African American mayor David Dinkins. Like Riordan, Giuliani built a center-right coalition without black voters, and won a surprising share of the votes of Jews and Latinos (Mollenkopf 1994).

Riordan's election was a signpost in a broad movement that reshaped city politics and government around the demands of largely white middle-class voters in the San Fernando Valley. Marginalized politically in the Bradley years, their comeback washed over into mayoral politics as well as secession movements. Riordan was the chief beneficiary of this movement. These shifts help explain how a white Republican got elected mayor in an increasingly diverse Democratic city.

Riordan was born in 1930 in Flushing, New York, and grew up in New Rochelle, a placid, affluent suburb of New York City. One of the city's most famous residents, Norman Rockwell, drew upon local residents for a number of his portraits (Fiore and Clifford 1993). The child of well-to-do

Irish Catholic parents, Riordan attended Princeton University, where he graduated with a degree in philosophy in 1952. Following service in the U.S. Army in the Korean War, he attended the University of Michigan Law School.

Building on a substantial family inheritance, Riordan made himself a wealthy man by investing in the stock market. At the age of twenty-six, still enrolled in law school, he bought stock in "four obscure, high-risk technology companies . . . and Riordan was halfway to making his first million by his 30th birthday" (Katches 1993a). The company that took off was Syntex Corp, which had marketed the first birth control pills.

When Riordan came to Los Angeles in the 1950s, he went to work for the politically connected law firm O'Melveny and Myers and continued to play the market (Katches 1993a). In 1975, Riordan founded his own law firm, Riordan and McKinzie, and then created a separate firm, Riordan, Freeman, Spogli and Company, to undertake corporate takeovers and restructurings. His big hit came with Convergent Technologies in 1978. In 1984, Riordan bought a large share of Mattel stock financed through Drexel Burnham junk bonds (Katches 1993a).

Riordan was not a businessman in the sense of running a company that made and sold a product. Rather, he was an investor, acquiring control of companies that were either bound to take off or targets for restructuring. Over time, he accumulated a fortune estimated at $100 million and became the owner of one of the city's most famous eateries, the Original Pantry on Figueroa Street. He was a pillar of the downtown establishment, and seemingly an unlikely candidate to become the tribune for Valley discontent.

Through his law and private investment careers, Riordan made one of the pivotal alliances of his career, with longtime Democratic power broker William Wardlaw. As Wardlaw (interview) recalled:

> I did something that was quite unusual at that time, which was to leave a very large, prestigious law firm to become a partner in March of 1984 in Dick Riordan's law firm. And from 1984 to 1988 I represented Dick's leverage buyout entity and I also became the managing partner of his law firm.

Wardlaw helped connect Riordan to the Bradley administration:

> Dick Riordan wanted to get on the Recreation and Parks Commission because he felt that there were vast areas of Los Angeles that were underserved, specifically the Eastside and South Central. And I, on his behalf, approached the Bradley administration, and that is how he became close to Tom Bradley.

In 1982, Riordan was the principal financial donor to Bradley's unsuccessful campaign for governor, providing a loan of $300,000 that was eventually repaid. The loan became an issue in the 1985 Los Angeles mayoral election, when Bradley's opponent, Council President John Ferraro, blasted Bradley for appointing Riordan to a city commission (Clayton 1985).

Riordan became a part of the Bradley administration, serving as president of the Coliseum Commission during tough negotiations with the Raiders football organization, and as a commissioner of Recreation and Parks. Riordan's role flowered during the years when Bradley was most oriented toward the centrist, probusiness stance that marked his two campaigns for governor in 1982 and 1986 (Sonenshein 1993). In 1988, the *Los Angeles Times* ran a profile of Riordan (Brownstein 1988), noting that "at 58, Riordan has become one of the most powerful unknown figures in Los Angeles."

Riordan was quietly accumulating a record of giving money to many Democratic politicians, including members of the Los Angeles city council. While Riordan was closely tied to a number of Democrats, he also paid some dues to his own Republican side. He helped to organize the fundraising for the controversial defeat of liberal State Supreme Court justices in 1986. As Wardlaw noted,

> Riordan, almost like no one else in the history of Los Angeles, was willing to put his own money behind his goals, whether it was to bring about political change by electing individuals, including himself, or whether it was to make structural changes or process changes, like charter reform. And I think when he was willing to show his friends that this was not just him speaking, but he made a personal commitment that allowed him to attract a group of very, very powerful people, very rich people, who shared his goals.

Unlike many millionaires in politics, who place vast sums into one or two of their own elections, Riordan's use of political money was tied to an informal network of campaign professionals and political candidates. A series of interlocking campaign committees funneled Riordan's political money to various causes, consultants, and candidates. As a strategic donor, Riordan developed a high capacity to leverage his influence in the community. The ability to target his personal funds and coordinate the money of others became a major asset during charter reform.

During the decades leading up to his run for mayor, Riordan became one of the city's most powerful private citizens. In a revealing statement, mayoral candidate Joel Wachs described Riordan in the 1993 mayoral campaign as "the biggest special interest in the city" (Katches 1993b). During that time, Riordan developed a powerful network of allies, constructed a well-funded political organization, and set the stage for a mayoral bid. But he did all these things largely outside the public eye, and when he ran for mayor in 1993, he had no visible mass base or public recognition.

Riordan's influence and reputation were further enhanced by his large financial donations to schools. Personally and through the Riordan Foundation, Riordan gave money for literacy and computer programs, and helped raise money from other sources as well. Riordan had dinner with Bradley in 1987 and mentioned his desire to help inner-city schoolchildren. Riordan received a call the next day from Rita Walters, president of the school board and future council adversary of Mayor Riordan. To Walters's joy, Riordan gave $275,000 worth of computers and other materials to the district (Woo 1987).

Riordan established himself as a negotiator and mediator during the Raiders' bitter battles with the city, and on the delicate issue of when and how Daryl Gates would leave as chief of police. He counseled the powerful Cardinal Mahoney, and later joined with media mogul Rupert Murdoch to raise money to build a new cathedral downtown.

As Riordan began to plan his run for mayor, his approach changed from the behind-the-scenes power broker to a more public, critical stance toward the city government. This transition alienated him from some of his allies in government, including Bradley and members of the council. It began to cut off some of his bridges to African Americans. But it also created the potential for a popular base for what had been largely an insider's career. Until that point, there was little evidence that he would emerge as the champion of the Valley and of white moderate and conservative voters alienated by urban liberalism.

Riordan placed his own interest in running for mayor in the context of what he called the breakdown of city leadership following the civil unrest of 1992. To some degree, Bradley had set the stage for Riordan's rise by creating an essentially private-sector response to the civil disorder, Rebuild LA (Jones-Correa 2001). Polling by the *Los Angeles Times* had found that large majorities of Los Angelenos of all races perceived things in the city to be going badly (*Los Angeles Times* Poll 1992). An economic recession, a vast and bloody civil disorder, and strained group relations all created a highly negative climate during the election year.

Before issuing any statements about his potential candidacy, Riordan founded a new civic leadership coalition consciously meant to be a more diverse version of the downtown power elites of earlier times. The new civic group included such African American allies as lawyer Virgil Roberts and community activist Sweet Alice Harris.

Wardlaw, who was Bill Clinton's campaign chairman in California in 1992, recruited Bill Carrick, one of the top political consultants in the Democratic party, to the Riordan camp after the 1993 mayoral primary election. As Carrick recalled (interview):

> [Wardlaw] was always good at reaching out to the other side, to cultivate potential allies. In 1993, for instance, when I was working for [mayoral candidate

Nick] Patsouris against Riordan, Bill and I often had lunch to talk things over. This style helped account for Riordan's ability to get endorsements in the general election from candidates who had opposed him in the primary.

With his ability to raise and leverage funds, Riordan proposed to create a voter initiative to limit all city elected officials to two terms. The measure would appear on the same ballot as the 1993 mayoral primary. A Republican political consultant noted, "What we have is a dysfunctional city government and all this talk of term limits is coming at the height of voter anger" (Orlov 1992a).

Foreshadowing the struggle over charter reform, Riordan "said he decided to put the measure before voters as an initiative because he did not believe the city council would place the measure on the ballot" (Orlov 1992a).

The council first considered placing a competing term-limits measure on the ballot that would apply only to the mayor. That approach drew a blistering response from Mayor Bradley's office, which called the council "hypocritical" (McGreevy 1992a). For different reasons, both Bradley and Riordan were now at odds with the council.

In late December 1992, the council voted to place a full term-limits measure on the ballot, which differed from Riordan's. The council's measure was based on a proposal originally made by Bradley to combine term limits with one of Bradley's defeated charter proposals, the removal of general managers from civil service. It was introduced by Mike Woo, Riordan's mayoral opponent. Woo withdrew his support when the council deleted the general manager change (Orlov 1992b).

One interpretation of Bradley's support for the council proposal is that it was meant to deflate Riordan's attempt to use it to catapult into the mayor's office (McGreevy, 1992b). Bradley was inclined to either run again for mayor or, once he withdrew from the race, to see a successor elected who, like Mike Woo, was part of his coalition.

In language that would reappear in the later charter debate, Riordan blasted the council: "The council was asked three months ago by me to adopt a similar resolution and they refused. Instead, what do they do? They wait to see what the citizens have done and then come up with their own plan to water it down" (Orlov 1992b). The council's measure would have allowed members elected in 1993 to run for two more terms, compared to Riordan's, which would not.

When the ballots were counted in 1993, it was the council's term limits measure that won. There were two lessons from the term-limits struggle that bear on charter reform. First, the council was able to beat back a Riordan measure it disliked, but only by creating a fully credible alternative measure. Second, while Riordan lost the battle when his own measure was beaten, he won the war in that term limits were implemented and he became identified as a reformer with a popular issue.

Even with these considerable assets, Riordan was still a white Republican running for mayor in a Democratic city with a nonwhite majority. How was he able to win?

The social context for Riordan's rise was the violence of 1992; an economic recession; the dislocations brought about by massive immigration; and the decline of the public schools. After the consensus building model of Tom Bradley, Riordan appealed to those who wanted a strong hand to turn things around.

Riordan ran for the mayoralty in 1993 as someone who would make major changes in a city that was experiencing a vast and disabling transition in its economy and politics. These changes were partly induced by global transformations, and their uncertainties were given voice by Riordan's campaign. While diversity was being increasingly celebrated in liberal circles, it was also creating insecurity and discomfort among major portions of the electorate.

By the end of the Bradley administration, the biracial coalition was itself fractured through internal disagreements and the simple passage of time. The 1992 civil disorder projected a sense of an out-of-control community. Even to Jewish voters, long accustomed to voting for Bradley, the socially moderate Riordan offered a reasonable way to slow down the slide toward disorder. He was in tune with some of the more liberal aspects of the Jewish community: prochoice on abortion and in favor of police reform.

As the campaign began, Riordan was virtually unknown to the electorate. The leading candidate was Woo, who seemed ideally suited to succeed Bradley's biracialism with a more youthful multiracialism. If social diversity was the path to a new progressive coalition, Woo was the presumed leader of the pack. Other strong candidates included two Jewish moderates, city councilman Joel Wachs and assemblymember Richard Katz.

Even without a strong African American candidate, racially oriented electoral patterns were likely to continue. Woo was able to mark out territory as the candidate of black voters. The liberal Woo had been the first city politician to call publicly for the resignation of Chief Daryl Gates, a position that endeared him to African Americans.

On the other hand, Riordan had a good chance of winning the votes of white conservatives and Republicans, long at odds with African Americans. With several Democrats in the race, Riordan's base among Republicans gave him a natural constituency for which he had little competition. According to Arnold Steinberg (interview), a Riordan ally and pollster, Riordan began the election campaign with overwhelming support from the 30 percent or so voters who were Republicans. This rock-solid base of support was available to no other candidate in the race, and in a crowded field earned Riordan a spot in the runoff against Woo. Republican votes would not be nearly enough to win a runoff election. Riordan would need to expand beyond his Republican base. If, however, Riordan could make inroads among moderate and even liberal whites and among Latinos, he could afford to lose African Americans.

The issue of race was delicate for both Woo and Riordan. In South Central, Woo called the 1992 violence a rebellion; in other parts of the city, he called it a riot (F. Seigel 1997). On the other side, Riordan found himself in trouble when he did not try to talk a San Fernando Valley voter out of a racist statement about blacks made during a precinct walk by the mayoral candidate.

With his own funds available for the campaign and a strong organization, Riordan developed a slogan that won many votes: "Tough enough to turn LA around." In the climate of the times, it had perfect pitch. Tough enough meant only tough *enough* and no more, but the slogan showed a determination toward change. As he campaigned around the city, Riordan painted a stark portrait of a city in trouble, and presented himself as a businessman-citizen who could bring fresh ideas to a "brain dead" system.

In the primary, Riordan finished first, with Woo in second place. Katz and Wachs had split a strong Jewish vote, and failed to reach the runoff. The final election would pit a conservative, white-led coalition against a liberal, multiracial alliance. In a sense, the contest came down to two visions of urban leadership in the 1990s, one ascendant and the other in decline. The ascendant one was a white-led, business-friendly reinventing-government view critical of the governmental status quo. The other was a more liberal, yet ironically also more status quo, approach built around minority voters, liberals, and labor unions. Riordan was drawing on the same electoral base that had undergirded Yorty's election victories (Allen 2000), while Woo sought to inherit the Bradley coalition of minorities and liberal whites.

In the runoff, Riordan was able to collect endorsements from candidates and political leaders who would never have endorsed Yorty. For example, J. Stanley Sanders, an African American mayoral candidate who had been close to Tom Bradley, backed Riordan, as did powerful Latino councilmember Richard Alatorrre. A number of city councilmembers crossed party lines to support Riordan instead of their colleague Michael Woo, an ironic development in light of the bitter conflicts Riordan was to have with the council after his election. Woo was disliked by a number of the councilmembers. Council president John Ferraro, a moderate Democrat, endorsed Riordan with a slap at his council colleague Woo, referring to him as "a snot-nosed kid."

Woo had considerable support from the liberal forces in Los Angeles, making him seriously competitive. Among councilmembers, he won the backing of those liberal members who were later to be the strongest opponents of Mayor Riordan: Mark Ridley-Thomas, Jackie Goldberg, and Mike Hernandez. By the end of the campaign, Woo had caught up with Riordan, and in an election week poll he was dead even.

Reports of several drunk driving arrests in Riordan's background emerged late in the campaign. The charges nearly derailed him, and caused his backers in the police union to reconsider their endorsement. The union stuck with him, though, and when Riordan's 101-year-old mother died, and he left town on election weekend for her funeral, the steam went out of the campaign and with it went Woo's surge (Fiore and Clifford 1993).

In the runoff election, Riordan defeated Woo by a solid 54 to 46 percent. Not surprisingly, and like both Daley in Chicago and Giuliani in New York City, Riordan received little support from African Africans in either the primary or the runoff elections.

Riordan received only about a third of Latino votes, but broke even among Jewish voters in the runoff. Jewish voters, who represented 19 percent of all voters, had been pillars of the Bradley coalition. Half of Jewish voters found Riordan's approach more appealing than Woo's (*Los Angeles Times* Poll 1993).

Riordan's winning electoral coalition was a mixture of the conservative white middle-class, nervous middle-class Jewish voters, and a minority of Latinos. This new center-right coalition, as in New York City and Chicago, was able to defeat a strong liberal coalition that could command nearly a majority of the vote. As a power broker with long ties to local Democrats, Riordan added a dimension to the Yorty coalition that allowed him access to a range of Democratic allies.

With Riordan's election, the key instigator for charter reform was in place. Those who spoke to Riordan at the time recall that he was talking about charter reform from the beginning—even before secession became a major threat. Civic activist Xandra Kayden (interview) remembered that Riordan spoke to her not long after his election about circumventing council opposition by going directly to the ballot with a reform measure.

Riordan's interest in charter reform to enhance mayoral authority was masked, however, by his early period of good relations with the city council. Riordan had enjoyed substantial support from the largely Democratic council in his mayoral campaign. To many of the more established members of the council, Riordan was a mensch they had dealt with and who they thought could be a successful mayor.

Riordan initially decided to put off charter reform until his second term. Wardlaw recalled that he had to argue against other Riordan allies who wanted to move immediately on charter reform. Wardlaw believed that the mayor needed the council to deliver on his promise of three thousand new police officers, and a battle over formal powers would be too costly while that goal was still short of completion (interview). But the timetable shifted when the winds of secession began to pick up in 1996.

Riordan ultimately alienated council members through his attitude toward them, and they alienated him by asserting their charter powers and their traditional authority over elements of city operations. What started as a lovefest soon turned into a long-running blood feud that animated much of the struggle over charter reform. An early issue was a reorganization plan that Riordan submitted with the 1994–95 budget. Deputy Mayor William Ouchi, a management professor on leave from UCLA, prepared a plan to restructure the city government. The approach was pure Riordan, bold in conception, vague in details, with a take-it-or-leave-it approach that was sure to anger the council. The council's response was pure council, burying the reorganization plan procedurally without bringing it to a vote.

The mayor wanted to reform government, but expected the council to fill in the blanks at the same time that he derided their influence. The council saw itself as the people's representatives, but instead of pursuing a public debate and building a constituency for its position, used its formal powers to simply bury the issue.

These battles reflected the unusual personal style that Riordan brought to city hall. Riordan saw himself as a negotiator and he kept his eye on his goal, but he was no coalition builder. Nor was he one to count votes on the council.

George Kieffer, an attorney and later chair of the Appointed Charter Reform Commission, had an introduction to Riordan's unusual business style several years before charter reform during complex negotiations involving rights of way for railroads:

> He had no patience for sitting at the table and going through a negotiating process. He had little grasp of the details of what the negotiation was about, and he often seemed to undercut his own client. The two things I saw about Riordan at that time was he was brilliant, way ahead of the rest of us, in his ability to project what the deal was, but was very limited in his ability to assess all these interest groups around the table, how to get them to where the deal was. (interview)

In governing style, Riordan was the mirror image of Bradley. Bradley loved the city government, in which he had worked for his whole professional career. He was a coalition builder who spent little time complaining about formal authority.

Riordan, by contrast, came from the private sector, and despite his long involvement with Los Angeles government, had little affection for the municipal government, whether its elected officials or its permanent employees. He wanted the sway that a CEO might have in a corporation. Riordan's determination to increase his formal authority often blinded him to his considerable existing powers, not to mention his vast ability to persuade and influence.

One case did a great deal to fracture the ties between mayor and council. In 1996, Riordan's counsel and close ally Michael Keeley presented information on the city's legal position to a legal adversary of the city.

Keeley's action created an uproar at city hall, and city attorney James K. Hahn publicly stated his refusal to have any professional contact with Keeley (Wilgoren 1996). Eventually Keeley resigned.

On a less dramatic level, Riordan outraged many government officials by hiring private consultants to explore policy and legal aspects of the city government, signaling his distrust of the council and of the city bureaucracy. The Keeley case signified Riordan's distrust of the city attorney's advice, and his belief that the mayor's office needed to keep its own legal options open.

Even a better coalition builder than Riordan might have found the climate daunting. When Riordan came into office, he both profited from and was buffeted by a more pluralistic set of forces than Bradley. Instead of a united growth machine, the city was dominated by newly assertive labor unions, a growing secession movement, active neighborhood groups able to block growth initiatives, and a community drastically reshaped by global forces and massive immigration. These changing forces fractured Bradley's coalition and made Riordan's coalition possible, but they also made it more difficult to build a stable dominant political coalition. Los Angeles was becoming more democratic and less manageable at the same time.

Even so, stable patterns developed in the Riordan era that were to have a great influence on the charter reform process. Riordan's coalition, while not as deep as Bradley's, was a politically effective, relatively stable confluence of political and economic forces. It was the Riordan coalition that set in motion the process of charter reform, but, consistent with Mollenkopf's view of urban power (1992), Riordan could not completely control the debate in the face of effective political actions by other members of the community.

Riordan had a steady and growing electoral base from which he could negotiate and bargain (two of his favorite activities). He was extremely popular in the San Fernando Valley. The secession movement that grew even stronger during Riordan's mayoralty was to Riordan what the Black Power movement had been to Bradley. Each was a radical view emanating from the political leader's core constituency, which would both empower the leader to deliver moderate change but place pressure on the leader as well.

Riordan's electoral coalition was bolstered by at first moderate and later enthusiastic support from the Westside white community, with its strong Jewish presence. Riordan was the first Republican politician in years to make any inroads at all into the Westside, heavily Democratic community. As a Westsider himself, living in a mansion in Brentwood, Riordan was much closer to the sophisticated Westside *culture* than Yorty had been. He was pro-choice on abortion, pro–gay rights, and a supporter of public education.

Like other white moderate mayors of the 1990s, Riordan managed to forge ties to the probusiness scholars and thinkers who shape ideas in public policy. The Milken Foundation, where one of the first charter reform conferences was held in January 1997, was an example of an institution from which Riordan was able to draw on outside expertise to advance his reform agenda.

Finegold (1995a, b) has shown that the success of progressive politics often depends on the linkage between working-class and minority voters on the one hand and the "expert" classes on the other. Riordan, like Giuliani and Daley, appealed to the expert group who sought to design new policies for city government, and moved the flag of reform leadership out of the hands of the liberal community.

In short, to liberal and moderate whites on the Westside, Riordan was no more frightening politically than Nelson Rockefeller had been to Jewish voters in New York State in the 1960s. One could be a registered Democrat, vote Democratic in every election, and still vote for Richard Riordan. Riordan's closest political advisers were Clinton Democrats, Bill Wardlaw and Bill Carrick, further cementing his ties to mainstream Los Angeles Democrats. In fact, when President Bill Clinton endorsed Woo in the mayoral race, he went out of his way to praise Riordan as well. As mayor, Riordan forged close ties to the Clinton administration, to the point of angering congressional Republicans. In 1994, he endorsed Democrat Dianne Feinstein for the U.S. Senate, a step comparable to Giuliani's endorsement of Democratic governor Mario Cuomo for reelection in the same year.

Jewish voters in Los Angeles remained Democrats, but to the extent that their fears of crime and disorder made them suspicious of some forms of liberalism, Riordan was a more than comfortable alternative. As Steven Windmueller, a leader in the Jewish community, described it: "Riordan was right where Jews were. He spoke directly to their concerns about the city falling apart" (interview).

Riordan was able to drive a wedge between African Americans and Latinos. He was soon able to appeal to some degree over the heads of Latino officeholders to Latino voters. Riordan had close ties to business leaders downtown through his many business and community activities. He had the close support of the *Los Angeles Times*. With his Valley base, he had the backing of the *Daily News*, the sworn journalistic enemy of the *Times*. He was close to the Cardinal, whom he had served as legal adviser.

Riordan became the vehicle for a temporary resurgence of business as a powerful force in city politics. His organizational ties to wealthy individuals and business corporations gave him a way to multiply his own resources. Unlike the puppet mayors of an earlier time manipulated by business leaders, however, Riordan was their leader and strategist. With their help, he revived and expanded various civic projects such as Disney Hall, renovations of the public library, and others.

His allies included developer Eli Broad and global capitalist and media mogul Rupert Murdoch. He maintained close relations with Valley business leaders, including David Fleming and Bert Boeckmann. Valley and downtown business leaders were much alienated from each other, and Riordan was a bridge between them. Riordan became a means by which these business leaders could collectively wield influence, although he was very much the glue holding them together.

In addition, Riordan had cultivated private-sector labor unions, and in particular the head of the County Federation of Labor, Miguel Contreras. The significance of this connection was more than personal. A probusiness mayor would draw support from construction unions and other private-sector unions. In fact, Riordan later became a key supporter of the janitors' union in its labor actions against hotels. This labor support helped Riordan counterbalance the places where he was politically weak, namely, the public-sector unions representing city and county employees.

Riordan had plenty of well-organized opponents. The most effective opposition to the Riordan coalition came from city employee unions. Increasingly powerful at city hall, where they had managed to supplant the business elite as the main force councilmembers feared, city unions were knowledgeable and dedicated. Riordan's problems with city labor helped explain his problems with the city council. Labor adviser Mark Siegel noted:

> City employee unions have always distrusted the mayor, since he originally ran on a platform of privatizing city services. In his campaign he characterized city employees as lazy good-for-nothings. So we were very suspicious. (interview)

Julie Butcher, general manager of the Service Employees International Union, Local 347, represented a large bloc of city workers, and she became one of Riordan's most effective adversaries. Butcher remembered that Riordan began his forays into privatization with refuse services. "Fortunately for us, refuse happens to be one of the most credible, best provided city services" (interview). The city employees out-organized Riordan on the ground, and beat him. They calculated that "a refuse route is about the same size as a precinct, and so we went door-to-door many Saturdays. We started in the twelfth council district, in the northwest end of town, and started talking to our customers. The most common question people asked, once they realized that at my door is not only a garbage man, he's *my* garbage man, was, 'Have you eaten?'"

Butcher noted that while Riordan did not count votes on the council, the city employees did: "Riordan never thought he had to count." The council, already sympathetic to labor, blocked Riordan's privatization plan. According to Butcher, this defeat motivated Riordan's group to push charter reform: "My sense is that when the privatization initiatives failed, this led him or his people on his staff toward: 'screw it, we'll just write new rules.'"

In electoral terms, the most solid opposition to the Riordan coalition resided in the African American community. In both 1993 and 1997, African American voters were the main group to vote against Riordan. Riordan never won more than 20 percent of black votes.

African American opposition provided a core base of opposition to Riordan's election and reelection or to such Riordan initiatives as charter reform. It sustained city attorney James Kenneth Hahn, Riordan's prime competitor in city government. With his base in the African American community, Hahn could safely fight with Riordan, and often did. With black support, Hahn defeated Riordan's endorsed candidate for city attorney, Ted Stein, in 1997 and for mayor, Antonio Villaraigosa, in 2001.

Riordan's antipathy to public employees had a particularly negative resonance for African Americans. One of the great achievements of the Bradley coalition was the improvement in the occupational status of blacks in city government employment (Sonenshein 1993). In fact, the existence of a black middle class in Los Angeles was both a cause and a consequence of the Bradley coalition. According to one study (Grant, Oliver, and James 1996), the key black employment niche was the public sector: "About one-fourth of all black men and nearly one-third of black women in the Los Angeles region worked for government in 1970, 1980, and 1990" (398). Over time, the black niche in the public sector grew in importance; it was much more critical in 1990 than in 1970 (398).

Between 1973 and 1991, the African American share of officials and administrators in Los Angeles city hall went from 1.3 percent to 10.5 percent; the black share of professional jobs also doubled (Sonenshein 1993). While Riordan's antigovernment rhetoric played well among white voters, it came across as a direct threat to the interests of the African American community. "Privatization" might sound efficient, but it also directly attacked the base of African American middle-class life in the city. African Americans comprised a significant bloc of membership in city employee unions, already hostile to Riordan.

Riordan's antipathy to African American police chief Willie Williams raised fears in the black community that Riordan was targeting top black officials. These concerns were amplified when Riordan challenged Franklin White, the head of the Metropolitan Transportation Authority. Riordan strongly denied that his motivations were anything but the improvement of government, but he was little trusted among blacks.

Another base of opposition was the progressive white community. Those whites who described themselves as ideologically liberal were more inclined to vote for Woo against Riordan, and to be suspicious of Riordan. Other than the alternative press, such as the *L.A. Weekly,* however, the white left had little organized base from which to mount attacks.

Liberals still constituted a potentially formidable opposition to Riordan, and were quite effective during the charter reform debate. Liberals often attacked Riordan for favoring big developers, but also on ethical grounds. When Riordan caused the firing of Ben Bycel, the executive director of the Ethics Commission, in 1997, he created great resentment among ethics reformers (H. Martin 1997).

Liberals were not without political weapons to use against Riordan. One was that, as with Bradley's coalition, the pieces of the Riordan alliance were not always allied with each other. For example, serious divisions between the Valley and downtown business communities created problems for Riordan. The difference was embodied in the competition between the *Times* and the *Daily News,* whose owners and top staff loathed each other. Partisan, cultural, and ideological divisions between Westside and Valley whites, and Jewish and non-Jewish whites provided openings for opposition.

Riordan's ability to create a political coalition out of the pieces left around after the blowup of the Bradley coalition created the conditions for comprehensive charter reform in Los Angeles. With his vision of reforming city government, Riordan captured the flag of city reform. His successful effort to help reform candidates win election to the Los Angeles Unified School District Board of Education against fierce opposition from the teachers' union solidified his reform credentials.

But with his inattention to details and to the bargaining required to turn ideas into reality, with strong and well-organized opponents, Riordan was certain to face major obstacles to implementing reform. Without some external rationale for change in government rules, he would be unlikely to win any additional authority under the charter.

Riordan's open contempt for the city government's other elected officials and for the bureaucrats who worked at city hall meant that he would have great difficulty creating a coalition linking outsiders and insiders. He would seek a charter that gave him greater formal authority over these other governmental actors. However, this strategy would be certain to narrow the reform coalition. Reforming government without involving government officials is a hard road.

Riordan's personality was an important factor in both his successes and the obstacles he faced. Riordan could be very charming, with a wide open smile and a warm manner. While a poor speaker, he was earnest and sincere in his public statements. In private meetings, he was alternately extremely focused and directive or at other times rambling. His friendships were eclectic, not limited by party or ideology. While seen as not very intellectual, he was an extraordinarily active reader, and possessed the largest private library in Los Angeles. While adopted by the Valley as the tribune of suburban conservatism, he was himself a cosmopolitan and socially liberal resident of Brentwood. His real feeling of being an outsider at city hall hurt him when it was time to get something done, but was well received by the public.

In any case, Riordan was the player with the most single-minded deter-mination to obtain comprehensive revision of the city charter. Riordan had the means and the motive to push charter reform. He had high pop-ularity, likely reelection, personal and allied financial resources that he was able to target effectively, and a strong desire to reform government and in particular to stick it to the city council. Secession was to provide his opportunity.

CHAPTER FIVE

Valley Secession and the Suburban Revolt

> Secession movements in Los Angeles are now a social project of the Right.
>
> —Julie-Anne Boudreau and Roger Keil, "Seceding from Responsibility? Secession Movements in Los Angeles"

THE SECESSION movement in the San Fernando Valley emerged out of a broad conservative political effort linking tax revolts, the battle against school busing, and the defense of the suburban ideal. Secession indirectly breathed life into the struggling good government movement in Los Angeles. Yet because of its conservative identity, secession would have to struggle to win the hearts and minds of the more liberal reform community of Los Angeles.

The San Fernando Valley became a part of Los Angeles during the struggle to bring water to Los Angeles at the turn of the twentieth century. As Los Angeles grew from a small town into a mighty metropolis, the chief engineer of the Department of Water and Power, William Mulholland, quietly facilitated the purchase of land surrounding the fertile Owens Valley in northern California. The city was then able to gain control of the Owens Valley water supply, and built a 223-mile-long aqueduct to transport its flow to Los Angeles (Reisner 1986).

The path of water from the Owens Valley that would allow Los Angeles to prosper passed through the arid San Fernando Valley north of the city. Under prevailing state law, Los Angeles did not have sufficient property value to issue bonds to build the aqueduct. The solution was to use Los Angeles's control of water to encourage annexation of the San Fernando Valley. With the Valley in the city's hands, there would be enough property value to issue bonds to build the aqueduct, and the water could irrigate the Valley as well as the city.

A syndicate of some of the most powerful private leaders of Los Angeles quietly bought up a considerable portion of the San Fernando Valley, blessed by insider knowledge of Mulholland's plan. The *Times*'s owner, Harrison Gray Otis, signed the papers for the group of speculators (Reisner 1993).

Not every community in the Valley was willing to join Los Angeles. Those that had their own water supplies—San Fernando, Burbank, and Glendale—

stayed out of the deal. But the rest of the Valley, in a lopsided vote, agreed to the annexation in a 1915 election. And, as a result, Los Angeles became a great city.

The water arrived in Los Angeles in a spectacular ceremony on November 5, 1913. A great mass of water gushed forth in front of an awed crowd, and Mulholland said, famously, "There it is. Take it." That the mayor of the city, Henry R. Rose, stood by while the city's leading bureaucrat spoke those famous words reinforces the relative standing of bureaucrats and elected officials in early Los Angeles. While the stated purpose of the water project was to allow Los Angeles to grow into a great city, in the short term most of the water went into the irrigation of the San Fernando Valley (Reisner 1986).

Not only did the water allow Los Angeles to grow; it also turned the Valley into a highly successful agricultural community. Yet agricultural uses could not long compete with land development. The huge flatland bordering the Santa Monica Mountains was irresistible to generations of developers. Little by little, the Valley turned from farming to tract homes, and the modern Valley emerged (Roderick 2001b). That Valley became the core of a new political constituency in Los Angeles politics.

World War Two turned the Valley into a suburban community. Returning veterans found that they could buy an inexpensive home, raise a family, send their children to good public schools, and live a suburban lifestyle in the heart of a great city. In so doing, they were replicating the original ideal of the midwesterners who had come to Los Angeles decades before in search of a small-town community in the framework of a great metropolis.

Even as the rest of Los Angeles was becoming more multiethnic and cosmopolitan, the Valley was solidifying its identity as a suburban community with its own traditional values. The Valley was not a place where African Americans felt welcome. Realtors made it difficult for blacks to buy homes outside Pacoima, and the Valley remained largely white and middle class. As Kevin Roderick noted, the pattern was clear by the 1950 census:

> While the black population of Los Angeles County swelled [in 1950] with the sons and daughters of the segregated South drawn to California by jobs and freedoms they had discovered during the war, of 402,538 Valley residents, only 2,654 were black and 2,189 were other nonwhites. Most of those lived in and around Pacoima, the Valley's unofficial minority district. (2001b, 140)

The most affluent whites lived in the western Valley; less affluent whites lived in the eastern part. Jews comprised a greater share of the Valley population from the 1950s on, moving into the southern portion of the Valley. Then, as now, the west valley was the most conservative part of Los Angeles (Roderick 2001b, 147).

The first Valley secession movement began in the 1920s (Hogen-Esch 2001), but became more galvanized in the World War Two era. Mayor Fletcher Bowron sought to respond to Valley pressures for secession by proposing a borough plan, but the council refused to place it on the ballot (Crouch and Dinerman 1963, 167–69).

In 1941, a group of Northridge ranchers petitioned the legislature for a secession bill, but failed (Roderick 2001b: 185). The first formal group, Valleywide Better Government Committee (VBGC), began meeting in the early 1960s. Led by business people, they complained about unfair tax burdens and poor services. In the 1970s, a new progrowth group, the Committee Investigating Valley Independent City/County (CIVICC), was formed. Hal Bernson, later a city councilman, was a key organizer. Home-owner groups were not part of the secession coalition until its most recent incarnation (Hogen-Esch 2001).

With its growing population, the Valley was soon entitled to more seats in the city council, and accommodating the Valley became a serious political problem. Racial politics intruded in 1961, when the council considered moving the biracial tenth district seat that eventually elected Tom Bradley into the Valley so that a white member could hold the seat (Sonenshein 1993).

The Valley burst into city politics in 1961, when a Studio City politician named Sam Yorty scored an upset victory over incumbent mayor Norris Poulson. As a Valley resident himself, and as an upstart against the downtown establishment, Yorty appealed to home-owner resentment against the downtown machine. Yorty sympathized with the Valley's concerns about land use (Hogen-Esch 2001). He found a wonderful issue to exemplify this stand when the council passed a measure to require home owners to separate their garbage. Yorty campaigned against the measure, promising "one can" to each household.

After his election in 1961, in which he drew support both from Valley home owners and from minority voters, Yorty moved to the right. As a former leftist turned conservative, he was much more closely attuned to Valley voters than to South Central Los Angeles. He positioned himself as the antiblack political spokesman in the city, and received a positive response from many Valley voters.

This ideological and racial dividing line defined the bitter 1969 mayoral race between Yorty and Tom Bradley. Using blatant racial appeals to draw a huge turnout from conservative white voters in the Valley, Yorty overcame Bradley's lead in the nonpartisan primary to win the runoff election. While Bradley won their rematch in 1973, it took Bradley many years to win over Valley voters. Only in 1985, in his fourth victory, did Bradley win the most conservative council district in the Valley, the northwestern twelfth district (Sonenshein 1993).

In the 1970s, the Valley became the heart and soul of two movements that brought together political and racial conservatism: the antibusing movement and the campaign for the tax-cutting measure, Proposition 13. When a court-ordered school-busing plan was announced for the Valley, the organization Bustop was formed to lead the opposition. Bustop spearheaded the recall of liberal members of the school board and their replacement by Valley-based Bustop activists Bobbie Fiedler and Roberta Weintraub.

The busing issue challenged the historic liberalism of Los Angeles Jews, especially in the Valley, and cast many into the conservative camp. In 1980 Fiedler upset Democratic congressman James Corman in a close election based on her opposition to school busing. A Jewish activist in Corman's camp noted that "we had the Jewish leaders, but they had the Jewish grass roots" (Sonenshein 1993).

Proposition 13 was another conservative political project whose roots lay in the home-owning Valley. Put together in 1978 by Howard Jarvis and Paul Gann, Proposition 13 galvanized taxpayer opposition to government spending and high property-tax rates. It soared in the Valley's precincts (Sonenshein 1993).

With Los Angeles government firmly in the hands of the moderately liberal Bradley coalition in the 1970s, however, the antibusing and antitax activists were on the outside at city hall. Valley voters represented the main obstacle to Bradley's moderately progressive agenda. Valley voters were the most likely to resist civilian oversight of the police, to vote against tax and bond measures, and in general to carry the banner of conservatism.

In the 1970s, Valley agitation for secession continued. Bradley sought the help of the state legislature, which in 1977 instituted a veto by the Los Angeles city council of any secession ballot measure. The council veto effectively removed the possibility of secession.

The idea of secession simply would not die. The enduring appeal of secession came from many sources: the long-standing political conservatism and racial homogeneity of the Valley, a desire to gain greater control over local land use, and a suburban vision (Hogen-Esch 2001; Purcell 1997). Physical geography also played a role. When viewed as a locale separated by mountains from the remainder of the city, the Valley has a physical and cultural coherence often lacking in Los Angeles (map 5).

THE RISE OF VALLEY VOTE

With Republican Pete Wilson in the governor's office, Valley activists believed that they had a real chance to break the council's veto power. Valley Republican state senator Paula Boland tried and failed to get a secession bill passed. Without help from powerful Democrats, nothing was possible.

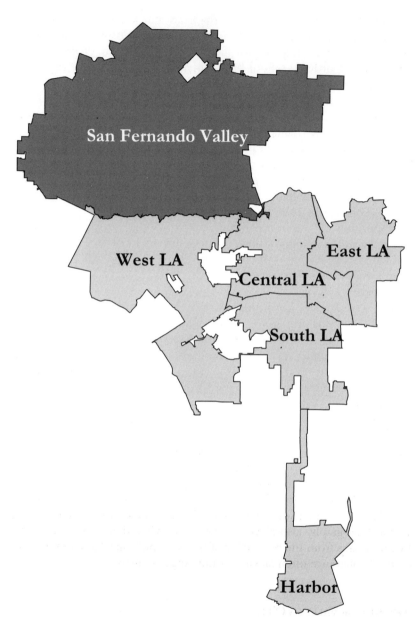

San Fernando Valley

West LA

East LA

Central LA

South LA

Harbor

Map 5. The Valley in the City of Los Angeles

Bob Hertzberg, Speaker of the Assembly and a Valley representative, eventually joined Republican assemblyman Tom McClintock in 1997 to craft new legislation governing "special reorganizations," the euphemism for secession. This bipartisan alliance broke the logjam.

The city of Los Angeles found itself playing catch-up, and worked hard to influence the final legislation. The city's position was that three requirements had to be met before the veto should be withdrawn: (a) the removal of the council veto applied to all cities in California; (b) a majority vote of both the city as a whole and the area seeking separation was required; and (c) secession had no negative fiscal impact on the remaining city (McHenry 2002). These demands were incorporated into the final legislation.

With the city's conditions met, the bill passed the legislature and was signed by Wilson in 1997. The council veto was eliminated. State law now required a showing that the new city would be fiscally viable and that secession would not harm the remaining city. Any fiscal harm would have to be mitigated by payments from the new city to the remaining city. A dual vote system was established. The seceding area would have to vote for secession, and a citywide majority would also have to approve it. Now, for the first time, Valley secessionists had a shot at winning.

In 2000, further legislative action created a set of rules to govern special reorganizations. The process of deciding whether a new city would be fiscally viable and whether mitigation was required was assigned to the Local Agency Formation Commission (LAFCO), a body whose composition would ultimately prove beneficial to secessionists. Made up of elected officials from the county of Los Angeles, small cities within Los Angeles county, and two representatives of the city of Los Angeles, LAFCO provided a majority unsympathetic to the city. Even more disturbing to the city was that the executive officer of LAFCO, Larry Calemine, was a founding member of one of the earlier secession organizations in the Valley.

Why did Democrats at the state level take an active role in facilitating the secession movement, whose base of support lay among Republicans? The answer lies in the complex social and political changes occurring in the Valley. The Valley, once the homogeneous white base of Los Angeles conservatism, was becoming more diverse and Democratic. State Democrats could see that the Valley's future was Democratic.

The largest single demographic change in Los Angeles between 1990 and 2000 was the increase in the Valley's Latino population. Even within the Latino community, this represented a shift. The 2000 census showed that roughly a third of the Valley's residents were foreign born, very close in proportion to the city as a whole. In that decade, the Eastside of Los Angeles, the traditional base of the Latino community, lost population. The fastest growing area of population was the East Valley, principally Latino. By 2003, there would be two Latino council seats in the Valley, and the

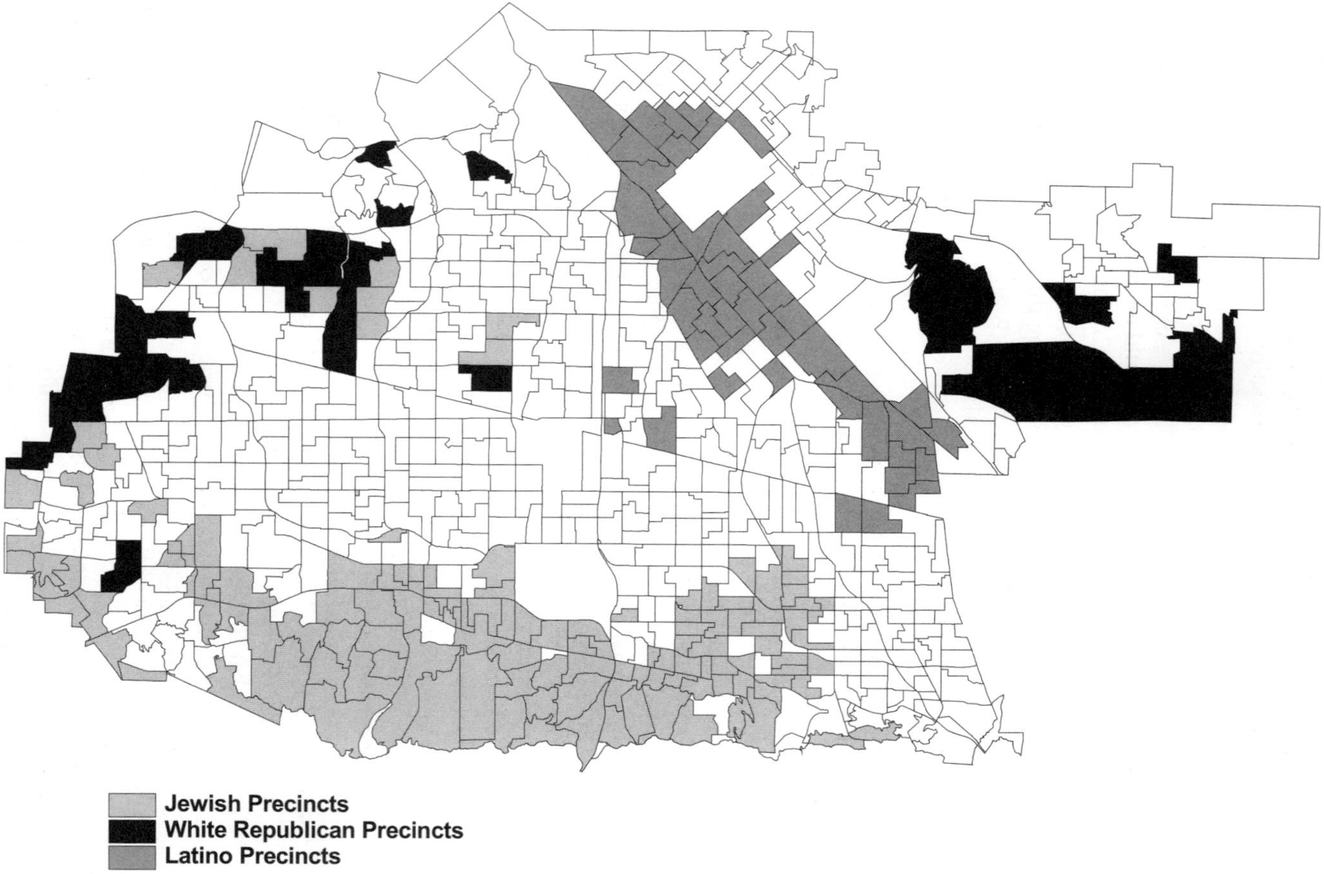

Map 6. Political Demographics, San Fernando Valley, 2000

council president, Alex Padilla, represented one of them. Politically, the Valley was divided among Jews, white Republicans, and Latinos (map 6).

Jews, another key Democratic constituency, were already a major force in the Valley. As early as the 1950s the westward migration of Los Angeles Jews spread over into the south side of the Valley. Today, half of Los Angeles's Jews live in the Valley. They are more likely to be Democrats than are white non-Jews in the Valley, but are more politically moderate than Westside Jews.

As white Republicans continued to decline in population, Jews remained a considerable force in the Valley. In 1993, Republicans had cast more than 30 percent of all votes for mayor; in 2001, they cast only 20 percent. Jews, by contrast, retained their percentage of the vote at roughly 18 percent (*Los Angeles Times* Poll 2001).

The rise of Latinos, the relative importance of Jews among Valley whites, and the declining numbers of Republicans suggested a more Democratic future for the Valley. Already most of the Valley delegation to the Legislature and to Congress were Democrats. The city council delegation was heavily Democratic, Latino or Jewish.

Two Democratic groups, Latinos and Jews, were likely to vie for leadership of the more urban, less conservative San Fernando Valley. Intimations of their possible conflict could be found in an intensely fought campaign: Richard Alarcon's election to the state senate over Richard Katz in 1998. In the 2002 redistricting, the most contentious battles were over the districts with Jewish and Latino populations.

State Democrats could certainly see the opportunity to eventually gain control of a more urbanized Valley. Such an opportunity could also respond to the challenge of term limits for the majority party. With seats changing hands, state party leaders had many mouths to feed, and the possibility of elective seats in the Valley could relieve some of the pressures created by mobile ambition.

Some Valley-based state legislators may have seen easing the path to a secession vote as meeting the demands of their constituents, without necessarily committing themselves to supporting such a secession measure. In fact, backing secession would be a very difficult proposition for state Democrats. Democratic politicians could not openly defy their party colleagues and lead a secession movement. Organized labor was vociferously opposed to secession. Among state Democrats, only Richard Katz, a former legislator, was willing to risk the ire of his peers by taking a key role in secession.

The interest shown by Valley-based state legislators placed Los Angeles city officials at a disadvantage. Without the council veto, a massive Valley vote for secession could outweigh a mild city vote against it. The potential sympathy of LAFCO for the secession forces meant that neutral-sounding fiscal analyses could disfavor Los Angeles.

Even though state Democrats played a key role in facilitating a new secession movement, the leadership of the secession movement that took advantage of bipartisan agreement in Sacramento did not arise from the Democrats. Nor did it draw the best-known conservative names. It reflected instead the peculiar alliance between home-owner associations and business groups that Hogen-Esch (2001) identified as the heart and soul of the new secession movement.

The latest, and by far the most successful incarnation of Valley secession was Valley VOTE. Unlike earlier secession attempts, Valley VOTE brought together two principal, and often opposed, political forces in the Valley: business groups and home-owner associations. Normally at odds over land use, these two groups found themselves allied in a coalition against "outside" control of land use (Hogen-Esch 2001). These strange bedfellows stayed together despite the obvious conflict between slow-growth home owners and progrowth business (Purcell 1997).

The new connection between the home-owner associations and Valley business played a major role in the movement's success. Hogen-Esch (2001) found that despite differences on growth policy, the home-owner groups and the Valley businesspeople shared a "suburban land use vision" that each thought could be better realized with a separate city.

Despite the strength of this alliance, the Valley secession movement was handicapped by a lack of experienced political leadership. The key organizers were Richard Close, president of the Sherman Oaks Homeowners Association, and Jeff Brain, a losing candidate in several city elections. Close and Brain eventually recruited former Democratic assemblyman Richard Katz to their cause.

Missing from the secession campaign were such key Republican politicians as Paula Boland and Bobbie Fiedler. None of the leaders of the Proposition 13 movement or the antibusing movement could be found. Were it not for the vocal, consistent support of the *Daily News,* the secession movement might have had difficulty gaining traction. On a regular basis, headlines in the *Daily News* excoriated the latest misbehavior at city hall, while the editorial page blistered city leaders and called for secession.

On the other hand, the case for secession was for the first time being presented in the context of governmental reform, rather than simply as a set of suburban complaints. Secessionists began to draw on a set of ideas about the proper size of local government to generate an intellectual rationale for a municipal breakup. Many of the ideas came from the world of economics. The hope for secession was that it would become a version of reform, even if an extreme one.

The "public choice" model became an element of the secession argument. The public choice school favors multiple, smaller governmental jurisdictions so that individual "consumers" can have the maximum choice of local government packages of taxes and services. In this view, consumers will create a market equilibrium as those who need fewer services gravitate to low-tax communities, and those who need greater levels of service head toward cities with higher taxes and more services. Those who move to these cities can control land use in the direction that they see fit (Peterson 1981; Oakerson 1999).

Public-choice theorists lean toward market-based reforms of government, such as vouchers and privatization of government services. The natural constituents of the public choice point of view are political conservatives, business leaders, and conservative intellectuals. In one of the most effective public-choice studies, Oakerson (1999) argued that the plethora of independent cities in California is not a problem for governance, but rather a positive setting for urban choices.

On the opposing side, a "collective goods" school argues that the public-choice environment advantages the well-to-do against the poor and working class. Multiple local governments simply encourage those with enough money to escape to other locales, taking their tax dollars with them and leaving the burden of the poor behind. Some argue that it is precisely the desire to avoid social "problems'" that led to large number of municipal incorporations. There are economies of scale for larger governments that make them more useful than imagined (Rusk 1993; Neiman 1999). Collective-goods theorists are drawn to even larger governments, including the regional, arguing that there is still a connection between suburb and city (Pastor, Dreier, Grigsby, and López-Garza 2000).

Collective-goods theorists are more likely to endorse positive government programs rather than market-based solutions, and fear that the fragmentation of land use among communities will make it difficult to achieve equity. The natural constituents of the collective-goods point of view are political liberals, minorities, public employee unions, and city government officials.

Secession provides a different angle on this long-standing debate. Usually, the issue has been the availability of new cities to which people may choose to move. Secession is different because it breaks the city itself up into pieces, without people having to move at all (Hogen-Esch 2001). Thus, it brings the debate about size away from the urban periphery, into the heart of the city itself. It is no longer a question of whether there should be many cities available so that dissatisfied city residents can opt out and move away. It is about whether big cities themselves should even exist.

The role of these ideas in the secession debate is notable in light of Finegold's view about experts (1995a, b); their role was important both for secession and for the right-leaning Riordan administration. A hothouse of ideas was just as valuable to this conservative project as it had been to the earlier, more progressive movements that Finegold studied.

As the driving force of secession, the discontent of white suburban voters merged with doctrines of reinventing and right-sizing government popular in the field of public choice into a neoconservative *vision* of urban governance.

The question was whether this reform vision of independent cities would be able to build a majority coalition in Los Angeles. If secession could be framed as a positive reform, it might weaken the opposition citywide. At the same time, this approach might trap secessionists into a debate over reform, where there were many ideas other than secession available for improving municipal governance.

Early polling on secession was mixed. In 1996, the *Times* conducted a poll on secession among city voters (*Los Angeles Times* Poll 1996). Valley voters and whites were the most likely to say that the quality of life in their communities had gotten worse over the past five years. Opinion on secession was split along racial lines. On the specific question of Valley secession, only 37 percent of all voters favored it. The idea was backed by only 43 percent of Valley voters, 49 percent of whites, 25 percent of blacks, and 27 percent of Latinos.

The *Times* also asked voters if they would support Valley secession if taxes and fees went up as a result. Only 14 percent of voters then favored secession, with 66 percent opposed. Even in the Valley, 68 percent opposed secession in that scenario.

In 1998, a poll of Valley voters was conducted under the auspices of the prosecession CIVICC Foundation. Analyzed by Svorny and Marcal (2000), this poll found majority support for secession in the Valley. According to Svorny and Marcal, blacks were 23 percent more likely to oppose secession than whites, and Latinos 7 percent more. Republicans were 15 percent more likely to support secession than Democrats and 10 percent more likely than independents.

Those who were most likely to support secession were white Republican long-standing residents of the Valley, and those who lived the farthest distance from the civic center of downtown Los Angeles. Of course, those factors are interrrelated, since the twelfth district in the northwest corner of the Valley has long had the largest share of Republicans and white conservatives in the city.

In short, the electoral core of Valley support for secession seemed to grow out of the same tradition as Proposition 13 and the conservative resistance to the Bradley regime. However, support for secession was broader than that definition would make it appear. After all, while most Valley voters are Democrats, many are Jewish and a large minority bloc are Latino, secession still drew strong Valley support in some polls.

Yet it remained a question whether secession as reform would win the backing of traditional reformers on the vote-rich Westside, or if there would be some other type of reform that would energize the civic reform coalition.

To become a citywide majority, the secession movement would have to join together the discontent of the twelfth district with the good-government fervor of the fifth and eleventh districts on the Westside. Conversely, to pass a comprehensive charter reform, long a dream of the civic-minded Westside, the support of the disgruntled Valley would be essential.

Neither would be an easy task. The political history of Los Angeles in the second half of the twentieth century was marked by a vast ideological gap between these two constituencies. The white Westside trended heavily Democratic and backed Tom Bradley. The northwest Valley was the government-in-exile during the Bradley years. The secessionists were profoundly anti–city government; the Westside wanted good government, but was not deeply alienated from the existing government.

The conservative Valley constituency was new to the politics of reform. For decades, they had been the principal obstacle to the passage of reforms that would increase the power of elected officials over the bureaucracy, or that would hold the police department accountable to civilians.

Perhaps reform could cross the borders of the Santa Monica Mountains; perhaps Richard Riordan, a westsider with his electoral base in the northwest Valley, could bridge it. But no one could foretell if it would happen. On previous reform issues, the fifth and eleventh districts almost always voted in favor of reform; the twelfth often voted against it. In 1990, the twelfth was the only one of the fifteen council districts in which the measure to create an ethics commission did not receive a majority.

Secession was likely to influence reform if it acted as an exogenous force on city leaders. It was difficult for city officials to assess just how serious a threat it was. Secession certainly offered a potential reason for city hall to explore governmental reform. Some city leaders felt that secession would never pass a citywide vote; others were very concerned. By itself, therefore, secession was unlikely to be the missing spur to the reform of Los Angeles government.

It took the active intervention of a key actor, Mayor Richard Riordan, to force the city's political leadership to engage in systematic reform. As Bowler, Donovan, and Karp (2002) indicated, the likelihood of reform is dramatically better if significant elite actors within the government see the value of reform. In Steinacker's term (2001), Riordan was the essential "policy entrepreneur." The threat of Riordan's proposals for change combined with the danger posed by secession would ultimately spur a major effort for governmental reform.

CHAPTER SIX

Charter Reform

THE CURE FOR SECESSION?

THE LINK BETWEEN secession and charter reform was made by a Riordan ally in the Valley, David Fleming. A wealthy attorney sympathetic to secession, Fleming argued that a better city charter would help reduce the calls for secession. In so doing, Fleming helped activate a hard-fought debate between competing visions of Los Angeles reform.

Armed with his idea to make charter reform the answer to secession, Fleming called Mike Feuer, the newly elected representative of the affluent and influential fifth district. Feuer's district rested half on the Westside and half in the San Fernando Valley. Like the equally affluent eleventh district, the fifth was therefore precariously balanced between two largely white power centers increasingly at odds with each other. What tied the areas together was the Jewish population, which predominated in the fifth district's two ends.

One of the most liberal members of the council, Feuer was also a dedicated reformer. While fifth-district voters would normally be expected to ally with the progovernment side in policy debates (such as on issuing bonds for education) against the Valley (with its reluctance to pay higher taxes), they also represented an alert and interested constituency in matters of governmental reform. The fifth district provided heavy backing for Proposition F, the 1992 measure to institute police reform.

Feuer and Fleming proposed that the council create an appointed charter commission, whose recommendations would go directly to the voters without passing through the city council. They assumed that the council would revise or block any fundamental charter change. Feuer brought their motion to the Rules and Elections Committee that he chaired. The city attorney argued that the city could not legally create an appointed commission with authority to go directly to the ballot. Reluctantly accepting this view, which the city attorney's office later changed, Feuer modified his motion to have an appointed commission with council review (Feuer interview).

Fleming broke off negotiations at this point and announced that he would pursue creating an *elected* charter reform commission under state law that could take its proposals directly to the ballot. In Mayor Richard Riordan, Fleming had an ally in this approach to charter reform. Xandra

Kayden recalled that she had first met Riordan in 1994 at a fund-raiser for the League of Women Voters: "He put his arm around me and asked, 'Is it true that I can put a charter proposal onto the ballot and get around the city council?'" (interview).

Meanwhile, the city attorney adjusted his opinion to say that it would be possible to have an appointed commission go directly to the ballot. With this new opinion in hand, Feuer worked with Mayor Riordan and council president John Ferraro to craft an agreement. Fleming did not endorse the pact, and continued to pursue an elected commission.

When Feuer brought his proposal to the council floor, he had reason to believe his measure would pass (interview). A deal had been brokered with the two most powerful officeholders in the city government. But he quickly discovered that the council was unwilling to go along. The council's powerful top staffer, chief legislative analyst Ronald Deaton came forward with a motion to be presented by Councilmember Ruth Galanter, calling for an appointed commission subject to council review. This commission would be similar to one envisioned by the Charter Study Group established by Mayor Tom Bradley and Galanter in 1991. The substitute motion passed by a ten-to-three margin.

The three members opposing the Galanter motion represented the three districts whose representatives, two and a half years later, supported the unified charter: Feuer (fifth district), Braude (eleventh district) and Joel Wachs (second district).

The council moved ahead to make its appointments to the commission. Feuer made a last stab at preventing two commissions. With signature-gathering already under way for a ballot measure to create the elected commission, he approached Riordan with a new compromise. On a Thursday, Riordan's office sent a message that the deal was on, but on Friday they took it back. And that was it. The city was now on the path toward two competing commissions, a remarkable development perhaps unique among American cities.

The commissions became the expression of two broad perspectives: the city hall view associated with the remnants of the Bradley coalition and organized labor, and the new suburban insurgents allied with Riordan and his experts and associates. With the reform of city government at stake, the two sides (and others that rotated around them) were in a position to compete for the position of reformer-in-chief, while also protecting and advancing their political interests. The creation of a citywide leadership coalition around charter reform that would bring diverse interests into the same movement seemed out of reach.

In early August, Riordan threw his support behind the elected commission concept. On September 11, Riordan announced that he would boycott the appointed commission by not making any appointments.

From the very first, the council and the mayor were engaged in trench warfare over the organization of the elected commission. The council used legislative and legal tactics to block the formation of the commission.

City attorney James K. Hahn challenged the mayor's plan for an at-large elected commission on the basis of minority vote dilution. Realizing that they could face voting rights problems, Riordan's people tried to change the at-large format to district elections *after* the petition for an elected commission had been filed. They had to go to court to win their case. The council argued that the format could not be changed after the petition had been filed, hoping that an at-large format would ultimately cause the petition to be ruled in violation of the Voting Rights Act. Riordan's argument prevailed in court.

Ironically, winning this particular tactical battle probably helped ensure that Riordan would lose control of the election itself. Riordan's opponents in organized labor would be much stronger in district races than in a city-wide election, where Riordan could gather and concentrate his forces.

Riordan's private fortune allowed him to do something Yorty had considered, but could not afford: to fund a citizen petition drive to get around council opposition. But by December, the mayor's petition drive seemed likely to fall short. The council hoped that the signature requirements would prevent the filing of the petition. The issue raised was whether the signature gatherers had to be Los Angeles residents. Finally, the city clerk certified that the petitions were valid.

In mid-December, a federal judge blasted city officials for blocking the elected commission. Finally, on December 20, a reluctant council approved the mayor's measure for the ballot. But on January 3, the council balked pending clarification of legal issues. Feuer called on the council to put it on the ballot. Finally, a federal judge ordered the measure onto the ballot on January 8.

The council did manage to insist that elections require a majority, rather than a plurality, vote. This change cost the elected commission several months, because runoff elections were inevitable with a majority requirement.

In February, a new controversy arose over the ballot wording of Prop. 8, the measure to create an elected commission. According to advocates of an elected commission, the council did not make clear that the work of such a commission would go directly to the voters (McGreevy 1997a). Riordan lost at first, as a federal judge refused to intervene on his behalf. But ultimately, the council dropped the controversial wording in an agreement with a superior court judge (McGreevy 1997b).

In addition to creating his own commission against severe council opposition, Riordan worked to delegitimize the appointed commission. Having refused to make his appointments to the council commission, he left them to council president John Ferraro to make as acting mayor. He disparaged the appointed commission, and put his sole focus on the elected commission. This tactic was effective in placing the appointed commission at an initial disadvantage. The *Daily News* blistered the council on a regular basis, solidifying its allegiance to Riordan's elected commission. Yet Riordan's opposition also bolstered the council's support for the appointed commission.

In this contentious environment, the appointed commission began its work. Ironically, in an attempt to create a unified commission that would be acceptable to the mayor, a relatively balanced, blue-ribbon commission emerged. The councilmembers made distinguished appointments, even as they tried to derail the process of an elected commission and expressed great skepticism about the need for major charter reform. It was a downtown-oriented group, suited to Riordan's core interest in charter reform: a business-centered focus on increasing mayoral authority. The mayor pulled out of the appointed process even as a commission was created that had many members sympathetic to his positions on mayoral authority.

The appointed commission met for the first time in November 1996. Brought together by the city clerk in a room at the Department of Water and Power, they were handed copies of the city charter and told that they were on their own. The members elected Linda Griego, a businesswoman and former deputy mayor, as temporary chair, and George Kieffer, an attorney, as temporary vice chair. In the methodical manner that characterized their work, the commissioners rejected proposals to immediately get into the substance of charter reform until hiring an executive director. They set to work drafting a mission statement and began a broad search for an executive director. I was hired for that position in the last week of February 1997.

A *Los Angeles Times* Poll (1997) conducted before the spring election showed the appointed commission's challenge. When asked whether voters preferred that the charter be rewritten "by an elected panel that has the power to put changes directly on the ballot" or "by a panel appointed by city officials that can recommend changes to the city council," 54 percent of the voters picked the elected option, and only 19 percent picked the appointed option.

The appointed commission would need to navigate very carefully through the political minefield created by Riordan's battles with the city council. The best, and only, argument for the appointed commission would be that it would take a more serious, thoughtful, and balanced approach than that of an elected panel. That argument would take a sustained effort over a long period of time. The appointed commission's above-the-battle stance eventually became the key to creating the civic coalition that helped bring Riordan to the negotiating table.

Griego chose not to pursue the permanent chairmanship and in April the commissioners selected George Kieffer. Kieffer brought to the commission a highly focused, strategic approach based on his experience in commissions, and outlined in his book *The Strategy of Meetings* (1988). The result was a commission that was quiet and steady, with a minimum of internal conflict.

The appointed commission had a start-up fund of $300,000. By April, Kieffer, commissioner Anton Calleia, and I were before the council asking for funding for the next fiscal year, in the amount of $1.125 million. We received our full funding. The council was pleased with the appointed commission (Greene 1999b). The money came out of the council's own budget, and did not require any mayoral approval.

One of my first assignments was to review the existing charter. I took it home for a weekend of sobering reading. After hundreds of amendments since its initial passage in 1924, the charter was a bewildering document. It was half employee contract, half governance document. There were references to sections that no long existed. There was a mind-numbing level of detail. In the middle of the section on the governance of the Police Department, for instance, there was a sudden detour into the financial details of the police pension system.

The level of detail on city elections was remarkable. On one page, there was an illustration of the correct form to be used to file for candidacy for city office (City of Los Angeles 1925, Section 317). I asked J. Michael Carey, the city clerk, to explain that one. Carey told an illuminating story. Long before Carey became city clerk, a candidate brought a petition to the city clerk on a large roller. The staff had to go out into the hall, unroll the petition and verify the names. The solution to the problem was to amend the charter to specify the form of the petition. Carey's story was indicative of the overuse of the charter as a detailed guide to city government.

While the two sides in the charter debate fought, the appointed commission went about its work, analyzing the charter and identifying problems that needed correcting. For some months, it would be the only commission, and would have a head start over its soon-to-be-created rival, the elected commission.

In addition to addressing its legitimacy problem, the appointed commission had to fill a role its members could never have anticipated and that did not become clear until the very end of the game. With the council battening down the hatches to protect the status quo, the appointed commission had to prove that a moderate alternative to the mayor's plans and to the proposals of the secessionists could improve city governance. It had to present a real alternative to mend the charter, and not end it. But with two commissions in the works, the appointed commission would also have to find a way to merge its work with a radically different elected commission.

The Lines of Charter Conflict

The charter debate divided the city's leaders and communities into two camps: one sympathetic to the Riordan- and Valley-centered view that the city government required fundamental change, against those, centered around organized labor, the remnants of the Bradley coalition, and city hall leaders who saw reform as preserving the long-standing elements of Los Angeles government. It was the conservative side that called for radical change, and the liberal side that sought to keep structural change within moderate bounds. It took two years to develop a charter that could win the support of the bulk of the leaders in both camps, and win popular support.

The "antigovernment" camp grew out of the same forces that elected Riordan in 1993, and operated on a set of reform principles that gave them a decided early edge in the debate. With a city government obviously under siege by secession, a case could be made that major change was needed. As Finegold (1995a, b) has shown in his study of urban reform, the alliance between politicians and "experts" greatly strengthened urban coalitions. That connection was clearly evident in the early success of the fundamental change camp.

With Riordan as the pivotal connection, Valley activists were linked to a series of private foundations, such as the Milken Foundation, and conservative public policy institutes such as the Reason Public Policy Institute. The set of interlocked "public choice" ideas includes a belief that large government is extremely inefficient and unresponsive. Additional concerns were raised about the ability of municipal labor unions to block presumed improvements in efficiency such as contracting for services.

With the electoral victories of Ed Rendell in Philadelphia and Rudolph Giuliani in New York City, this fundamental change network was linked *nationally* to a group of centrist reformers. Often Democrats, in some cases sympathetic to the Clinton administration's Reinventing Government initiative, this group provided further intellectual support and confidence to local reformers.

These groups came together in an early charter reform seminar in January 1997 at the Milken Institute. The fundamental-change side offered a coherent analysis of the problem—big government and an interfering city council—and a set of solutions.

The solutions from the antigovernment side involved major devolution of city authority such as empowered neighborhood councils or boroughs (in David Fleming's formulation). The inside-game solution was greater authority to the mayor and less to the council.

While the secessionists were willing to work with Riordan in the inside game, however, it was never their main concern. They agreed with Riordan that the council was the enemy, but Riordan was far more interested in winning the inside game of mayoral authority than they were, and less interested in the outside game of neighborhood participation. Riordan's business allies also favored more power to the mayor but were mortified by the idea of any neighborhood councils, especially elected ones with decision-making authority over land use. Notwithstanding these internal divisions, the common enemies (the city council, labor) drew a strong alliance together.

On the other side were arrayed a group of forces that seemed initially to be behind the curve on government reform. While the Bradley coalition had its roots in the reform movement of the Democratic party, its leaders now held public office or major private-sector jobs. Bradley himself was not a major structural reformer, except in the area of police reform. He changed the policies and personnel of city government to open up doors to minorities and progressives, but it was only on police and civil service issues that he sought major change in the city charter.

Bradley liked and respected the city government he had served since 1940, first as a police officer and then as councilmember and mayor. His allies had worked in the government as staff members, as elected officials, as union activists, as business leaders, as lobbyists, and as consultants. They were, in essence, the progovernment party in Los Angeles and their main base was downtown. The *Los Angeles Times,* the media power in the city, was torn. It was promayor (whether Bradley or Riordan) but highly suspicious of the secession movement and nervous about neighborhood democracy. It was both part of the system and suspicious of city hall bureaucracy.

There were few ideas or theoretical movements afoot that could anchor the progovernment side in the emerging charter debate. What they did have was considerable leverage over the means of implementing reform (with the council's power to place measures on the ballot), and an understanding and knowledge of the existing system of government. Unlike the fundamental reformers, they knew the charter line by line.

While the connection between these assets and a reform philosophy was not immediately apparent to either side, the debate eventually brought the progovernment side to see its own connection to the local tradition of charter reform. In addition to their desire to protect their own turf, they greatly feared that the antigovernment outsider Riordan would do profound damage to the city government if left to rewrite the charter on his own. It was only when that connection to ideas of reform was made, relatively late in the game, that the dynamics of the battle dramatically changed. At that point, the considerable edge in expertise and accumulated experience began to weigh heavily on the progovernment side.

The key elected official on the progovernment side was city attorney James K. Hahn. Heir to a well-known political family in Los Angeles, Hahn had also inherited his father Kenneth Hahn's massive support in the

African American community. Elected citywide both as city controller and city attorney, Hahn was the highest ranking remnant of the Bradley coalition in city government. With his close ties to the government, he was the main competitor to Riordan's outsider alliance, and a thorn in Riordan's side.

THE ROLE OF LATINOS

A big question was the role of Latinos. Would they join the fundamental-change side headed by Riordan or the progovernment side headed by the city council? As a relatively new entrant onto the center stage of Los Angeles politics, the Latino community could make a considerable difference. They could provide not only numbers, but legitimacy. For Riordan, Latino support could prove that his reform agenda was not only built around the preferences of conservative whites. For the progovernment side, Latino backing could mean a broader rainbow coalition and a bigger alliance than African Americans and organized labor. With Latino numbers rising in the electorate, there was sure to be an impact on the secession and reform coalitions.

In the 1993 mayoral election, 72 percent of all runoff votes were cast by whites, and 84 percent of all votes by either whites or blacks. It was still accurate to describe Los Angeles politics as "politics in black and white." That was to stand as the last such municipal election.

Proposition 187 began the historic mobilization of Latino voters that transformed Los Angeles and California politics. Citizenship applications grew, as did voter registration among Latinos. The newer Latino registrants were younger, poorer, and more Democratic than earlier Latino voters. Roughly one million new Latino voters joined the California electorate in the 1990s (Field Poll 2000).

In Los Angeles, Latino participation in city elections grew steadily. According to *Los Angeles Times* exit polls, Latinos increased from 10 percent of the vote in 1993 to 17 percent in 1997, and then 22 percent in 2001. A Latino candidate was nearly elected mayor in 2001. In addition, the aggressive organizing of Latino immigrant workers brought a new dimension to Latino participation. Miguel Contreras, the secretary-treasurer of the County Federation of Labor, became a major power broker at city hall.

It would remain unknown almost until the end whether Latinos would join one coalition or the other or neither. Few issues in charter reform directly addressed Latinos, with the exception of proposals to increase the size of the city council. Latino voters would be key to a close vote on the charter, and the large number of Latinos in the San Fernando Valley might hold the key to the vote on secession.

PART THREE

The Battle over the Charter

CHAPTER SEVEN

The 1997 Municipal Elections and the Politics of Charter Reform

IN APRIL 1997, the voters reshaped charter reform. Riordan won a smashing reelection victory, Latino participation surged, a massive school bond issue was passed, and Riordan's elected charter reform commission won voter approval.

The principal feature of the election was Riordan's sweeping reelection. Running against a liberal opponent, Democratic state senator Tom Hayden, Riordan dominated the voting in all but the African American community. The likelihood that Riordan would be emboldened to move forcefully on his reform agenda, not only in the charter but with school reform, was greatly magnified.

Riordan's victory established a framework for charter reform by reinforcing and expanding his electoral coalition. His reelection coalition was much broader than his base had been in his first election in 1993.

Riordan's initial victory had been constructed around the mobilization of moderate and conservative white voters. He managed to break even with historically liberal Jewish voters, and won a respectable minority of Latino voters. In 1997, he swept both Jewish and Latino voters with solid majorities. According to the *Times* exit poll, Riordan won more than 60 percent of Latinos and more than 70 percent of Jews (table 4).

Riordan's ability to win Jewish and Latino support gave him control of the vast middle of an emerging Los Angeles politics still polarized between African Americans on the left and white conservatives on the right. The scope of Riordan's support could also be seen in the short-lived endorsement he received from the County Federation of Labor. Only the vehement objections of city employee unions led the Federation to backtrack and remain neutral.

Polling by the *Times* had indicated that between 1993 and 1997 Riordan had built increasing support among Latinos. Even though the Latino voting population had changed by 1997, and was more likely to be Democratic and working class, Riordan still managed to do very well.

By 1997, Riordan's overall popularity and political resources preempted strong opposition. A 1996 *Times* poll of Los Angeles voters had found that Riordan's approval rating citywide was a relatively anemic 46 percent. Sixty percent of whites approved, but only 30 percent of blacks and 34

TABLE 4
Riordan Support in Two Mayoral Elections (percentage)

	1993[a]		1997[b]	
	Riordan Vote	Share of All Votes	Riordan Vote	Share of All Votes
Blacks	14	12	19	13
Jews	49	19	71	15
Latinos	43	10	60	15
Asian Americans	31	4	62	4
Whites (including Jews)	67	72	70	65

Sources: [a]Los Angeles Times Poll no. 316, general election, 1993
[b] Los Angeles Times Poll no. 394, primary election, 1997.
Note: Percentages of vote shares do not add up to 100 percent because Jews are included in the white category.

percent of Latinos (study #346). Nearly half of blacks (46 percent) disapproved, with 27 percent strongly disapproving.

By early 1997, these dynamics had shifted in Riordan's favor. A February Times poll found that Riordan's overall support was 57 percent (table 5). His performance was endorsed by 66 percent of whites, 38 percent of blacks, and 52 percent of Latinos. A month later, another Times poll found that his rating was 58 percent, backed by 66 percent of whites, 24 percent of blacks, and now an impressive 65 percent of Latinos.

A union poll, privately conducted for the Service Employees International Union by GLS Research (#97301) in January 1997, revealed Riordan's strong position. Voters listed crime, violence, and gangs (key Riordan issues) as the main issue complex for the city (49 percent); the next highest was public education, with 9 percent. Riordan's favorability rating stood at 62 percent, with 21 percent strongly favorable. Riordan's personal popularity did not translate into public support for his privatization ideas, a fact that eventually played an important role in charter reform. The people "who collect the garbage and recycling from your home" were seen favorably by 84 percent of voters. Refuse privatization was strongly opposed by 38 percent and overall opposition was 57 percent.

In the union poll, Riordan defeated Hayden, 45 percent to 20 percent. By a fifty-three-to-nine margin, voters blamed the council instead of Riordan for the city's problems. Only 33 percent had heard anything about charter reform. When voters were made aware that Riordan was spending

TABLE 5
Riordan's Approval Rating in *Times* Polls, 1993–1999 (percentage)

October 1993	45
June 1994	59
June 1995	46
June 1996	46
February 1997	57
March 1997	58
April 1997	54
March 1999	57

Source: Los Angeles Times Poll, no. 424

his own money to create a charter commission and elect its members, however, voters reacted negatively. Thirty-five percent were much more likely and 24 percent somewhat more likely to oppose Proposition 8, for an elected charter commission. At the same time, Prop. 8 retained majority support. When voters were told about the existing appointed charter reform commission, however, a majority felt that Prop. 8 was not necessary.

Jewish and Latino voters, and Riordan's backing (a formula that helped pass charter reform two years later), also helped ensure the two-thirds majority needed to pass Proposition BB, a huge bond issue for the schools. Prop. BB was driven by Latinos and Jews, followed by African Americans.

Prop. BB became one of the great coalition campaigns of all time in Los Angeles, and the moderate Riordan was in the middle of it. The fundraising base for the proposition was large and varied. Angelenos for Better Classrooms—Yes on BB included Riordan's business allies as well as the interracial Bradley forces. It included developers friendly to Riordan and city employee groups hostile to Riordan. It tied together the district's chief critic, Riordan, and the school unions against which his efforts were directed in school reform. Money came from Riordan ally Jerry Perenchino ($10,000), but also from Riordan foes Jackie Goldberg and school board member Jeff Horton. The Times-Mirror Corporation, parent corporation of the *Los Angeles Times,* put in $10,000. In its breadth it resembled what would later be the coalition against secession in 2002.

Clearly, with his own reelection and the passage of Proposition BB, Riordan was in a formidable position. But the limits of Riordan's hold on this vast middle were illuminated in the race for city attorney. Riordan supported Ted Stein against incumbent James K. Hahn, and saw Stein go down to a crushing defeat. Hahn's campaign was chaired by George Kieffer, soon to be the chair of the appointed charter reform commission that was to face off against the Riordan-financed elected charter reform commission. Hahn clearly commanded a political base independent of Riordan and almost a mirror image of Riordan's. Starting with African American support, Hahn was reasonably strong everywhere else.

The voters passed Proposition 8, financed by Riordan, to create an elected charter reform commission. But this was not to be the clear-cut victory Riordan's people had anticipated. Tactically it was a success. The Riordan forces were able to move quickly with little time available for candidates to sign up to run. In addition, voters were not told on the ballot that there was already a tax-supported appointed charter commission in operation, information that they might have considered relevant to their vote.

The Riordan strategy on Prop. 8 was a quiet one: lots of money, short time for access to the ballot, and a quick campaign for the measure and for individual seats. Riordan created Citizens for a Better Los Angeles, one of the array of Riordan-allied campaign committees that raised money for a number of charter-reform candidates. Bill Carrick was paid by these Riordan committees to run several charter candidate campaigns. Corporate allies of Riordan provided large donations.

Riordan's forces, however, did not count on organized labor at the ballot box. Labor was very alarmed by the prospect of a Riordan-controlled elected commission. Although Riordan had the initiative, labor organized on very short notice and put together a list of strong candidates.

According to SEIU Local 347's Julie Butcher, the private-sector and public-sector unions were united in the campaign. A series of meetings were held among labor groups, and in a pivotal conclave attended by councilmembers Jackie Goldberg and Ruth Galanter, it was decided that Prop. 8 was likely to pass, and that a backup plan was necessary (M. Siegel interview). Based on polling conducted for SEIU, the decision was made to not put funds into opposing Prop. 8, but to field labor candidates. According to Siegel:

> We made the decision that this was going to be a minor blip on the political radar, that the people wouldn't know who to vote for, and there wouldn't be well-funded campaigns. Our gambit was to pick candidates with high name ID and so we sat around the table thinking of candidates. And then we basically called them up and interested them in charter reform. Nobody turned us down.

According to Siegel, the lead role among city employees was played by SEIU, which represents about 40 percent of city workers. Each labor-endorsed candidate received a package of aid, as had Riordan's candidates from the mayor. Siegel's estimate was that the labor campaign cost about $150,000.

Jackie Goldberg recruited Erwin Chemerinsky, a law professor at the University of Southern California, and one of the best known liberal activists in Los Angeles. Chemerinsky recalled that he refused to do any fundraising, insisting that labor deliver the money. They largely did (interview). He also sought Riordan's endorsement, having concluded that he was much closer to Riordan's views on charter reform than he had imagined. However, his repeated calls to Wardlaw were never returned, and Riordan endorsed a Valley real estate attorney in the fifth district. Chemerinsky, who was widely known through his television commentaries on the O. J. Simpson trial, crushed his opposition, winning easily without a runoff.

The labor campaign did not attack the popular Riordan. Labor did promise to "protect firefighters" and to support neighborhood councils. (The firefighters theme turned up again in the opposition to the charter in 1999.) As Siegel pointed out, "You couldn't really run on defending the status quo. So we ran on neighborhood councils and participation."

Riordan tried to avoid the charge of boss politics. As Bill Wardlaw, Riordan's closest ally, recalled, a decision was made not to join the Riordan re-election, Prop. 8, and the individual charter commissioner campaigns into one big unified effort: "I did not want to give people an argument that Riordan's trying to impose fifteen mini-Riordans on the populace."

Wardlaw (interview) met early with the County Federation of Labor's Miguel Contreras to reassure him that the mayor's interest in charter reform would not lead to reopening the painful issues of privatization and other hot-button labor issues: "They would never have to worry about what Dick Riordan was going to do in charter reform. . . . We were hoping that labor would not take a lot of interest."

In the primary election, Riordan won a major victory when Proposition 8 passed with 61.1 percent of the vote. But labor had done extremely well with its endorsed candidates. The Riordan forces virtually conceded three seats in the African American community, where Riordan was unpopular. Of the eight candidates elected outright with a majority in the primary, all had been endorsed by labor. Of the seven remaining races, labor was to win three more in the runoff election (see table 6).

Labor was "feeling pretty powerful," according to Siegel. Now labor had to confront the fact that in its desire to block Riordan, it had seemingly won control of the elected commission. Riordan had his commission in place, but his opponents in labor seemed to be in charge of it. Kieffer noted the irony: "Since the appointed commission had been selected in part to appeal to the mayor, Riordan at that moment probably had more friends on the appointed commission than on his own elected commission" (interview).

TABLE 6
Labor Slate in 1997 Charter Reform Commission Election

District	Candidate	Outcome
1.	Gloria Romero	**elected** in primary (ran unopposed; also endorsed by Riordan)
2.	Anne Finn	**elected** in primary
3.	Dennis Zine	**elected** in primary
4.	Charlie Mims	defeated by Riordan candidate, Bill Weinberger, in runoff
5.	Erwin Chemerinsky	**elected** in primary
6.	Jimmie Woods Gray	defeated by Riordan candidate, Chet Widom, in runoff
7.	Marcos Castenada	**elected** in primary (also endorsed by Riordan)
8.	Marguerite Archie-Hudson	**elected** in primary
9.	Woody Fleming	**elected** in runoff
10.	Jackie Dupont-Walker	**elected** in primary
11.	Maureen Kindel	defeated by Rob Glushon (Riordan candidate)
12.	Paula Boland	**elected** in primary
13.	Bennett Keyser	**elected** in runoff
14.	David Tokofsky	defeated by Nick Pacheco
15.	Janice Hahn	**elected** in runoff

Labor's goal had been to block Riordan from accumulating too much power in city government. They never expected to win control; they only expected to make it harder for Riordan to hold unchallenged sway over the charter process. Their main hope had been to do well where Riordan was weak, especially in the black community, and to be competitive elsewhere.

According to Siegel, "There was no consensus in the labor community as to what the program should be and there was never that great dissatisfaction with the current charter, and so we never developed a labor program. Labor can unite around labor issues, pensions, privatization, job security, economic issues. But whether or not there should be neighborhood councils, whether or not there should be area planning commissions, whether or not there should be the CAO's office or empower the mayor's office, you get a lot of different points of view."

Labor's ambivalence toward reform helped account for what happened next: Riordan's remarkable success in retaking control of the elected commission. In contrast to labor, Riordan certainly had a program for government reform and knew exactly where he wanted the commission to go.

Labor had both an opportunity and a problem. A blocking strategy had worked beyond their expectations, and they had a new baby to raise. They were unsure how to raise it. Miguel Contreras, who was a member of the appointed commission, contacted me and explained that he was considering leaving the appointed commission because now that labor had a commission, he had to do his best to make it work. Kieffer talked him into staying a little while longer, but Contreras eventually quit and put his efforts into the elected commission.

The council's position was also thrown into disarray. Labor was close to the council; the council hated the idea of an elected commission. Now there was an elected commission, but it seemed to be controlled by labor. Should the council abandon its own appointed commission and do what Contreras had done—and try to make the elected one a success? But as Siegel noted, "Even though the labor slate won, the council never fully trusted the elected commission, so it never really gave them the resources. The candidates were chosen on name ID alone, so there was no real discussion of where they stood on the charter."

Tensions were inevitable between the two charter commissions. Shortly after the April election, I received a call from a labor attorney who described himself as a key adviser to the new elected commission. He demanded that the appointed commission give half our city funds immediately to the elected commission or face being taken to federal court. He indicated that he had been encouraged in this strategy by Mike Keeley, Riordan's ally. Naturally, I rejected this demand.

The elected commission could not take office until all members were elected, and with runoffs set for June, it would be July 1997 before the full commission could be seated. The appointed commission used the time to build its credibility in substantive areas and with the media and other stakeholders. The appointed commission developed its work plan, conducted study sessions with the city attorney, created study groups and reports on participation, management, and institutions. Kieffer and I made numerous visits to editorial boards and interest groups.

But with Riordan hostile to the appointed commission, it was difficult for the appointed commission to get traction, especially with the influential *Times.* The appointed commission was well respected among insiders, including city bureaucrats, elected officials, reporters, and editorial writers. But it was difficult to shake the impression that the council would control its product and that the other commission was, after all, elected.

To a greater degree than was appreciated at the time, Riordan had options with the elected commission. Riordan believed that he was the main force in charter reform. I was summoned to meet with the mayor's strategy group in mid-April, and told their view of charter reform: "You wouldn't be here if it were not for the mayor."

Right after the runoff, Riordan held a press conference to welcome the formation of the elected commission. According to Siegel, Michael Keeley was assessing the commissioners, and said, "I think we can work with some of these commissioners." The elected commissioners were generally hostile to the city council, seeing it as obstructing their creation and funding. Even though the council and labor were close, this presented a wedge that Riordan very effectively utilized. "They wanted to go their own way," according to Siegel.

Wardlaw said that the mayor's people "could still see how you could make it work." Woody Fleming, an African American candidate on the labor slate, was endorsed by Riordan in the runoff election. Contreras of the AFL-CIO was not unfriendly to the mayor. Those not allied with the city employees were amenable to working with Riordan. The fundamental strategic decision that may have made the most difference was described by Wardlaw:

> We would not spend any time with the appointed commission. We wanted the elected commission to know that we loved them to death, they were our favorites, they were champions of the people. Dick Riordan worked so hard personally on virtually every one of those commissioners. And so at the end of the day, Dick Riordan had significant influence over that elected commission. (interview)

In adopting this strategy, Riordan obtained a horse in the race that he could ride to the end. Riordan had an additional advantage in his power to appoint commissioners to fill vacancies on the elected commission. After some confusion, it was established that Riordan had the sole authority to fill seats.

This power helped swing the balance to Riordan when Marguerite Archie-Hudson, the only commissioner to serve simultaneously on both the elected and appointed panels, resigned in December 1998. Riordan replaced her with Ken Lombard, a close ally who provided a reliable vote for the mayor. Earlier, he replaced Gloria Romero with Richard Macias, one of his appointed city commissioners. (Critics of the commission began to refer to it as "the appointed elected commission.")

Even though the elected commission was in disarray, without a staff or funding, and torn between labor and Riordan, they represented a fundamental threat to the survival of the appointed commission. Kieffer thought "we were at risk for the next two months. Unless we established ourselves with the *LA Times* in particular and with a few people, we were at real risk of being eliminated."

In June, the final races were decided and the elected commission prepared to take office on July 7, 1997. They had no money—Riordan having pulled back on his earlier dollar commitment—no office, no phones. Filled with labor appointees recruited to block the mayor, they had no affirmative agenda. And labor was in no position to give them one.

Here, Riordan's ability to divide labor came into play (Orlov 1999). Riordan would be able to play on internal labor divisions throughout the process. Step by step, Riordan's warm embrace of the troubled elected commissioners brought a majority into his fold. Riordan managed to slowly but surely take control of the elected commission. Riordan provided attention, support, and an agenda to a commission that was shell-shocked, isolated, and angry.

For better and for worse, the city of Los Angeles now had two legally valid charter reform commissions operating simultaneously, with different legal bases but the same charge to conduct charter reform. They each developed their own culture and style, and it seemed impossible that they would ever come together.

CHAPTER EIGHT

The Charter Reform Commissions

> The charter commission, a distinctly American contribution to the art
> and practice of local government . . . has a unique and important service
> to perform. . . . Free from the necessity of engaging in actual government
> and party strife, it can turn its full attention to the improvement of
> governmental machinery. If its work is well done and forward-looking,
> and if the voters choose to adopt it, the commission may have a positive
> influence for decades to come.
> —National Civic League, *Guide for Charter Commissions*

FOR TWO YEARS, two commissions in Los Angeles pursued charter reform,
each with its own assets, liabilities, and base of support. The situation only
reinforced the view that in this fragmented city, even a good-government
policy like charter reform will inevitably fall apart.

The charter battles were fought on two fields: the inside game and the
outside game. The inside game was the taut, edgy battle over the structure
of the central government, hard fought between Mayor Riordan and the
city council. The outside game concerned the relationship between the
central government and the neighborhoods of Los Angeles. The fields of
battle overlapped and intersected, but were also distinct.

As the two commissions began working on substantive issues of charter
reform, they came from different perspectives (Greene 1998c, 1999b).
Their differing styles made compromise extremely difficult, because they
differed not only on what they concluded but on how they got there.

In general, the elected commission saw itself as an outsider body alienated from city hall. The commissioners believed that they were writing a
new charter from scratch, and that the official forces at city hall were their
enemies. In this respect, they took Riordan's style much farther than even
Riordan did. Inevitably, they leaned toward his point of view on key issues
of authority. When they voted to name themselves, the elected commissioners decided to italicize the word "elected," a none-too-subtle dig at
the appointed commission (Greene 1999b).

The appointed commission was established in the pattern of the traditional charter reform commission. The appointed commission saw itself as
an official city commission. The appointed commissioners did not operate
from the premise that they were writing a charter from scratch, and were
often sympathetic to concerns expressed by city officials about potential
changes.

In stylistic terms, the commissions could not have been more different. The appointed commission was a tightly run body that made few waves. It met once every two weeks. It was hierarchically organized, with the chair in the lead role and with staff providing research and analysis directly to the commission. Kieffer organized the appointed commission to largely avoid committees so that the whole body could deliberate with the same base of knowledge. His approach was intended to avoid the problem of committee chairs becoming too committed to their own solutions.

The elected commission met every week, often until late at night, in sessions marked by wide and passionate debate. Virtually all work was done by committees of elected commissioners, with staff consultants providing research to the committees but not presenting recommendations directly to the full commission. Because the commissioners had been elected and because so many were planning runs for office in the near future, they were constant targets for pressure from interest groups.

If the appointed commission was built on the model of the traditional citizen commission (as described in the National League of Cities *Guide to Charter Commissions*), the elected commission was much more like a legislature, with powerful committee chairs and active interest groups.

As the substantive issues emerged, certain fault lines came through. The elected commission generally put bold ideas on the table: elected, decision-making neighborhood councils; a bill of rights; broad new powers for the mayor. These ideas could emerge quickly and dramatically on the elected commission because in the legislative model, any member's idea would have legitimacy and would have to be respected. The appointed commission was more cautious, and was more dedicated to keeping what was good in the existing charter. Built around staff research, the appointed model channeled virtually all ideas and proposals through the staff before being presented to the commissioners. Commissioners generally responded to, amended, and voted on staff recommendations.

The elected commissioners were more likely to see themselves as founders of a new constitution; they once held a press conference wearing tricornered hats. As appointed commissioner Alexandra Glickman put it, in a bicameral system, the appointed commission was the Senate, and the elected commission was the House (Greene 1999b).

The elected commission had to operate in the face of profound organizational problems. While the mayor portrayed the elected body as the only legitimate commission, and the appointed body as an interloper set up only to block change, in organizational terms, the appointed commission looked much more stable. It had funding, staff, and strong organization.

From the start, the two commissions were like competing siblings. Both had a mission that would have made more sense with only one commission, and each operated with an eye on the other. At the organizational level, there was a great difference in terms of organizational stability that began with the nature of how they were created, organized, and funded. Each tended to its political base in the search for a winning coalition.

Kieffer put considerable effort into cultivating the business leadership of the city: the *Times* publisher, Mark Willes, the Central City Association, the Chamber of Commerce, and the Los Angeles Business Advisers. Looking toward the end game, Kieffer wanted to be certain that business understood the appointed commission and respected its work. Otherwise, they would rely on Riordan's negative view of the appointed commission (Kieffer interview).

As a former council deputy, I devoted considerable time to keeping close ties with councilmembers, their staffs, community groups, and the city employee unions. Both Kieffer and I concentrated on the civic sector, the citizen organizations that would weigh in on a major reform project. In every case, we were trying to build a supportive constituency, and working desperately to avoid being isolated and marginalized by Riordan.

Kieffer and I made unflagging attempts to repair our image as the commission disfavored by the mayor through visits to media outlets. We spent time talking to the *Times* editorial staff. We visited the *Daily News* and other papers, and KNX News Radio.

The appointed commission faced a continuing challenge of legitimacy. As the day neared when the elected commission would take office, the issue of legitimacy became more and more acute.

The world of the elected commission could not have been more different. From the very start, the elected commission had to fight for its right to exist and for the resources to operate, and had to find a way to organize itself effectively. And at every stage, the elected commissioners could see what they considered the easier practical path of the appointed commission. On the other hand, they had the mayor, and they were elected. While their competence was often questioned, few contested their basic legitimacy.

It was clear from the start that there would be two major forces operating on the elected commission: the mayor and organized labor. The main labor force, Miguel Contreras, was at times allied with the mayor and at other times opposed, while SEIU and the city employees it represented were opposed to the mayor. At the first meeting, on July 7, 1997, Gloria Romero (who had been supported both by Riordan and labor in the election) was chosen as interim chair, after lobbying by Contreras (Chemerinsky interview). Chemerinsky insisted that the chair selection be temporary, earning enmity from Romero and Contreras (interview).

After several months, Romero resigned to pursue a successful state assembly campaign. The commission turned to Chemerinsky. A well-known legal scholar and commentator, Chemerinsky was a political liberal, and a recognized and popular figure in Los Angeles. On civil liberties issues, Chemerinsky was a nationally known figure and his name recognition was among the highest of all members of both charter commissions.

Chemerinsky's selection was a mixed blessing for the Riordan forces. As an ideological liberal, he was on the wrong side of the Riordan people. He was, however, an excellent public leader for the elected commission, always putting forward a positive perspective of even the most difficult meeting of his group. Well known to the local media as a commentator, he had no trouble getting on the air or in print with his commission's views.

Chemerinsky ran the elected commission with great deference to the electoral needs of his members. It was in any case nearly impossible to impose a hierarchical structure on a body whose members were elected officials. Chemerinsky was always counting votes and mollifying angry elected commissioners. Meetings went on until late hours so that each commissioner could speak.

When the elected commission was finally seated in July, the next battle was over money and organization. Riordan had said or implied on several occasions that he would fund the elected commission. Riordan's ally David Fleming had been even clearer, specifically promising that Riordan would provide the money (McGreevy 1997c). Yet as soon as the commission was in place, Riordan called on the council to provide public funds. The mayor promised to deliver an additional bloc of money to the commission, but only if proper documentation and budget projections were presented.

At the first meeting, the commission divided over whether to seek public funds. Chemerinsky favored it from the start, but the commission voted to seek the mayor's promised money instead. Dennis Zine, head of the police union, and secessionist Paula Boland, among others, were strongly opposed to public funding.

On August 4, 1997, the mayor offered the commission $30,000, the acceptance of which was legally dependent on council approval. The commission then voted to seek council funding, despite continuing opposition from several commissioners.

Riordan managed to place the council in a corner, arguing that if the appointed commission was funded, so should an elected commission be. An angry council president John Ferraro wrote to Riordan, "You delivered the message, loud and clear, that the commission would be funded through private sources" (1997). With great reluctance, however, the council came across with the funds. While Riordan won the battle, he generated further enmity from the council, which felt that it had been double-crossed in light of the promises Riordan had made or implied about private support for the elected commission.

Meanwhile, even with the promise of public funds, the elected commission struggled mightily to pull itself together. The commission advertised for an executive director starting in August, and received ninety-eight applications.

Labor vetoed Riordan's choice, former state assemblyman Mike Roos, the head of the school reform program, Project Learn, and a close Riordan ally. With Riordan still envisioned as the key source of funds for an executive director's salary, the mayor's endorsement of Roos carried considerable weight. But labor was reluctant to support a candidate so clearly tied to Riordan.

As August proceeded, the elected commission was still without funds. Only in late August did the council allow the commission to accept the first $30,000. The commission still had no staff. At the September 2, 1997 meeting, Erwin Chemerinsky was elected permanent chair.

The impact that Chemerinsky's intellect and energy had on a divided and demoralized commission was startling. Immediately a series of memos began to emerge from the chair, calling for a calendar and for immediate work on the substance of charter reform. Chemerinsky had only a week earlier sent a memo pushing the commission to get going on substantive charter issues, rather than bogging itself down in organizational detail. Chemerinsky was conscious of the positive reception for the appointed commission's first major report, *Road to Decision,* released to the public in early September (interview).

Finally, the commission found an executive director, C. Edward Dilkes, and $300,000 was made available by the council. Dilkes was a municipal attorney and a charter expert, but his organizational approach was a disappointment to the commission. Elected commission meetings between September and December were dominated by commissioner complaints about nonworking phones, the lack of office space, and lagging behind the appointed commission. Three months after his hiring, Dilkes was fired by the elected commission.

The commission then decided to hire political scientist H. Eric Schockman of the University of Southern California, a well-known expert on Los Angeles who seemed likely to put them on a substantive path. Schockman was trusted by labor. Schockman and I were colleagues in the study of urban politics. The path to a joint approach would have been smoother with his appointment. But Schockman's leave was vetoed by top officials at USC.

Now the elected commission decided to create an unusual staff structure, hiring former police union official Geoffrey Garfield as administrative director and Schockman as the volunteer part-time policy director. But the structure may not have mattered, because in any case the elected commissioners were not about to be "staff driven," their perception of how the appointed commission operated. Despite the strange organizational structure, Garfield immediately solved most of the commission's organizational problems and allowed the commission to get down to the business of recommendations for reform (Chemerinsky interview).

By early 1998, both commissions were on a path to making preliminary decisions about what should be in the charter. The appointed commission had used 1997 to develop a set of questions and to conduct research on

topics. The elected commission had used the time to get its footing orga-
nizationally. For the first time, the two commissions were roughly on a
similar time path.

The appointed commission kicked off this period with a report, entitled
Deliberations. The report moved past *Road to Decision* and laid out a set
of decisions to be made, rather than issues to be addressed. My task was to
prepare a staff report on each topic, and Kieffer directed me to make recommendations for decisions by the commission.

The elected commission set out a schedule of deliberations to be held in
public forums throughout the community. Each commissioner expected
to have a meeting in his or her district. According to Chemerinsky, each
commissioner wanted to have the discussion on the popular topic of
neighborhood councils. Chemerinsky had to patiently devise a plan that
would advance the individual interests of the commissioners while getting
substantive work done. The staff work was to be done in committees run
by commissioners, with policy consultants assigned to each committee.

As the year ended and the commissions got down to work, Riordan
maintained his policy toward the two commissions. In his year-end review,
he pointedly indicated that he was "working with the elected commission
and communicating with the appointed commission."

CHAPTER NINE

The Inside Game

MAYORAL AUTHORITY

> The sheer inactivity of the mayor's office is stunning. I have never been
> given so much help and so much attention so quickly by so many press
> officers with so little to do. Unlike New York's mayor, who makes
> headlines almost daily, the L.A. mayor, currently Richard Riordan, can
> go unsighted for weeks.
> —Fred Siegel, *The Future Once Happened Here*

> "People here have not the faintest interest in taking anything but maybe
> pizza and bagels from New York," said Los Angeles city employee labor
> leader Julie Butcher. . . . Laura Lake, a Westside activist who was a leader
> of the 1980's slow growth movement, which she called Not Yet New
> York, said she still has leftover buttons, if anyone needs some. . . . Lake
> observed: "The way I view New York is as the Old Country. It's as if
> someone were coming from Europe to tell us how to run a democracy."
> —Ted Rohrlich, "Charter Panel Compares Big Orange
> to Big Apple," *Los Angeles Times*

FROM THE beginning to the end of charter reform, the process was driven
ahead and at other times nearly derailed by Richard Riordan's desire to increase mayoral authority in the city charter. Unlike the New York City
charter reform of 1986–89, which was driven by a federal court order de-
claring the Board of Estimate unconstitutional, the Los Angeles charter
reform was essentially driven by political, not legal, pressure. And the political actor whose agenda set the tone for support and opposition was
Riordan. Had Riordan decided to withdraw from the process, charter reform would have undoubtedly ground to a halt.

The intensity of Riordan's agenda was such that it drew other political
actors into the charter reform debate, even if only to block Riordan. Other
political actors saw advantages for their own goals in the process, and either through alliance with Riordan or conflict with him pursued their own
charter reforms.

The single most persistent and consistent goal Riordan pursued in charter
reform was the augmentation of the formal powers of the mayor and the

reduction in the power of the city council. Riordan could point to the trend in California's larger cities, such as San Francisco and San Jose, toward stronger mayors. In particular, Riordan could watch with envy as the mayors of Chicago and New York City, moderate reformers like himself, wielded great power.

A consensus had emerged from a series of charter reform commissions as far back as 1934 that the mayor of Los Angeles should have enhanced authority, but there was disagreement among the various commissions about the nature and extent of such changes (Appointed Commission 1997a). Thus the two commissions in 1997 were left with a general view that the mayor needed more authority, but with serious disagreements about the nature of that change. A number of reforms were possible, as outlined in table 7.

TABLE 7
Potential Ways to Increase the Authority of the Mayor

- Add detail to the charter about the mayor's role, compared to the spare paragraph in the existing charter.

- Change the reporting relationship of the CAO from mayor and council to simply mayor.

- Alter the process of reorganizing city departments to give the mayor control, instead of the council having the main role and the mayor a lesser one.

- Give the mayor a role in litigation, currently kept in the hands of the council.

- Strengthen the mayor's appointment and removal powers for city commissioners and managers of departments.

- Reduce the number of matters that can be done by the council by resolution compared to ordinance, requiring the mayor's involvement.

- Transfer control of intergovernmental relations from council to mayor.

- Specify that the mayor is in charge of emergency operations.

- Increase the number of positions exempt from civil service and enhance the mayor's role in filling exempt positions.

- Eliminate or reduce the council's ability to override decisions made by city commissions (Prop. 5).

- Eliminate the council's designation as the city's governing body.

- Allow the mayor to appoint the city attorney.

- Give the mayor, instead of the controller, "pre-audit" authority over spending.

Taken individually, these were relatively small changes. Taken collectively, they would have dramatically enhanced mayoral authority along the lines of New York City's government. There were major fights on each proposal, but at the end of the day the key battles were fought over the power of the mayor to fire general managers of city departments without council review and the reporting relationship of the city administrative officer.

Riordan's agenda evolved over time as he searched for a practical, politically viable set of proposals. By the time charter reform got under way, he had been bloodied by city unions and the council on privatization, and the intensity of labor's commitment to the civil service provisions of the charter had become evident.

City employees were profoundly concerned about the civil service system. The existing charter contained a vast array of highly sensitive provisions having to do with employment conditions. City unions were fearful that Riordan wanted to use charter reform to restore the vigor of his earlier attempts at privatization. They would fight greater mayoral authority, believing that they were in better shape with the council than with Riordan.

But labor was not unified. The broader County Federation of Labor was more favorable to Riordan than the city employees. City workers might see Riordan as a jobs killer; but a progrowth mayor would be seen as a jobs creator (like Tom Bradley) by many other unions.

To an important degree, Riordan's high investment in the charter meant that the debate was framed as a response to what he wanted. This dynamic placed Riordan in a good position from which to bargain and negotiate. He enthusiastically bluffed, bargained, and negotiated from the first day until the last, and on through the implementation phase.

But if Riordan were to get everything he wanted in the charter proposal, he might end up with nothing that he wanted. Even popular mayors can be defeated by the voters on measures principally designed to increase their own formal powers. At the same time, the charter commissions needed Riordan to campaign for the charter. No one in the city could match his resources citywide, and a weak campaign would be easy pickings for those who were comfortable with the existing charter.

The crucial dividing issue for the city's power brokers became the power of the mayor. And here the perception of New York City government emerged strongly as a factor in the debate.

In fighting hard to increase the power of the mayor, Riordan was proposing to make Los Angeles government more like that of New York City. The New York City analogy energized the opposing progovernment coalition. It gave them a chance to take the high ground of reform for the first time by referring to the perceived corruption of New York City government.

It was inevitable that Riordan, a businessman with little patience for leg-islative politics, would find appealing the mayor-centered governments of New York City and Chicago. He saw Richard M. Daley and Rudolph Giu-liani seem to dominate and reshape their local school systems (a core in-terest of Riordan's) and shuffle and reshuffle their governments with barely an effective squeal from other power brokers in the system.

Riordan frequently referred to the mayor's office as weak and powerless. His argument resonated among business leaders and to some degree in the San Fernando Valley, where his many political supporters regarded him as a friendly force in an unfriendly government. Others argued that the mayor's office in Los Angeles, while not nearly as strong as in New York City and Chicago, was much stronger than believed (McCarthy, Erie, and Reichardt 1998; Greene 1998b).

The mayor had considerable influence and power under the 1925 charter, but that power was hemmed in by the council. For example, the mayor appointed and removed general managers of city departments, but in each case required a majority vote of the fifteen-member council. The city administrative officer, a position established in 1951, served both the mayor and the council, and provided neutral budget numbers. There is no equivalent office in New York City.

Even under the 1925 charter, the Los Angeles mayor had great authority in the development of the city budget. It was difficult for the council to in-terfere with the mayor's budget. If the council did not act by a set date, the mayor's budget took effect. Even the governor of California has no such power. (The new charter largely retained the mayor's budget authority.)

Riordan set out three main goals for charter reform: (1) to have the mayor appoint the city attorney, instead of the attorney being elected as under the old charter; (2) to change the role of the city administrative of-ficer, which reported both to the mayor and council under the old charter, to report only to the mayor, or to weaken the CAO drastically; and (3) to give the mayor the authority to unilaterally fire general managers of city departments. In all three areas, Riordan's proposals would have aligned Los Angeles practice with that of New York City. There were a host of less important Riordan priorities, most aimed at reducing the council's influ-ence and increasing that of the mayor (Rohrlich 1997).

While the final charter proposal made significant adjustments in a number of areas to increase mayoral authority, and was attacked by oppo-nents of the charter for that reason, Riordan gained none of the three core goals he originally set forth. But the city gained, as a by-product of Riordan's search for authority, a new system of citizen participation, and the mayor did receive considerable increases in authority.

As the charter debate continued, Riordan further called for granting performance audit authority to the elected controller, in an apparent move to reduce the authority of the CAO, who had the power to conduct management audits. He aligned himself with Police Chief Bernard C. Parks, who wanted more positions exempt from civil service, and Riordan called for greater flexibility in the creation of exempt positions generally. He sought mayoral authority for emergency powers management, and the authority to represent the city in intergovernmental relations.

On April 28, 1997, Kieffer and I had our first official meeting with Riordan to discuss his charter agenda. Riordan began by telling us that he understood labor's fear of changes in civil service, and that he had no intention of opening that issue. The mayor complained that general managers were "emasculated." He urged greater authority for the mayor in emergency management. He called for breaking up the elected city attorney's office, with the civil side appointed. When I asked Riordan about appointed city commissions overseeing city departments, he spoke highly of the existing system. He said that Prop. 5, which allowed the council to temporarily assume the powers of a city commission, was the real problem.

By early 1998, the two commissions began to take preliminary votes on charter proposals. At its February 25, 1998, meeting, the appointed commission began with the structure of the charter. It voted to eliminate long descriptions of formal powers of the city council, and to replace those provisions with broad grants of authority. The commission also voted to move civil service provisions to a second volume of the charter and in general to clean up and update the charter. The creation of two volumes with equal legal force allowed the development of a much more accessible first volume, but raised considerable fear among city unions that their protections would be weakened. Try as I might, I could not shake the embarrassing habit of referring to the first volume as the "main volume"; whenever I did so, I would be severely chastised by union officials.

At its March 25, 1998, meeting, the appointed commission endorsed a staff recommendation to assign principal management authority to the mayor; to share policy between mayor and council; and to lodge oversight authority in the council. This became the basic theory of the appointed commission. If the mayor were to receive additional authority, it would not be because the mayor was the *executive*, like a governor or president. It would be because the mayor would be the chief *manager*, within a policy and oversight framework that centrally involved the city council.

As part of this approach, the appointed commission decided that citizen commissions should generally not manage departments. Furthermore, the commission voted to lodge the power to remove general managers unilaterally in the mayor's hands, and to have the mayor, instead of both mayor and council, conduct merit pay reviews. Unlike the elected commission, however, the appointed commission voted that reorganization of departments was a policy, not a management matter, and that the existing mayor-council framework should remain. The appointed commission did vote to make it more difficult for the council to bury reorganization proposals submitted by the mayor. The council was required to vote on such proposals within a set time period.

The mayor's office was pleased with the appointed commission's vote on general manager removal, and according to Deputy Mayor Kelly Martin (interview), relaxed its oversight of the process. If, after all, both commissions were going to give the mayor what he wanted on the general manager firing, there should be no problem.

Alongside the issues of mayoral authority lay another one that created some interesting alliances: the question of financial management. While arcane to the public, the control of the financial management of the city government was important to people at city hall. It became another vehicle for Riordan to reorient the charter in the direction of mayoral authority, and also gave him a means to form a charter alliance with the popular elected controller, Rick Tuttle. It provided further grist for Riordan's ongoing battle with Keith Comrie, the CAO.

The issue had been identified early by both commissions. In *Road to Decision*, the appointed commission set forth a question whether the financial management of the city should be changed. Riordan wanted to create a mayoral department on finance that would incorporate most of the functions of the CAO and centralize all financial functions under the authority of the mayor.

Riordan was willing to cede some of these functions to the elected controller, and Tuttle had written publicly of his support for the unilateral mayoral firing authority of general managers. Tuttle wanted the charter to require the controller to conduct "performance audits" of city departments. Under the existing charter, no such provision existed, and Tuttle found it difficult to win council budget support for his performance audits. His goal was to create a requirement that would make it easier to win council funding.

On another financial front, however, Riordan and Tuttle were at odds. Riordan wanted to split the preaudit and postaudit functions of the controller, and reserve the preaudit function to the mayor and his budget advisers. The significance of this idea was that it would change the city's long-standing practice of having checks reviewed by the controller before they were sent, and would let the mayor go ahead and authorize them to be paid. To this proposal, Tuttle was adamantly opposed.

In *Road to Decision* (Appointed Commission 1997b), the appointed commission staff presented a critique that was somewhat consistent with Riordan's: "Many offices are involved in the City's financial management structure, including the City Clerk, Purchasing Agent, Mayor, council, controller, City Administrative Officer, Treasurer, City Attorney and departments administering pension and retirement systems" (39). The staff report leaned toward the creation of a Department of Finance, and recommended that the appointed commission contract with the Government Finance Officers Association (GFOA) to make a study and recommend charter changes.

The GFOA study was approved by the appointed commission, and resulted in a series of interviews with city officials and a GFOA report. The report was presented both to the commission and to a panel consisting of the city's top financial management: the deputy mayor, the controller, the treasurer, and the CAO. A number of elements of the GFOA study eventually found their way into the new city charter. But Riordan did not win the full finance authority he sought.

On the appointed commission, easy votes for Riordan's platform soon became rarer, as his arguments began to be countered and questioned. Riordan tended to win charter battles fought on theoretical grounds, but as the debates turned toward practical questions, his position seemed to erode. He and his staff rarely acknowledged the powers he already possessed as mayor and were not always able to cite examples of real obstacles to mayoral action. Here the strengths of the progovernment side began to emerge.

By March 1998, the elected commission had begun to vote at its meetings in the community. The mayor's success in wresting control of the elected commission away from organized labor, especially the city employees who had engineered the election of a majority of the commission, became clear.

The Committee on Allocation of Power between Mayor and Council presented a report that went largely with the mayor's position. A small minority of labor allies on the commission, led by Janice Hahn (the city attorney's sister), Jackie Dupont-Walker, and Bennett Keyser, strongly opposed increased mayoral authority. Ironically, Hahn was also one of the most vocal members calling for the abolition of the appointed commission. On a series of straw votes, the commission voted to give the mayor the power to fire general managers unilaterally, to reorganize departments, and to have a central role in litigation. SEIU's Julie Butcher strongly opposed the votes, and could see the city employees' hold on the commission weakening.

Yet labor was not initially unified on the question of mayor authority to fire general managers. According to Chemerinsky (interview), Miguel Contreras at first indicated that the County Federation of Labor could support Riordan's position:

> I remember before my commission took up the issue for the first time, and this would have been around March of '98, being called to a meeting in the mayor's office, and the mayor saying, "I want unilateral authority to fire general managers," and Miguel says, "I think that's good for labor and I favor that." I didn't realize at the time that Miguel didn't speak for all of the unions.

The apparent calm on the two commissions about the unilateral firing authority was to change dramatically in the coming months.

Despite the strong majority in Riordan's corner, the elected commission was at first badly split on one of Riordan's key issues: the reporting relationship of the CAO. They could not muster a majority position, given their requirement of eight affirmative votes for any proposal to pass. Only later did the elected commission go with the mayor's position on the CAO.

On its weekly pace, the elected commission was flooded with information, with public speakers, and with committee reports. They plowed ahead, in contrast to the more stately twice-a-month pace of the appointed commission.

Chemerinsky churned the waters by proposing that the charter contain a Bill of Rights. A committee of the elected commission unanimously endorsed the proposal, but it engendered great conflict with other commissioners. It included "the right of each person to make choices concerning reproductive autonomy." Paula Boland, representing the conservative twelfth district, was adamantly opposed to that and other elements of the proposal. Dennis Zine, of the Valley's third district, added sarcastically, "I think this is a wonderful document, if you want to form a new nation" (Greene 1998a).

At the March 30, 1998, meeting, Bobbie Fiedler, former member of Congress, blasted Chemerinsky's proposal to place a Bill of Rights in the charter. This idea was becoming a serious problem for the commission, although it made labor and the liberal community very happy.

On June 25, 1998, the elected commission took up the city attorney issue. Labor was mobilized in the persons of Miguel Contreras and James Hahn. The committee report supported Riordan's position, but Chemerinsky spoke against the idea. On an eleven-to-two vote, the commission authorized the mayor to control litigation, with Janice Hahn and Keyser opposed. But on a ten-to-two vote (Romero and Widom opposed), the commission voted to keep the city attorney's office undivided and elected. Following this round, James Hahn proposed a complicated compromise to the elected commission on litigation, which was included in the final charter.

Thus by spring, the elected commission had largely endorsed the mayor's agenda on the inside game. The labor majority of July 1997 had become a rearguard minority fighting on the margins against expanded mayoral authority. The city labor unions seemed to have lost.

On July 20, 1998, Riordan addressed the elected commission. His call for greater mayoral authority was vehemently opposed by Julie Butcher. But the commission, on a unanimous vote, passed the mayor's proposal on reorganizing departments, which was strongly opposed by an increasingly frustrated labor contingent. By now, the battle lines between the two commissions were drawn.

On August 24, 1998, the elected commission voted to transfer many of the CAO's functions to the mayor. The appointed commission, meanwhile, largely endorsed retaining the CAO in its existing form.

Keith Comrie, the CAO since his appointment to the post by Mayor Tom Bradley in 1978, now entered the debate. He issued public denunciations of the mayor's position, bringing into the open a battle that had been developing between himself and Riordan since 1993. Irritated with the CAO's dual reporting relationship, Riordan had long ago abandoned reliance on the CAO, and personal relations between the mayor and Comrie were poor.

The image of New York City government now became a key part of the local debate. Comrie cited New York City government as the model that Los Angeles had consciously rejected, and argued that the mayor's proposals, if enacted, would bring East Coast corruption to Los Angeles and take Los Angeles back to the days of the Shaw regime (Greene, 1998c).

Comrie's charges for the first time mobilized the progovernment forces around a reform-oriented agenda, rather than simple self-protection. He provided the beginning of a public argument for what had largely been seen as a status quo point of view.

Comrie was joined in his assault on the elected commission by city employee unions which blasted increases in mayoral power and called for retaining the CAO. Comrie maintained the New York City theme: "progressive governments don't look to New York for good government and leadership. . . . Does it make good common sense to look to New York, the only large city that went bankrupt, as a model that we want to follow?" (McGreevy 1998b; Newton 1998a).

SEIU prepared a leaflet to attack Riordan's approach to charter reform. It asked: "Does the Mayor need more power? To do what? Does the Office of the Mayor need more power? Where are the checks and balances of a progressive western City? What is this really about?" Mobilizing labor forces on charter issues, Butcher faxed out the message: "the labor and progressive communities of this town don't want the mayor to have MORE power. Not yet New York? Not EVER New York!"

On September 10, 1998, Comrie attacked the proposals of the elected commission regarding mayoral authority and the CAO's office. He announced that he would delay his January retirement because "I consider this such a threat to honest and good government that I'm going to stay on." An aide in Riordan's office blasted back, "Keith is just proving that he's denying a village somewhere in the world its idiot" (Newton 1998b).

But Comrie had hit a nerve: the fear that East Coast corruption would arise, the very corruption that many people had fled the East Coast to avoid. And the role of the CAO as nonpartisan servant of both mayor and council had been powerful before in charter reform, when former CAO

Sam Leask had attacked similar recommendations of the Reining Commissions three decades earlier (Rigby 1974).

The New York image became more entrenched as Comrie spoke about the staff of the elected commission. The executive director, Geoffrey Garfield, was from New York City. He brought with him as legal drafter and most trusted staffer a close friend from New York, Steven Presberg. Together, they were open, avowed fans of the New York City government system. Garfield described New York politics:

> New York politics is a spectator sport. Unlike here. Politics here is subterranean. In New York, it's in your blood. There are Democratic clubs, Republican clubs, in your neighborhood. That's how you get things done. There are five, six daily newspapers (Greene 1999g).

Comrie blasted both Garfield and Presberg, and blamed them for the drift of the elected commission toward the mayor's position, relying on what Comrie called "the New York model."

On September 17, 1998, Comrie's office released a study contending that consolidating power in the mayor's office would severely damage good government. His report was entitled "Prescription for Incompetence and Corruption."

For key political actors, the general manager firing and the CAO began to shape up as do-or-die issues. Councilmembers were adamant about the general manager firing, and were also fearful of losing access to the research role of the CAO. Organized labor was vehement in its opposition to changing the rules on firing general managers as well as in its support of the CAO.

The majority on the appointed commission to grant the mayor unilateral firing authority over general managers began to weaken. The appointed commission had voted to give the mayor this power on March 25, 1998, matching a similar action by the elected commission in the same week.

At that time, the mayor's arguments for unilateral firing authority had been well received by the appointed commission. UCLA vice-chancellor Joe Mandel, generally a supporter of mayoral authority, strongly endorsed the recommendation. Charley Mims, a labor representative on most issues, called for a compromise. Other members worried about the implications. Andrew Henderson, generally suspicious of mayoral authority, said, "We've got a current mayor who has said that it's better to ask forgiveness than permission. And there's a risk that there would be one day a mayor who actually believes in that philosophy and carries it out" (Appointed Commission 1998a; 177). His concerns, however, did not carry the day. Kieffer later recalled that he did not see the vote as particularly important because it was only a preliminary decision; furthermore, "I saw it as a means of reaching a compromise with the elected commission."

Not long after the appointed commission's vote, Kieffer and I began to receive feedback from councilmembers and from organized labor that they considered giving the unilateral firing authority to the mayor to be a critical issue. Their opposition did not mean we were going to change our position, but it sensitized us to the issue's importance.

On August 12, 1998, the appointed commission voted to place on the agenda the possible reconsideration of the removal of general managers. When the appointed commission's policy positions on the draft charter were released for public comment, however, the unilateral firing authority for the mayor was still included. A series of interactive open houses were held around the city to assess public comment on the preliminary decisions of the commission.

At the first open house, held in the San Fernando Valley, I stood with commissioner Charley Mims and, out of the corner of my eye, watched the "votes" being placed on posters with individual commission proposals. People who attended (of whom there were more than one hundred) could mark the pro side or the con side. On each issue, the commission's proposals were winning overwhelming support, including proposals that strengthened the mayor.

One board seemed to contradict that view, and I walked closer to see which one it was. It turned out to be the general manager firing, and the con side was flooded with stickers and strong negative comments in this bastion of Riordan's electoral support. This was the first indication that the voters in Los Angeles might not be ready to give more formal power to even a very popular mayor. The pattern continued in other open houses throughout the city. In the harbor, the Eastside, South Central, and in midcity those who attended open houses were strongly opposed to the general manager firing in contrast to strong support for most of the other recommendations.

When the appointed commission convened on October 7, 1998, in the middle of the open house period, a staff report indicated that among eight hundred persons who attended open houses, there was overwhelming support for most of the commission's recommendations. There was great division on council size. There was nearly unanimous support for leaving the city attorney's office unchanged. There was, however, a very solid bloc of opposition to the mayor's unilateral firing authority.

The appointed commission's survey found that 61 percent of all respondents opposed the unilateral firing authority, with 34 percent in favor. Fully a third of all participants expressed strong disapproval of the proposed change to the charter on firing of general managers (Appointed Commission 1998d).

I recommended a reversal of the commission's earlier recommendation, or as a second choice, a two-thirds appellate compromise. Under this proposal, the mayor could remove a general manager, but the manager could appeal to the city council, which could by a two-thirds vote reinstate the employee. While the unilateral firing may have had theoretical support, it seemed increasingly to be out of sync with the local political culture and with traditions of Los Angeles government.

Keith Comrie, the CAO, spoke in support of the staff recommendation, citing Mayor Giuliani in New York City and his apparently arbitrary firing of a successful police chief: "not the type of government we want in Los Angeles." (Ironically, that fired chief, William Bratton, turned up as chief in Los Angeles several years later.) Bob Duncan, of the coalition of city employee unions, echoed the argument.

Theresa Patzakis of the mayor's office spoke against the staff recommendation, questioning the validity of the public comment analysis. She further argued that the current situation made it hard for Los Angeles to attract top-notch administrators.

The commission's debate showed that there had been a significant shift in thinking since March. It was difficult for the mayor's office to come up with specific problems in governance that were caused by the current provisions. Their arguments were usually stronger theoretically (the mayor *ought* to have this power) than as a response to a practical problem (the mayor must have this power in order to prevent a particular, proven problem).

As the discussion continued, it was clear that the mayor's most sympathetic commissioners were themselves now unconvinced by the mayor's position. Alexandra Glickman, a businesswoman friendly to Riordan's views, worried about whether general managers, working without a contract, would be subject to arbitrary dismissal. Joseph Mandel, who generally voted to expand mayoral authority, now said he was changing his mind and liked the two-thirds compromise.

Kieffer, who rarely stated a position in commission debates, spoke at length. He said that he disagreed with the staff recommendation to maintain the current charter provisions, but said that over time he had become persuaded that there needed to be protections for the "permanent government" of Los Angeles. As a result, he favored the backup staff recommendation of the two-thirds compromise.

When the vote was taken, the shift of the appointed commission was complete. There were eight votes for the existing charter provisions and six votes opposed. An informal estimate was that most of the 6 votes were for the two-thirds compromise. In other words, the mayor had lost the appointed commission on an issue near and dear to him.

The shift was long in coming, but received some negative publicity. The *Times* ran a story about the appointed commission "flip-flopping" (Newton 1998d). The mayor's office was extremely unhappy, and Kelly Martin later recalled that this sealed their view of the appointed commission as lackeys of the council (interview).

Kieffer (1998) explained his position in an op-ed article: "the mayor's office is not as weak as it has been portrayed. . . . The authority of the mayor of Los Angeles should be increased. But the sole and unfettered authority to remove general managers is not so necessary to effective leadership as to outweigh the risks of mischief, incompetence and political abuse."

The general manager issue now represented a fundamental area of disagreement between the two commissions. On November 16, 1998, Mayor Riordan transmitted a letter to the elected commission defending his case for unilateral removal authority. Council president John Ferraro responded with a letter on December 4th (Ferraro 1998, emphasis in original) stating: "**I am absolutely and unequivocally opposed to giving any mayor of the City the unilateral authority to remove its general managers**. . . . The Mayor feels that the involvement of the Council will have a corrupting influence on the process, but allowing the Mayor to act alone will not. I don't find that to be a valid argument. It seems that it would be easier to corrupt one person than 15."

The two-thirds compromise proposal on general managers soon began to gather support on both charter reform commissions, among city councilmembers and other elected officials, business, and labor. A union poll (SEIU 1998) found very strong support for both the current firing provisions and the two-thirds compromise. Even in areas of the city where Riordan's political approval was highest, the unilateral firing appealed to only a minority of voters. But the mayor remained adamantly opposed, and the unilateral firing authority remained his bottom line until the end.

CHAPTER TEN

The Inside Game

POLICE REFORM

IN ONE ASPECT of the inside game of charter reform, the roles of initiator of reform and protector of the status quo were reversed. The nature of reform as a contested value was demonstrated. On police reform, liberal forces were on the attack, moving to increase civilian oversight of the LAPD. Not surprisingly for a law-and-order mayor whose base of support rested in the conservative San Fernando Valley, Riordan resisted the charge for police reform.

In an era when reform was the leading edge of a revived, white-led conservatism, police reform provided a reminder that the liberal coalition and its goals had not disappeared. On this issue, the progressive side had the initiative, the energy, and the high ground.

One of the most profound problems for Los Angeles democracy has been the Los Angeles Police Department. Police reform has long been the most contentious aspect of Los Angeles politics. During the Bradley years, opposing coalitions were built around police accountability. Civilian control of the police became the rallying cry of progressive forces, while maintenance of the LAPD's autonomy unified conservatives.

While Bradley made significant progress in police reform, it was at best an even match until the televised beating of an African American motorist in 1991. The Rodney King beating altered the lines of political power on police reform. For the first time, the reformers had the upper hand, and they used their advantage to implement a series of far-reaching charter reforms. The Christopher Commission appointed by Bradley proposed charter amendments to eliminate the civil service protection for the chief of police and to strengthen the civilian police commission.

Many of the recommendations of the Christopher Commission were rammed through the city council in a long closed session. Several were left out, including the important recommendation for a civilian inspector general to oversee department investigations of police misconduct. The inspector general recommendation was finally placed on the ballot and passed in 1995.

The main Christopher recommendations were placed on the ballot for June 1992, which turned out to be a very difficult time to hold an election on police reform. In April, a Simi Valley jury acquitted the officers in the King case, and the city exploded in massive violence. There was every reason to be concerned that conservative forces, ever vigilant to restore order, would argue that this was the wrong time to "tie the hands of the police." Even so, the voters clearly wanted reform, and Proposition F passed easily. The liberal reform coalition held fast even in the ashes of a divisive urban disorder. African Americans and white liberals, particularly Jews, overwhelmingly backed Proposition F.

Proposition F amended the charter to create a new procedure to hire and fire the police chief and to remove the chief's civil service protection. The key line in the amended charter stated: "The Chief of Police shall serve at the pleasure of the City . . . and shall not attain any property interest in the position of Chief of Police" (City of Los Angeles 1925: sec. 199[b][4]) The chief was now to be appointed to a five-year term, renewable one time only; no chief could serve for more than two terms. The chief must apply for reappointment to the Police Commission near the end of the first term. In addition, provisions that gave virtually insurmountable advantages to insider candidates for chief were removed.

In 1995, another charter amendment implemented one of the key Christopher Commission recommendations, the creation of an inspector general, to "audit, investigate, and oversee the Police Department's handling of complaints of misconduct by police officers and civilian employees" (City of Los Angeles 1925: sec. 206[d]). Katherine Mader was hired in 1996 as the first inspector general.

In addition to Proposition F, Bradley's other legacy to Riordan was a new police chief, appointed in 1992 to replace Daryl Gates. Willie Williams, the African American chief in Philadelphia, came to Los Angeles with rave reviews for community policing. Bradley's Police Commission was able to appoint Williams because of the new provisions under Proposition F that gave outsiders a chance. Previously, no outsider who did not finish ahead of all other candidates in the written exam could even be interviewed.

Williams became extraordinarily popular in Los Angeles, and was a highly visible advocate for community-based policing. But his luck ran out when Riordan defeated Woo in 1993. While Woo favored police reform, Riordan emphasized his pledge to increase the police force by three thousand officers. It was a classic matchup of the historic police debate in Los Angeles: public safety versus police accountability.

Facing a mayor with an agenda completely different from his own, Williams publicly challenged Riordan's hiring plan. He continued to call for community-based policing, and questioned the fiscal and organizational logic behind the Riordan police buildup. Despite Williams's high popularity ratings, it was difficult to see how he was going to block the main proposal of the winning mayoral candidate.

Behind the scenes, Williams was being challenged by an African American insider, Bernard C. Parks. A highly regarded department veteran, Parks had sought the chief's job and finished behind Williams. Parks was extremely well connected in city politics, a close friend of William Wardlaw, Riordan's political adviser, and solidly allied with key members of the city council. Complaining that Parks was undermining him, Williams got the Police Commission to demote Parks. Parks threatened a lawsuit and eventually compelled Williams to back down. While many of the councilmembers liked Williams, he did not have Parks's local history, and members were increasingly worried about Williams's approach to the job of police chief.

Riordan did not move to have the Police Commission fire the popular Williams. However, the commission began to exercise close oversight over Williams's work, and increasingly found fault with it. The police union, which had supported Riordan in 1993, detested Williams, and the union's newsletter regularly issued vitriolic criticism of the chief.

The Police Commission conducted an investigation of Williams and his wife for gambling trips to Las Vegas. Believing that Williams had lied in his testimony, the commission formally disciplined the chief for misrepresentations. The council, however, utilized its power under Proposition 5 (City of Los Angeles 1925: sec. 32.3) to overturn the commission's disciplinary action. While members were increasingly concerned about Williams, there was a general feeling that Riordan was trying to get rid of the chief, and the councilmembers were reluctant to help Riordan use the Las Vegas case to do it. Two leading police commissioners resigned in protest of the council's action.

With Williams and the Police Commission constantly at odds, Williams applied for a second term in 1997 and was rejected. The commissioners then recommended a list of alternatives to the mayor, who selected Parks. Parks was extremely well regarded among blacks, especially in middle-class professional circles, and at the same time was in tune with Riordan's priorities on public safety.

With Parks's selection the transition from Bradley to Riordan was complete. The momentum for police reform that began with the Rodney King beating stalled.

Riordan fought a rearguard action to narrow the scope of police reform. Yet because the leadership of the department was in the hands of a close ally, Chief Bernard C. Parks, who was highly popular in the African American community, the liberal coalition was not as strong and united as it had been on this issue under Tom Bradley.

Parks soon eliminated the highly popular Senior Lead Officer program that had placed top officers in close contact with the community. Parks took this action without the authority of the Police Commission, even though it was a policy matter of great public importance. In addition, he moved to restrict the access of the inspector general, Katherine Mader, to information regarding investigations of police misconduct.

Parks was able to undertake these moves because, with the resignation over the Las Vegas matter of the highly regarded commission president Gary Greenebaum, the Police Commission became completely subservient to the chief. Edith Perez, the new commission president, seemed to regard Parks with awe and helped turn the commission into a cheerleading body that Parks simply ran right over.

In contrast to his enmity with Williams, Mayor Riordan was enthusiastically committed to Parks. Parks facilitated Riordan's plan to increase manpower and shared Riordan's distaste for internal reform or civilian review.

The already shaky reputation of the Police Commission fell even lower during the Perez presidency. Perez refused to back Mader against Parks, making the inspector general's position virtually untenable. With Riordan, the chief, and the leadership of the commission against her, Mader was isolated, and she eventually resigned.

The disastrous Perez presidency rotated between the implausible and the outrageous. In October 1997, Perez intervened when Parks was criticized for treating a police sergeant in a manner that seemed to violate a court order. Perez held a press conference to announce that she had conducted her own independent review of the matter, and that Parks had done nothing wrong.

Perez's actions in this matter so troubled the *Daily News,* a long-time supporter of Riordan and Parks, that it ran an editorial accusing her of "rubberstamping the actions of the police chief. . . . For years, Los Angeles suffered because the police chief was never questioned or challenged by a rubber-stamp civilian oversight board. The result was a kind of infallible and omnipotent police chief for life. After all the pain the city and the LAPD have been through because of that, it should be clear we must not go down that path again" (*Los Angeles Daily News* 1997b).

The low point of the Perez presidency came during charter reform. Packages containing letters condemning Mader and praising the police commission were sent in mysterious, anonymous form marked with the mailing stamp of Perez's law firm to those invited to testify before the charter commissions (Lait 1998). Perez resigned not long after.

Police reform was in trouble, and there was concern that the priorities established by the Christopher Commission were in serious danger of being lost and even reversed. As a result, police reform came to the charter reform commissions.

In charter reform as a whole, Riordan was the reformer fighting against the status quo. In the broad context of charter reform, the city council and organized labor and many progressive groups in the community saw themselves fighting a holding action against Riordan largely in defense of existing political and institutional structures.

On police reform, the roles were reversed. The mayor, his police chief, and his Police Commission president were the main obstacles to reform, and strong sentiment for change emerged on the city council, in organized labor, and ultimately on the two charter reform commissions. Indeed, Riordan's favored commission, the elected body, was even more adamant about specific police reforms than the appointed commission.

During Mader's tenure as inspector general, the mayor's police commission appointed a new executive director to run the commission's staff. They chose Joe Gunn, a close friend of the mayor, for the position. Gunn immediately went to the city council and demanded that his pay be increased to at least that of the inspector general, since the charter technically made him her supervisor. The council went along. When Gunn began to edit and block Mader's reports from being received by the Police Commission, however, the charter commissions became involved.

An example of the problems with the inspector general and the chief was brought before the city council in January 1999. A police sergeant wanted to file a complaint with the inspector general about a comment made by Chief Parks regarding the police union. Katherine Mader was out of town. Joe Gunn, the executive director, intercepted and handled the complaint, and then on his own initiative dismissed it. With Gunn's close ties to Riordan and the chief, councilmembers expressed great concern about the complaint process (Shuster and McGreevy 1999).

As the inspector general suffered greater and greater distress at the hands of the chief and the chief's allies, requests began to flow into the charter commissions to do something about the situation. Liberals on the council and in the labor movement were calling for change in the charter. Chemerinsky, chair of the elected commission, was himself a strong civil libertarian and police reformer. Dennis Zine, head of the police union, was an elected commissioner, and the police union was coming to loathe Parks despite their election support for Riordan. Geoffrey Garfield, administrative director of the elected commission, was a former communications director for the police union and a close ally of Zine.

Sentiment for the Christopher Commission reforms was very strong on both commissions, and these reforms had a great reputation in the community at large. One of the appointed commissioners, Andrew Henderson, was the son-in-law of Warren Christopher. Chemerinsky was an active civil rights lawyer with ties to the police reform community. Riordan and Parks could count on neither commission to carry their water for them against the inspector general.

On February 9, 1998, Parks attended a meeting of the elected commission and asked for several things in the charter. He wanted the power to remove command staff. Parks asked the commission to reduce the authority of the inspector general. He offered an even more remarkable proposal: to eliminate the Christopher Commission's two-term limit on the police chief (McGreevy, 1998a). The *Daily News* (1998c), generally supportive of Parks, criticized his ideas for weakening the oversight authority of the inspector general, noting, "Parks does not need to turn back the clock to move the LAPD ahead."

Both commissions were looking for ways to prevent the executive director from standing between the commission and the inspector general. A proposal emerged that the charter be amended to have the inspector general report directly to the commission. The proposal was opposed by the chief, by Joe Gunn, and by the Police Commission and its president, Edith Perez.

When the appointed commission took up this issue, the staff report strongly supported the proposal that the charter be amended to have the inspector general report directly to the Police Commission.

In testimony before the appointed commission, Joe Gunn spoke in opposition to the staff recommendation. Gunn, a flamboyant character known for fighting corruption many decades ago as an LAPD officer and writing a book about it, told the skeptical members of the commission that his personal involvement was essential to make sure that Mader's reports were first-rate in quality.

When Gunn commented that his actions relative to Mader were consistent with the spirit of the Christopher Commission, Andrew Henderson, Christopher's son-in-law and a volunteer attorney on the Christopher Commission, spoke up. Henderson said, "I worked on the Christopher Commission, and I can tell you unequivocally that the Christopher Commission intended that the reports of the Inspector General would go directly to the Police Commission" (Appointed Commission 1998e). Shortly after Gunn finished his presentation, the commission adopted the staff recommendation by a unanimous vote.

The elected commission reached a similar conclusion not long after. However, they went further and considered a range of specific protections for the inspector general. Ultimately, the proposals were ironed out during the compromise phase. Under the new charter, the IG would report directly to the Police Commission and "have the same access to Police Department information as the Board of Police Commissioners." The IG was also given the power to undertake investigations unless blocked by a majority of the commission, and could hire and fire his or her own staff (City of Los Angeles 1999, sec. 573).

Police issues were not finished. The police union, now at war with the chief, asked the charter commissions to change the charter in the area of police discipline. The existing charter lodged the authority over police discipline solely with the chief and not the Police Commission.

The police union asked the commissions to change the methods by which misconduct charges were reviewed within the department. One union request was to prevent the chief from interfering with the rulings of a disciplinary body. The union complained that Parks was intimidating command officers about their votes in disciplinary hearings. The commissions agreed to prohibit "Ex Parte communication with members of a Board of Rights regarding the subject matter of the hearing while proceedings are pending" (City of Los Angeles 1999, sec. 1070(k)).

The discipline question split the liberal community. Supporters of the Christopher Commission argued that the chief's authority and accountability for discipline were essential to civilian oversight of police brutality. Pro-union liberals thought that Parks's discipline had become arbitrary. Others believed that the union would resist any significant discipline. The commissions ultimately maintained the chief's overall authority over discipline. But the commissions ruled against Parks on the question of creating a unified police command to incorporate Harbor and Airport police. Neighborhood organizations fought to keep these forces autonomous, and the commissions agreed.

The commissions voted to exempt all deputy chiefs of police from civil service. The last provision was agreed to near the end of the joint committee process after a personal appearance by Parks. The change gave Parks authority available to no other general manager, even with the enhanced openings for civil service exemptions in the new charter.

The struggle over police reform in the new charter revealed some important aspects of Los Angeles reform. The tremendous reputation earned by the Christopher Commission was a great asset to police reformers. Being consistent with the Christopher Commission reforms was a position sought by both sides in the debate. Even the changes wrought by the King beating could not ensure that the path to police reform would be easy or steady. With a mayor more committed to police manpower than reform, and with a chief resistant to civilian oversight, the challenge of reform was very great. That the commissions chose to at least keep the ball rolling in police reform, however, was an important contribution to the long-term prospects of police reform in Los Angeles.

CHAPTER ELEVEN

The Outside Game

THE POLITICS OF PARTICIPATION

> If corruption was the great fear in 1925, then public disaffection from a government often seen as inefficient and unresponsive, and the tension between neighborhoods and the greater community are the concerns we must address today and in the future.
> —Appointed Los Angeles Charter Reform Commission,
> *Road to Decision*

THE FUNDAMENTAL issue of charter reform for the community was not the power of the mayor. Participation—the outside game—was the key to public interest in the charter reform debate. The roots of the charter reform battle came from the secession movement, which was far more concerned about decentralizing power than about the roles of actors within the central government. Any charter reform that failed to deal with these democratic issues would be doomed to failure or irrelevance.

Low participation had become a characteristic feature of Los Angeles politics. The mixture of great geographic size and lack of connection to city hall was widely noted. A fifteen-member city council to represent more than 3.6 million residents created a constituent/officeholder ratio that ranked as the largest in the nation.

Voter turnout remained low, with the exception of the racially polarized 1969 and 1973 mayoral elections between Sam Yorty and Tom Bradley. Even in a tightly contested runoff election in 1993 between two ideologically opposed candidates, turnout was less than half of registered voters.

The long-standing problem of low participation in Los Angeles was exacerbated by the massive rise of immigration. Immigration had not been matched by a rise in citizenship, and there remained a vast and disturbing gap between the population and the voters. In the early 1990s, more than a third of the city's adults were noncitizens, raising basic questions of fairness and representation.

The charter commissioners learned directly from residents during public hearings that many did not feel heard in their dealings with city officials. A resident in the western San Fernando Valley with a relatively minor zoning matter might take the long ride on the crowded 101 freeway at rush hour to make a 10 A.M. meeting of a city commission. Upon arrival at city hall, he or she might be informed that the item had been moved to another day. Or, the item might be acted on very quickly without significant public input.

Most immediately, the discontent that drove charter reform came from those communities in the San Fernando Valley and in the Harbor area that sought to secede from the city. But the sentiment for secession hid a quieter alienation that kept Los Angeles from achieving its democratic potential.

The central role of participation issues altered the structure of the charter debate and opened new opportunities for groups to influence the result. In the inside game at city hall, the players were clustered around those who favored and those who opposed the mayor's position. In the outside game, there were more players with diverse perspectives, and those who were fighting the inside game tried to orient themselves to the outside game debate. Side deals across the inside and outside games that Norton Long (1958) would have recognized as an urban "ecology of games" were common.

The outside game was fought around several different alternatives to neighborhood participation. How much authority would the new charter grant to neighborhoods? How would the electoral system be changed, if at all?

Los Angeles had had so little experience with participatory mechanisms that the community had to educate itself on the state of the art. A hodge-podge of theoretical and practical models was available. *The Rebirth of American Democracy* (Berry, Portnoy, and Thompson 1993) was read widely during charter reform, and provided a baseline of neighborhood participation efforts in other cities. The appointed commission staff took a strong interest in the New York City community boards. New York's size seemed more apt as a model for Los Angeles than the smaller cities in *The Rebirth of Urban Democracy*. Research that showed a great influence by these advisory appointed bodies in land use matters (Pecorrela 1989) was an indication to the appointed commission staff that advisory bodies could develop power.

There were several local experiments in neighborhood participation. Mark Ridley-Thomas, councilmember of the eighth district in South Central Los Angeles, had established an extraordinarily successful Empowerment Congress. The congress, whose members were appointed by Ridley-Thomas, was divided into four geographic areas. They met regularly, provided advice to Ridley-Thomas and city bureaucrats, and recommended community priorities for police and other services. At the congress's annual meeting, it was not unusual for six hundred or more people to attend. Ridley-Thomas devoted up to one-third of his council office budget to the support of the congress.

Several councilmembers had created appointed neighborhood advisory bodies. Michael Feuer developed a strong group in the Robertson area that later became a model for new neighborhood councils. Hal Bernson had a local advisory group in the twelfth councilmanic district. In an irony that did not go unnoticed by his colleagues, the most vocal advocate of neighborhood councils, Joel Wachs of the second district, had never established an advisory council in his own district.

The status quo, therefore, was a system in which councilmembers could, on a voluntary basis, create advisory councils within their own districts. This status quo was appealing to the council members, but fell far short of the aspirations of reformers.

The framework of the debate was whether neighborhood councils should be established; whether or not they should be elected; and whether or not they should have decision-making authority. There were those, including elements of downtown business and members of the city council, who opposed any sort of neighborhood councils. But the campaigns for elected charter reform commissioners had shown significant public interest in some form of neighborhood councils.

The debate parameters ranged from appointed neighborhood councils with advisory powers to elected neighborhood councils with decision-making authority over land use. There was great confusion within the community over the different alternatives.

Politically, the greatest bang came from advocating the strongest possible alternative (short of secession). As a result, it was sometimes difficult to decode the actual structure a politician supported. The rhetoric did not always match up to the actual proposals (e.g., "I support neighborhood councils with decision-making authority," but "I intend to take their advice into account.").

The outside game intersected with the inside game at an angle. In other words, one could not completely predict a player's position on one game from his or her view on the other.

For Riordan, the outside game was secondary to his primary interest in mayoral authority, the heart of the inside game. Riordan took the most radical view of enhancing mayoral authority, but favored advisory neighborhood councils.

For home-owner associations in the Valley, giving a mayor they supported more authority was useful, but not as important as winning the most radical model of local authority over land use. For still others, like Bennett Keyser of the elected commission, opposition to mayoral authority went hand in hand with enthusiastic support for elected decision-making neighborhood councils. The *Daily News*, on the other end of the ideological spectrum from Keyser, was equally strong in favoring elected decision-making neighborhood councils and mayoral authority.

Riordan's allies in the downtown business community were adamantly opposed to decision-making neighborhood councils. Twenty-four downtown business leaders came together to influence charter reform through the Los Angeles Business Advisers (LABA). Comprised of top executives of downtown companies, including the publisher of the *Los Angeles Times,* LABA sought to move the charter debate away from neighborhood participation. These business leaders feared that neighborhood councils would block growth and development. Instead, they pushed for a much larger city council, both to divert support from neighborhood councils and to strengthen the hand of the mayor within the city government.

Valley business leaders were closely tied to the secession movement, and their mouthpiece was the *Daily News.* In fact, a war developed between the *Times* and the *News,* with each corporation making donations. The *Daily News* put money into secession; the *Times* helped back LABA.

The debate on neighborhood councils might have split the secession movement's two wings of home-owner associations and business interests. Business people in the Valley were heavily progrowth and saw secession as a way to avoid government regulation of land use. Home-owner associations wanted to control land use so that they could block growth (Purcell 1997). Home-owner associations, especially in the Valley, favored elected, decision-making neighborhood councils with authority over land use and were suspicious of developers. Valley business leaders were strongly in favor of secession, but ambivalent about giving community bodies land-use authority if the city stayed together. The best solution was to keep the discussion of land use in a future Valley city vague (Hogen-Esch 2001).

Another set of players in the outside game were Latino voting-rights activists who saw an opportunity to boost minority representation by increasing the size of the city council. This issue split minority communities. African Americans were opposed to any change that might dilute their council representation. Latino activists, however, had powerful allies in the downtown business community and the *Los Angeles Times,* which supported a larger city council in order to head off neighborhood councils.

The downtown business leaders saw a larger council as a way to forestall decision-making neighborhood councils, which they feared above all, and also as a way to weaken the council and strengthen the mayor. Riordan's political advisers favored council expansion, at least until popular opposition became clear. As Wardlaw candidly indicated, "We thought a larger council would be a good idea because it would weaken the council" (interview).

City employees, who were on the defensive in the inside game at city hall against Riordan's restructuring proposals, went on the offensive in the neighborhood council debate. Proposals for strong elected decision-making neighborhood councils came from the left: from Tom Hayden in his 1997 mayoral campaign against Riordan, from councilmember Jackie Goldberg, from Julie Butcher of the SEIU, and from Bennett Keyser of the elected commission. Meanwhile, construction unions and other private-sector labor groups, who were amenable to mayoral authority, feared antigrowth neighborhood councils.

Had there been a clear point of view from the voting public, the list of alternatives might have changed. However, focus groups funded jointly by the appointed and elected commissions revealed that while there was broad enthusiasm for the idea of neighborhood councils, there was great disagreement on how they should look. No single alternative emerged as uniquely compelling to the voters interviewed. Yet the idea itself was a formidable force, meaning that in political terms, the only alternative that would disappoint the public would be the status quo.

On February 23, 1998, Councilmember Jackie Goldberg presented to the elected commission a plan, which she later presented to the appointed commission, for a system of elected neighborhood councils with decision-making authority. These elected bodies would operate within council districts, with as many as five elected bodies per district. The Goldberg plan bore some similarities to plans for local elections presented by the Valley Industry and Commerce Association (VICA) and by David Fleming.

The appointed commission took up these issues first on April 8, 1998, when the staff presented a report entitled "Barriers to Access." Two strong advocates of neighborhood councils, Doris Nelson and Jerry Gaines, were the leading voices on the appointed commission calling for neighborhood councils.

At almost every commission meeting, Doris Nelson asked speakers to comment on the potential for neighborhood councils. Gaines had been appointed to the commission after his defeat by Janice Hahn for the elected commission in the fifteenth district Harbor area, where secession sentiment ran very high. Gaines ran with Riordan's endorsement, and ironically ended up on the commission Riordan opposed. Gaines sent a stream of memos to both charter commissions calling for further action in the direction of neighborhood empowerment.

While the appointed commission staff favored neighborhood councils, both for substantive and political reasons, our inclination was to first research what other cities had done. The review revealed some surprising results. It had been widely assumed in the local debate that there were elected, decision-making neighborhood councils in other cities. A survey of the literature and telephone calls to those cities that had neighborhood councils brought forth the clear conclusion that every city with neighborhood councils, with the temporary exception of a Washington, D.C. provision on liquor stores, granted them only advisory powers. Neighborhood councils with decision-making authority would be a radical change, unprecedented in the United States.

The second conclusion that emerged from the staff research was that advisory neighborhood councils were remarkably influential in the planning process. Ironically, given New York City's unpopularity in the local political culture, the example of New York City's community boards was influential with the appointed commission. Over 80 percent of recommendations on land use made by community boards were approved by the New York city council (Pecorello 1989). Besides, New York City was an appropriate comparison to Los Angeles because of its size and complexity.

The multicity review also elicited the information that other cities were less likely to view neighborhood democracy as an outgrowth of a hostile relationship to the city government, but rather saw it as an expansion of the government's relationship to the community. Despite the polarized debate surrounding secession and Riordan's battles with the city council, an effective system of neighborhood democracy seemed more likely to succeed if it were to be built more around a cooperative than a confrontational approach to city government.

After the staff report at the April 8, 1998, meeting, the appointed commission made preliminary decisions on participation at the April 22, 1998, meeting. The staff report presented several alternatives, including the status quo with voluntary creation of advisory neighborhood councils by members of the city council; formal neighborhood councils with procedural authority to be heard on city issues; and decision-making neighborhood councils. This listing clarified that a system of advisory neighborhood councils with procedural authority was not the status quo, despite widespread impressions to the contrary in Los Angeles. In my oral report to the commission, I said:

> Alternative 1 is to leave the charter silent on the question of power. But this also implies the continuation of a current system which is a voluntary system of truly advisory powers in which people in government can choose to listen to comments or not and can choose to establish systems or not. Alternative 2 is a mandatory procedural system of input. And for those cities that have systems of neighborhood councils, this is by far the system that is most widely adopted in New York, Portland, St. Paul, other cities. . . . If we're looking at an experimental system that is going to evolve, the staff's belief is that it would be a serious mistake to begin that system with a formal delegation of powers with substantial legal liability for the city by creating another level of review that has not been done in other cities in a city that has almost no track record of its own of citizen participation. (Appointed Commission 1998b, 232–35)

The commissioners voted eleven to one to adopt the staff recommendation for a mandatory system of advisory neighborhood councils. The next question was what the charter should say about the subjects on which neighborhood councils should be heard. The commission was split between those who wanted to leave this question open and those who felt it crucial to spell out such areas as land use. A number of commissioners believed that especially in light of the vote against decision-making neighborhood councils, it was urgent to specify in the charter the areas of purview. As labor leader Charley Mims said, "If we put something in the proposed charter that has no form and apparently no substance, people are going to look at it as a sham."

Doris Nelson added, "Land use issues are critical, and if we don't put anything in the charter, no one will know for sure whether that's going to be real. People are not going to be involved if they think that the issues are not going to be important. As it is, advisory is going to seem very weak, but I think, clearly, if there were some procedural authority that is in the charter, that would show people that this is an important thing to get involved in." Andrew Henderson expressed concern that if the issues over which neighborhood councils held sway were left to ordinance, the council might not act: "I think there should be a nonexclusive list of advisory powers as a minimum."

While the question was put over to a later meeting, the direction of the appointed commission was toward a formal advisory system in the charter, and with procedural input on specific issues at a minimum. Finally, the commissioners took the important step of placing a Department of Neighborhoods in the charter, with room for the council, by ordinance, to flesh it out.

The appointed commission was strongly imbued with the philosophy that the charter should be a broad, enabling document and that detail should be left to ordinance. On the other hand, advocates of participation feared that the government would not encourage neighborhood councils if there were insufficient detail in the charter. In the end, this debate was worked out in the final negotiations on the unified charter.

The power of the outside game to create strange bedfellows was shown by the fact that the direction of the appointed commission was highly compatible with that being developed by Mayor Riordan. On neighborhood councils, the appointed commission was closer than the elected commission to Riordan's view.

Only the week before the deliberations meeting, Riordan sent a letter to Kieffer outlining his views on neighborhood councils. He proposed a system of "neighborhood councils consisting of members annually elected by caucus." While this method was not particularly clear, it was specifically presented as an alternative to formal elections, "which would increase the cost and politicization of the process, while appointing members goes against the idea of a local independent body." Riordan's letter called for advisory councils and a formal process of input. Consistent with the appointed commission's research, Riordan argued against decision-making councils as inconsistent with practice in other cities, and pointed out that advisory councils had become strongly influential in other cities. One difference is that the mayor favored the creation of a Department of Neighborhoods by ordinance, not by placing it in the charter.

By the spring of 1998, Riordan and the appointed commission, opponents in the charter process, were largely on the same page on the nature of neighborhood councils. The elected commission was in the midst of its own process of evolution. While the elected body was supportive of Riordan's goal of enhancing mayoral authority, its predilections on neighborhood councils were far from Riordan's approach. Riordan did have some assets on the elected commission on this issue, including allies Chet Widom and Bill Weinberger, the Building Trades Union, and a business community fearful of neighborhood councils.

From the very start, the elected commission was avidly interested in neighborhood councils. Virtually every winning candidate (and many of the losing ones) for the elected commission had promised to create strong neighborhood councils. Once elected, that was the topic they wanted to talk about. When the commission voted to hold its deliberations meetings in each council district, Chemerinsky had to beg members to allow the topics of the meeting they hosted in their districts to be other than neighborhood councils. Nobody wanted to host a meeting in his or her own district on the subject of financial management.

At the start, a majority of the elected commissioners favored elected neighborhood councils with authority over land use. Chemerinsky said that he did not favor advisory councils, the model used in other cities. Recalling his days in student government, he said, "I don't see any point in institutionalizing student government" (Rohrlich 1998b).

But this interest in neighborhood councils masked internal disagreements among the elected commissioners over the shape of neighborhood councils. Two of the mayor's closest allies on the commission, architect Chet Widom and attorney Bill Weinberger, were the most skeptical.

A survey of the elected commissioners by the *Los Angeles Times* (Rohrlich 1998b) found that most were developing serious doubts about giving land use authority to neighborhood councils. Opposition from business, from Riordan, and from construction unions was having an effect. Ironically, the four members who still strongly favored giving councils such authority were not from secessionist territory, but were labor Democrats: Marguerite Archie-Hudson, Marcos Casteneda, Janice Hahn, and Bennett Keyser.

On the other hand, progressives were ambivalent about certain features of the elected decision-making model. First, formal elections would not allow noncitizens to participate, since the California Constitution limits voting to citizens. Second, nonprofit organizations expressed the fear that powerful neighborhood councils would block social service programs for unpopular groups.

Participation proposals could be equally perilous if they stirred up conservatives. A comment by Chemerinsky concerning participation by undocumented residents outraged conservatives, including commissioners Boland and Zine. The *Daily News,* the principal media supporter for the elected commission, issued an angry editorial (1998b):

> Welcome to Sillyville, USA. The goofball republic of wayout ideas. Chemerinsky all but killed hopes for reforming the incomprehensible City charter with his recent idea for a bill of rights granting an inalienable right to abortion. Now, Chemerinsky and charter Commissioner Gloria Romero are entertaining the notion that if the city creates official neighborhood councils, then immigrants—legal and illegal—ought to be able to sit on them.

In early May, divisions on neighborhood councils began to surface on the elected commission. Bennett Keyser's committee on participation received a draft report on neighborhood councils from its consultants. The report was strongly tilted toward elected, decision-making neighborhood councils. Advisory neighborhood councils were characterized as the status quo in Los Angeles.

This analysis differed sharply from that of the appointed commission, which drew a distinction between a voluntary system currently in place and a mandatory program of neighborhood councils with procedural authority. The draft report incorrectly indicated that a number of cities had decision-making neighborhood councils. I took the unusual step of calling the staff of the elected commission to correct this critical misstatement.

The draft report raised questions within the elected commission. Weinberger prepared a detailed memo dated May 4, 1998, complaining about "a lack of balance and depth in the report's analysis. . . . It is incomplete, and, at times, contains conclusions that are not reflective of the views expressed by the Committee." Weinberger's memo not only revealed splits on the commission, but on the committee headed by Keyser. The final revised report was more balanced and corrected the statement about the systems in other cities.

Weinberger was one of the mayor's strongest allies on mayoral authority, and Keyser was to be one of the mayor's strongest opponents on those issues. But on the issue of neighborhood councils, Weinberger was closer to the appointed commission's view than to the early consensus on his own commission, and Keyser, who was later to become a key ally of the appointed commission on the unified charter, was far from the appointed commission's view on neighborhood councils. I faxed Weinberger's memo to Kieffer, with a note that "you might consider talking with him about this."

On May 30, 1998, the elected commission considered the amended committee report. Sam Bell of LABA presented the business community's view against strong neighborhood councils. The position of the downtown business community had been that if they were to be created at all, neighborhood councils should be advisory and appointed. LABA's leaders said they would campaign against any charter that included elected decision-making neighborhood councils. On May 18, the *Times* (1998a) editorialized in favor of a larger city council, arguing that a system of neighborhood councils would "layer an expensive new bureaucracy onto the city's already top-heavy structure without solving the problem."

At the same meeting, State Senator Tom Hayden and Jackie Goldberg spoke in favor of elected decision-making neighborhood councils. Julie Butcher of SEIU concurred. Chet Widom expressed concerns about this direction, and Bill Weinberger called for advisory bodies. By an eight-to-two margin, the commission endorsed elected neighborhood councils. By an eight-to-one margin, voting on neighborhood councils was limited to eligible voters (thereby ruling out noncitizens). This issue was to resurface during negotiations on the unified charter, because of its massive implications in a city where one-third of the adults were not citizens.

In the process of decision, however, commissioners were confronted with Weinberger's memo analyzing the report produced by the committee and the consultants. The Weinberger memo questioned a number of key aspects of the argument made by the committee, and indicated that there would be articulate opposition within the commission to the proposals it had already endorsed. The elected commission voted to endorse elected decision-making neighborhood councils with authority over only some city funds and services, a considerable step back from power over land use.

Weinberger and Widom's opposition seemed to signal that Riordan would fight elected decision-making neighborhood councils. But how hard would he fight? Riordan's business allies expected him to use his clout with the elected commission to kill the idea. Riordan's position could be summed up as mayoral authority, and as much neighborhood participation as would be necessary to win mayoral authority. There was therefore no assurance that he would use *every* resource he possessed to block neighborhood councils in the interest of his business allies. Despite his opposition to decision-making neighborhood councils, no one could be certain he would not make a trade to get the power to fire general managers.

The labor side was once again divided between city employees and the County Federation of Labor. SEIU 347 came out in favor of elected decision-making neighborhood councils. Along with Jackie Goldberg and Tom Hayden, the "left" position emerged as opposition to mayoral authority along with support for elected decision-making neighborhood councils.

On neighborhood councils, the County Federation of Labor and the Building Trades were very likely to be concerned about the NIMBYism of home-owner groups, and to be suspicious of the left-led move for neighborhood empowerment.

Business continued to be divided, with downtown business dead-set against neighborhood councils, but Valley business organizations not opposing the call of home-owner associations for a devolution of power.

In an analysis of the debate on neighborhood councils, Jim Bickhardt, an experienced council deputy, found the downtown business approach "myopic." "After all, it is the specter of land developer and big business influence that has fueled several successful insurrectionist city council and initiative campaigns in Los Angeles since the mid 1980s." He continued:

> While business interests would likely mount the best-funded campaign on whatever side of a charter reform ballot measure they chose to advocate, they would also be an easy target for the barbs of their opposition. A headstrong, big-money effort by business interests to scuttle charter reform could well come to resemble the sorry, sadistic, sight of pre–Revolutionary War British soldiers marching down the middle of a Massachusetts road while rebels sniped away at them from behind every tree and boulder. (1998, 10–11)

There were therefore at least three broad positions on neighborhood councils: the downtown business-Riordan-*Times*-Building Trades "conservative" group; the Goldberg-Hayden-SEIU "left" group; and the populist Valley, Valley business, home-owner association, *Daily News* group. It was up to the two charter commissions to craft a proposal on neighborhood councils in light of these three hovering coalitions.

Faced with these divergent opinions, Chemerinsky proposed a "summit" to bring stakeholders together for a common position. This plan placed the appointed commission in a vulnerable position, in that it positioned the elected commission as the mediator among community power brokers. As it turned out, the summit was less than successful.

The meeting began with Chemerinsky stating that elected decision-making neighborhood councils were going to happen; the only question on the table was how. Under the Brown Act rules on open meetings, a majority of elected commissioners could not attend and conduct business. So he and the other elected commissioners then left the room. This approach outraged those in the room from the conservative bloc who intended to fight against the elected decision-making model of neighborhood councils.

Meanwhile, the elected commission was going through a final transformation on neighborhood councils. If one argument for the new charter was to broaden participation in a diverse city, and if the current structures of voter registration did not reflect the city's diversity, how could a system of elected neighborhood councils where voting was open only to citizens expand democracy?

A related argument was brought to the elected commission by nonprofit social service organizations, which feared that voters organized in majorities could block the activities of their agencies within the borders of neighborhood councils (Orlov 1998).

These contradictions, quite important to progressives, could only be resolved by abandoning the elected decision-making model.

There had been a slow but steady shift on the elected commission from its apparent support for elected decision-making neighborhood councils to its ultimate recommendation for advisory councils. Kieffer believed that a compromise on neighborhood councils and other issues would be essential, but was further convinced

> that we couldn't make progress together until they made progress alone. They had such clear divisions. They hadn't reached conclusions that we had reached. They were heading toward a direction that was going to be a better place to negotiate with them from than where they were on that particular day. We had to wait.

The real difficulty was not bridging the question of advisory or decision-making powers, because the elected commission eventually came around to the view of the appointed commission. The more difficult question became how to select neighborhood councils.

While the elected commission had changed its position, there was still considerable support for elected neighborhood councils on that body. The appointed commission wanted to leave the process of selection to ordinance.

Those suspicious of the city government wanted detailed protections in the charter. The appointed commission adamantly opposed what it considered excessive charter detail, believing that the ability of interest groups to get their provisions into the charter where they could not be changed without a vote of the people had created the mess that the charter had become. Yet the appointed commissioners would eventually have to give considerable ground to the elected commission on neighborhood councils.

Once again, there would be a debate between the two commissions about the council, which the appointed panel trusted somewhat and which the elected body loathed. Greg Nelson, chief deputy to councilmember Joel Wachs, pursued a different alternative: self-selection, championed early by Riordan. This idea helped bridge the difference at least in part by obscuring it. It did, however, offer a constructive way out of the impasse. The self-selection idea had already been incorporated into the appointed commission's draft charter, as a result of the efforts of Doris Nelson. It offered a flexible, community-based approach to designing neighborhood councils.

Under the self-selection model, neighborhood councils would devise their own method of selecting members and officers as part of their application to a new Department of Neighborhoods. Neighborhood councils could utilize elected members, a caucus method, appointment, or a mixture. It was more autonomous than New York City's community boards, whose members are chosen by borough presidents and city council members. This self-selection system avoided the pitfalls of formal elections by allowing noncitizens to participate and removed control from the city council. Ultimately, both commissions were able to accept it.

AREA PLANNING COMMISSIONS EMERGE

On September 22, 1998, Anton Calleia sent a letter to his fellow appointed commissioners that called for further work in the area of participation:

> The changes we have tentatively endorsed, though modest in their scope, will help create a more agile organization, capable of restructuring itself if necessary to meet emerging public needs. However, *we have not done as much as we might to bring the City's government closer to the people.* (emphasis in original)

Calleia concluded that "the disappointment we have caused in some quarters by our rejection of decision-making neighborhood councils can be remedied by our recommending a new procedure for dealing with land-use decisions. . . . We should propose creation of several regional planning commissions . . . which would be the first to hear and *decide* land-use issues" (emphasis in original).

On September 23, 1998, the appointed commission adopted the concept of area planning commissions, largely as proposed by Calleia. Although it was not recognized at the time, the appointed commission's decision laid the groundwork for a relatively easy agreement with the elected commission, which had already adopted a similar idea proposed by Chet Widom.

On June 29, 1998, Widom had proposed to the elected commission the creation of District Planning Commissions, which would have significant decision-making authority over land use. In Widom's proposal, the DPCs would replace the citywide City Planning Commission. In the appointed commission's model, area planning commissions would supplement the City Planning Commission.

Area planning commissions were among the most important elements of the new charter. There was no model on which to base them. Neither commission was aware of any other city that had created them. Yet they seemed to have potential to fill in one of the missing blanks in the Los Angeles system of participation: the lack of intermediate decision-making bodies that could cut the distance from city hall to the neighborhoods. By designing bodies regional rather than neighborhood in focus, the commissions hoped to avoid creating a large number of new institutions, so that they could be more easily held accountable to city laws and procedures.

If area planning commissions worked well, they could reduce one of the biggest complaints against Los Angeles government: the long ride to downtown to handle a relatively small land use matter that could more easily be dealt with locally. One other virtue that was discovered later was that area planning commissions could become the basis for further decentralizing reforms. Borough proposals could be generated by electing, instead of appointing, members of these commissions. The areas designed to be at least five in number could be the basis for decentralization of city services, as proposed in 2002 by both Mayor James Hahn and Councilmember Tom LaBonge.

COUNCIL SIZE

If the debate over participation led to advisory neighborhood councils and area planning commissions—two major steps toward participatory democracy and decentralized government—another approach to enhanced democracy through *representative* democracy failed to win enactment by the voters. The idea of increasing the size of the city council drew together the two charter reform commissions, the business community, and representatives of some civil rights organizations representing immigrant communities. But it also generated furious, ultimately unresolvable conflicts.

On the surface, increasing the size of the council seemed to be a no-brainer. No city council in the country had as many people served by as few city council members (table 8).

Each councilmember served a quarter of a million people, well above what any reasonable person would consider a small-sized district. While both commissions hoped to expand the council, there were three obstacles. One was their inability to agree on a single number. The second was conflict among minority groups, who were presumed beneficiaries of a larger council. The third, and ultimately the most important, was vigorous voter resistance to any proposal that would create more elected officials at city hall.

The debate over the size of the city council engaged minority communities in a way that a number of other charter issues did not. A close alliance emerged among those who favored a strong mayor and feared neighborhood councils in the business community and those minority activists who wanted greater representation. They converged in their support for a substantially larger city council.

This debate mobilized Latino civil rights organizations, and to some degree those representing Asian Americans and African Americans. However, there was significant political conflict between the position of African Americans on the one hand and Latinos and Asian Americans on the other. There could be no single minority position on council size.

TABLE 8

City	Population	District Size
Los Angeles	3,448,613	229,908
New York	7,333,253	143,789
Phoenix	1,048,949	131,119
San Diego	1,151,977	143,997
Houston	1,702,086	189,121
Detroit	992,038	at-large elections
San Antonio	998,905	99,981
Philadelphia	1,524,249	152,425
Dallas	1,022,830	at-large elections
Chicago	2,731,743	54,635

Source: Adapted from McCarthy, Erie, Reichhardt, and Ingram 1997, table 5, p. 90.

As Latino voters became a larger part of the electorate, Latino activists sought to broadly expand the number of elective offices. The Los Angeles City/County Redistricting Coalition established the ambitious goals of creating more L.A. city council and school board seats, expanding the size of the county board of supervisors, and changing community college board elections from at-large to district. Latino groups were not in complete agreement among themselves, with the established Mexican-American Legal Defense and Education Fund (MALDEF) holding back from supporting some of these measures until further discussion of school board governance (Rohrlich 1998d).

As Muzzio and Tompkins (1989) demonstrate in their analysis of council size in the New York City charter reform of 1989, manipulation of the size of the council in traditional cities like New York had been a battle between reformers and party regulars for many years. In brief, party regulars wanted big councils elected by district and reformers wanted smaller councils elected at large. Traditional reformers feared that a large council, elected by district, would represent "parochial" interests. Modern reformers, of course, are looking to increase the access of the public to legislative bodies, and no longer favor small councils. The New York city council was already quite large in 1989 (thirty-five members) and charter reformers increased it to fifty-one in 1989.

From the start, the Los Angeles business community was the strongest advocate for a much larger city council. They were backed in this approach by the *Los Angeles Times*. Both feared not only neighborhood councils of the variety being pursued by the elected commission, but even the milder version pursued by the appointed commission.

The business group hired a voting-rights expert to look at council size from the angle of minority representation. As tended to occur in the Riordan years, there were the beginnings of an alliance among business, Riordan-type centrist reformers, and some Latinos against African Americans.

The LABA analysis claimed that a much larger council would be a boon to minority communities and neighborhoods in general. In a slick brochure and publicity packet, LABA contrasted the presumed benefits of a larger city council with those of neighborhood councils. With more council-members there would be smaller districts, and therefore greater representation. The LABA study offered a way to keep the cost of a larger council from rising, and that was to reduce council staffs. The number of council members that these groups tended to favor was thirty-five.

The other agenda of the LABA study, beyond blocking neighborhood councils, was revealed by a close analysis of the presumed benefits: that the council would exercise more legislative than executive power. Not surprisingly, the two very large councils, New York City and Chicago, operate in cities with very strong mayoral structures.

The report was based on the assumption that there would be no net cost of a larger council "if each council member had approximately 6 staff members, instead of the 17 person staff each has today." This assumption was in turn based on the notion that in smaller districts, there would be fewer demands for constituent service.

There were serious problems with this analysis. If the purpose of the larger council would be to strengthen responsiveness to neighborhoods, there would actually be greater expectations of constituent service with fewer staff members to provide it. Jointly funded focus groups on participation conducted by the firm Fairbank, Maslin, Maullin and Associates under contract to the two charter reform commissions had found that staff members for city councilmembers, not the members themselves, were the "go-to" people for residents with a problem to be solved.

Initially, the elected commission leaned toward the larger number. Some, but not all, minority organizations agreed. However, the elected commission soon ran into the issue of race. African American members of the commission, particularly Woody Fleming, were adamant that council size remain at fifteen in order to preserve the black community's stake in the council. Since 1963, African Americans had held the same three out of fifteen seats. Janice Hahn and Woody Fleming warned commissioners on March 16, 1998, about the public outcry that would confront a recommendation for a larger council.

As former outsiders edging toward the inside, Latinos had no stake in maintaining the current percentages on the council. Richard Fajardo, of

MALDEF, presented a series of maps in support of the larger city council. Fajardo told a meeting of the joint charter reform commissions that a twenty-five-member council would increase Latino representation from three to six, and African American representation from three to four (Orlov 1999a). The elected group now leaned to twenty-five.

On the appointed commission, the staff's research suggested that a large increase could lead to unforeseen consequences, such as the diminution of the authority of individual councilmembers and the rise of an inside leadership clique. As a result, the staff recommended a smaller increase, to twenty-one members.

With the proposed increases in both commissions, to twenty-five by the elected, twenty-one by the appointed, the issue seemed to be only over numbers. It seemed at the time that a larger council would be created along with neighborhood councils, rather than, as business hoped, as an alternative to neighborhood councils.

The proposals for neighborhood democracy that emerged from the two charter reform commissions were meant to address the lack of participation that had long characterized Los Angeles government. Through a vigorous local debate, the reformers had proposed a system that was substantially more independent of city politicians than the system of New York City community boards.

In New York City, the community boards were very much integrated within the city political system. Appointments to the boards were made by borough presidents and members of the city council. This alternative was rejected in Los Angeles in favor of a system of "self-selection" that left the election of officers to local people and that did not connect the boundaries of neighborhood councils to city council districts.

This plan held the promise of an extension of participation without direct control by city politicians, a fact that was not lost on councilmembers. Hal Bernson castigated the charter chairs at the city council hearings on the new charter, indicating that he already had neighborhood councils in his district, by which he meant advisory bodies that he had appointed.

Advisory councils were created to respond to progressive, as well as business, concerns. Nonprofit organizations serving disadvantaged communities lobbied the elected charter reform commission against decision-making neighborhood councils. They feared that the groups they served would be kept out of the neighborhoods by such bodies. Further, the commissions were concerned that decision-making councils would require formal elections, thereby disenfranchising noncitizens. Third, the commissions were influenced by research showing that all other cities with neighborhood councils had advisory, not decision-making, bodies.

Downtown business did not have the ability to block neighborhood councils. Despite its reputation as an unstoppable force, downtown business had fallen back of the curve in charter reform. It had neither the resources nor the political power to stop a popular proposal in its tracks.

In reality, charter reform had created odd alignments inconsistent with simplistic views of the absolute power of the downtown business establishment. By now, the inside and outside games had created a complicated, cross-cutting set of proposals that generated numerous possibilities for alliance and conflict. The problem would be finding a way to reconcile the interests and beliefs that were driving these proposals into a unified program of reform.

PART FOUR

The Unified Charter

CHAPTER TWELVE

The Creation of the Unified Charter

ON JULY 13, 1998, the *Los Angeles Times* carried a story by reporter Jim Newton (1998a) that compared and contrasted the working styles of the appointed and elected charter reform commissions. The story brought into public view for the first time their long-standing differences about the government of Los Angeles. What had been an insider discussion for many months was now out in print. Based on interviews with commissioners and staff members from both commissions, the *Times* story served to drive the commissions even farther apart.

In the *Times* article, the two chairs defended their commissions. Newton noted, "The elected commission and its staff tend to see the appointed group as conservative tinkerers, bent on incremental change and resistant to major reform. The appointed panel and its staff, meanwhile, question the depth of the elected group's research and the thoughtfulness of some of its proposals." Geoffrey Garfield, the executive director of the elected commission, added, "They're editing; we're writing a new charter." I retorted, "We are neither status quo nor radical; we're just cautious."

I ran into Chemerinsky that evening as the elected commission prepared for its meeting, held in the same Department of Water and Power Building where our offices were located. He held up a copy of the *Times* article and pointed out our negative comments. I reached over and pointed to the parts where his group was downgrading us. Each of us saw only the insults from the other side.

As Chemerinsky later recalled it, the *Times* article was the low point of the search for a unified charter, and eroded the trust that would be needed to complete the job. "I can't tell you how many calls I got from elected commissioners saying, 'Why should we work with them if that's how they feel about us?' And there's the tendency naturally on our side to ignore the quotes from our side." Kieffer commented that "the appointed commission was getting blamed in part because of the reputations of the two commissions that had been established by then among those in the inside of the policy process."

To pass the proposed charter, the commissions had to settle their own rivalry with each other. The *Times* article made it clear that even if the policy conflicts were settled, the animosity between the two commissions could by itself doom charter reform.

Perhaps the most critical variable was that the two chairs, Chemerinsky and Kieffer, believed from the start that there had to be a single charter. As outsiders to city hall, both were able to stand outside the mayor-council conflict and hear what people in the community had to say. Neither met anyone not involved in the inside game at city hall who thought it was a good idea to have two charters on the ballot.

But how could they get there? The mutual distrust between the commissions and the staffs was serious. After Chemerinsky became chair of the elected commission, there was the beginning of a thawing in the relationship at the chairs' level. The two commissions decided to create a liaison committee to keep the lines of communication open. The first meeting of the liaison committee took place before one of the appointed commission's public hearings in the fall of 1997 at an elementary school in South Central Los Angeles. The liaison committee continued to meet on a sporadic basis.

By early January 1998, the elected commission had begun to right its ship, and both commissions were moving toward preliminary decisions. At this point, the chairs decided to move toward a more formal working relationship between the commissions in the form of a conference committee.

The chairs created a committee of five members of each commission. Riding herd on fourteen other elected commissioners, Chemerinsky rotated his commissioners onto the conference committee. Kieffer preferred five permanent members, with the hope that the body would become an active decision-making force. The permanent members chosen by Kieffer tended toward the mayor's position on a number of key issues, allowing flexibility for compromise. Chemerinsky wanted to handle decisions one at a time as they were being taken up by the full commissions. Kieffer wanted each commission to work through its preliminary decisions before seeking to compromise.

The meetings did not go well. By the summer of 1998, it became harder and harder to schedule meetings of the Joint Conference Committee. The meetings ground to a halt, well short of their target.

Through the summer months of 1998, the relationship between the two commissions languished. There were other complications. In September, the charter news was dominated by CAO Keith Comrie's attacks on the elected commission and its staff for supporting the strong mayor model. Speculation was growing that the joint committee was breaking apart. Several of the appointed commissioners heard that the elected commission was going to be ready for the April ballot instead of June and called me to be sure that we would be ready with our charter just in case. We were keeping our powder dry, and would be ready for April, if need be.

The appointed commission sought to keep its lines open to labor and to the public. On September 23, 1998, the appointed commission reversed an earlier decision to eliminate the employee representative's veto on investments by pension funds. It had seemed a minor issue the first time, but there had been a vociferous reaction from labor. The commission also changed the Department of Neighborhoods to the Office of Neighborhood Empowerment in response to public comments that reflected a suspicion of city hall bureaucracy.

In early to mid-November 1998, with progress stalled and increasing indications of a ballot battle between two charters, the two chairs spoke about what to do. Their conclusion: "it's us or nobody; it's now or never." According to Chemerinsky, Kieffer proposed a package deal in which the chairs would handle all the issues. The chairs asked my staff to prepare a list of all outstanding issues between the two commissions. It was a daunting collection. We could not tell how many additional policy disagreements were embedded in the secretive draft of the elected commission.

The plan was that the two chairs would divide all the issues into four or five meetings of the Joint Conference Committee, and that the two of them would make chairs' recommendations to the committee. The idea was well received by both commissions as a way to break the logjam. Kieffer had more leeway with his commission than Chemerinsky had with his, and the support the elected commissioners provided at the start was an important boost. Many involved in the process were alternately enthusiastic and terrified over this high-wire act, knowing that very important agreements on the city's charter were going to be made by the two chairs without staff or other commissioners present. But there was clearly no other way, and anything was preferable to the agony of the wandering, tense meetings of the Joint Conference Committee.

The strategy was intended to replace the absent trust between the two commissions with trust between the two chairs. The effort of the two chairs was consistent with the view of leadership in coalitions presented two decades ago by Barbara Hinckley (1981). Hinckley framed the survival of coalitions as a very human phenomenon, not merely a calculation of costs and benefits:

> A player, faced with uncertainty and many other things to do, seeks a trustworthy partner as the quickest, easiest, surest way to maximize a share of returns. Historical memory, repetition of the game—all suggest who is to be trusted. (1981, 74)

There was no trust between mayor and council, and the road to trust among the commissions was blocked. A new path had to be constructed very quickly. The trust that developed between the two chairs led to agreements that would, hopefully, feed back through the system to the commissioners, to the elected officials, and to the public.

The element of trust among leaders, a critical feature of the twenty-year Bradley coalition (Sonenshein 1993), was emerging again in charter reform.

The coalition for charter reform was now centered around the trust between the two chairs. Both chairs noted that it took a long time to build this trust. Kieffer recalled, "From the very beginning, we had to feel each other out. I can remember early on we debated some things, and they did not go that well. It was not worth debating substantive issues early on."

One key method of building trust between the chairs was to speak to the media together. The commissions had long been media competitors, with each commission wanting to get the best media coverage. Under the new framework, Kieffer and Chemerinsky reached agreements and then together called reporters from the *Times* and the *Daily News*. It was quite a sight to see the two of them standing next to each other, passing the phone back and forth while talking with reporters.

This remarkable plan had two months in which to be completed.

As the two chairs moved toward a process that could create a unified charter, the autonomous role of the commissions temporarily expanded. Because agreement on a unified charter was now at least theoretically possible, the leverage of both commissions temporarily increased. If there were two charters, one would be the mayor's and the other would be the council's. The mayor would greatly influence "his" charter since he would be its main, perhaps its sole, supporter. With a mayor's charter ready for the ballot, the council could then take the appointed commission's charter and rework it in a manner that could best achieve the council majority's goal of blocking the mayor's charter. Once that dynamic had played out, the commissions themselves would have little to do with the final outcome. There was every reason to think that both charters would fail at the polls.

On the other hand, the possibility of a unified charter greatly expanded the scope and role of the commissions. With a single charter, the elected commission could prevent the mayor from dictating the final form of the document. The appointed commission could prevent the council from taking its product and reworking it as it pleased, since the option remained for the appointed commission to go directly to the ballot with the elected commission. At the symbolic level, a single charter would also allow the commissions to dominate the high ground of the debate, even without the formal powers of the mayor and the council.

Riordan could see the danger to his own position in a unified charter, and moved to solidify his support for the elected commission. On November 2, Riordan called a press conference to announce his full support for the elected commission and his distaste for the appointed commission's work. His staff referred to the appointed commission's soon-to-be-released draft charter as moving around the deck chairs on the Titanic. The idea presumably was to undercut the scheduled release of the appointed commission's draft charter on November 16.

During a four-month period between November 1998 and late February 1999, the commissions became remarkably close to authoritative governing bodies on the matter of the city charter. Neither before that period nor after it did that situation hold, but during the critical period when the final charter was produced, it was the commission chairs, the commissioners, and the staffs who were making the actual line-by-line, word-by-word decisions about the charter. The continuing conflict between mayor and council, and the emergence of the idea of the unified charter, combined to create this extraordinary opening.

The vehicle for this temporary shift in authority was a series of eleven memos jointly produced by Chemerinsky and Kieffer and presented to the Joint Conference Committee, and later to a smaller Drafting Committee of commissioners. The memos reflected a temporary, threefold shift of authority: to the commissions, from the mayor and council; from the commissioners to the chairs; and to a full alliance between the two chairs.

The mayor and council were frustrated by the rising authority of the commissions. Commissioners in both camps were extremely nervous about the scope of the deals and agreements being negotiated by the two chairs. Interest groups that had earlier been able to play the two commissions against each other found it harder to do so. But more and more it became clear that this was the only possible way the goal could be accomplished, short of a complete about-face by either the mayor or the council on the structure of authority at city hall.

The chairs had to work hard to justify their authority and to maintain the support of their commissions. As always, this was a more perilous task for Chemerinsky than Kieffer. In their first memo, the chairs set forth an overall approach:

> We are committed to doing all we can to reach an agreement between the Appointed and the Elected Commissions on the many issues on which we disagree. If adopted by you, these would be considered tentative positions for the Conference Committee. We propose that these decisions be presented for approval by the respective Commissions at some point in the near future after a number of decisions have been made.

The language was Chemerinsky's, seeking to reassure his commissioners that they could take this step without losing their autonomy. The strategy was Kieffer's, holding all the proposals together as a package, and preventing mutinies on individual issues. The chairs agreed that in order to create momentum, the first set of proposals should be relatively painless, and that in general they should be giving and taking roughly equal amounts from the dearly held positions of each commission.

The chairs went off either in person or by telephone and walked through a set of issues. They drafted a memo. Then Chemerinsky, whose energy and writing speed seemed limitless, would type up a memo to the committee, often within a day or two of the upcoming meeting. According to Kieffer, "we were always trying to get a balance. It was less a negotiation per se than it was seeing how we can reach a common ground and maintain principles."

The chairs' negotiations were a mixture of hard bargaining, mutual agreement, and light moments. After many hours on many topics, they evolved a way to describe their most important issues in terms of baseball cards. Chemerinsky remembered saying, "I'm giving you my Mickey Mantle and you're giving me your Orlando Cepeda, your Maury Wills." Neither chair could give ground beyond where his commission would go. Ultimately, the chairs developed, in Chemerinsky's term, "a mind meld."

I worked closely with both chairs for the first time, and my staff became the staff for both chairs. I began to see Chemerinsky as part of a team that was led by the two chairs. For the first time, his political problems became our political problems, and vice versa. But the positions of the two chairs were not mirror images. We understood his difficult standing with his own commission, and the precariousness of his position compared with Kieffer's.

Kieffer's main concern was to keep close touch with the most experienced people at city hall: "If we lost Ron Deaton and Keith Comrie and a few other key people in the government on anything that we did, it would undermine the credibility of what we did. So as we entered these negotiations with Erwin, I let Deaton know what I was doing and wanted to hear from Deaton as to where he would scream about something." Both Kieffer and I spoke frequently with Theresa Patzakis of the mayor's staff to see what issues were critical to the mayor.

In the first memo, the chairs gave the elected controller the authority to conduct performance audits of city departments. This was the elected commission (EC) position, and had been rejected by only one vote on the appointed commission (AC). The close vote meant it was a feasible first bargain for Kieffer to make.

The mayor was given the authority held by the CAO in the existing charter to approve transfers of personnel and funds between and within departments. On the heavily criticized Board of Public Works, the city's only paid, full-time citizens' commission, the chairs recommended the modest step of creating a general manager. Finally, the chairs went with the AC position on an advisory, instead of decision-making, independent redistricting commission.

The proposals were presented on December 19, 1998, and all held their breaths. The chairs' first presentation to the Joint Conference Committee was a nervous moment, because if they could not get support for their agreements from the Joint Conference Committee, the whole process would fail.

The members of the Joint Conference Committee rather amiably discussed the chairs' proposals, made some relatively minor changes and asked for some items to be deferred. Then they voted unanimously to approve the list, with some items to be carried over. The process had taken its first step, and authority was now moving toward the chairs. After months of failure to reach agreement, this plan seemed as if it might work.

In a December 2, 1998, memo the chairs took on the issues of representation and responsiveness of the government. They reminded the commissioners that they were approving broad policies, not charter language, a way of putting off the contested question of who would actually write the final charter.

On neighborhood councils, the chairs indicated that the commissions now agreed on advisory, self-selected councils, and differed only on whether there should be a separate ballot measure calling for elected decision-making neighborhood councils. The chairs recommended against that option.

The two commissions were in close accord on area planning commissions, an innovation that had sparked excitement in both camps. On elections and on the governance of the Los Angeles Unified School District (LAUSD), the chairs compromised. Each commission had pet ideas on these issues, so the chairs simply recommended dropping them all. There would be no significant changes in either area.

On the size of the city council, the first of a series of compromises was proposed. The appointed commission's goal of twenty-one members would be placed in the main charter, but to please those who wanted the voters to be able to choose the existing 15, that option would be a separate measure. But trouble was emerging already, and, as was to happen again and again, council size was put off until the next meeting.

At the December 9, 1998, meeting, it was time for the big compromise on the removal of general managers. The idea of having the council exercise a two-thirds vote to overturn the removal of a general manager, in place of the existing system under which a majority of the council would have to approve a removal, had gathered considerable support. Chemerinsky and Kieffer spearheaded the search for community backing of the compromise. A key person in the Chamber of Commerce told me that the downtown business community was ready to back the two-thirds compromise, even if Riordan was opposed.

The chairs wrote, "If the two Commissions are to agree on a single charter proposal, a compromise must be reached on this issue." The compromise proposal moved through without major objection, belying the extreme sensitivity it would engender in the days to come. A reminder of the urgency of charter reform occurred on December 9, when Valley secessionists delivered twenty boxes containing 205,000 signatures on petitions calling for a study of the feasibility of secession (*Los Angeles Times* 1998b).

The mayor was given the authority to direct emergency powers and intergovernmental relations, as called for by the EC. Mayoral succession, which had been redesigned by the EC to keep it out of the hands of the council president, was to be conducted under the AC format that left the existing provisions largely intact.

The chairs compromised on what branch of government should be the city's governing body. The existing charter designated the council as the governing body. The EC wanted the mayor and council to share the governing authority. The AC wanted to leave the charter's designation of the council as governing body intact. The chairs wrote, "We recommend that the charter be silent as to governing body. We recommend this, in part, as a needed compromise. It is very unlikely that either Commission would accept the approach of the other Commission."

On the various issues involving city commissions, the chairs gave some to the EC, some to the AC. The removal of commissioners would be by the two-thirds appeal, rather than the existing method of requiring approval by a majority of the council. The EC would have its way in that the mayor could unilaterally remove commissioners of nonmanaging, noncharter commissions. With some reservations about detailed language, this set of compromises sailed through.

As the commissions moved toward deadlines to decide on the unified charter, the chairs presented a memo on December 16, 1998. On Prop. 5, the two chairs agreed on the principle that the council should not be able to modify commission decisions but should be able to veto them.

On the critical issue of the CAO, the chairs largely chose the AC approach. The CAO, renamed the head of the Office of Administrative Research Services (OARS), would report to the mayor and the council, rather than to the mayor, as the EC strongly desired. While the mayor's budget authority and flexibility would be strengthened, and the OARS would not have any line authority, the agreement clearly kept the main elements of the office intact.

The chairs wrote, "We believe that this compromise has many virtues. It strengthens the Mayor's authority to formulate the budget. It continues to have an independent reporting office that can produce independent, professional estimates of revenues and costs. It provides accountability by using the same mechanism for appointing and removing department heads that the Conference committee has approved in other areas."

Once again, the council size issue could not be resolved. The chairs proposed fifteen in the charter and twenty-three on the separate measure. "This will keep people who do not want a larger Council from having a reason to vote against the charter." We were already receiving phone calls from knowledgeable people in politics who were livid about the increase in the size of the council. Kieffer recalled: "I was in bed reading one night when the phone rang. On the other end was (county supervisor) Zev Yaroslavsky. He asked me what I thought we were doing on council size.

Zev was very clear: 'If it's in the charter—hidden from the public—I will oppose the charter and campaign against it.' "

While the general manager question seemed to have the greatest potential to derail the unified charter, council size emerged as a near deal-breaker. Later, we were to hear uniformly from pollsters that the issue was a disaster with the voters. Not reaching agreement and, most of all, keeping fifteen in the charter, may have ultimately saved the charter at the polls.

After months of internal debate, the elected commission had settled on a twenty-five member body, while the appointed commission, more concerned about the dynamics of a very large council, went with twenty-one. This did not seem to be a very troublesome issue. Both commissions favored a larger council; only the number was at stake. But it turned out to be unresolvable. One reason was that the number twenty-three, the obvious numerical compromise, was satisfactory to neither side. And neither side wanted to adopt the other's number, a very human and expected continuation of the sibling rivalry that had been part of the charter story from the beginning.

Things took a turn for the worse at one JCC meeting, when appointed commissioner Joseph Mandel explained that the appointed commission had decided on twenty-one members not by trying to find seats for every group, but by seeking to create a well-governed council. Elected commissioner Woody Fleming, who was substituting that day for Jackie Dupont-Walker, angrily accused the appointed commissioners of racial insensitivity, and contrasted the diversity of the appointed commission to his own commissioners.

When it was obvious that no number was going to be acceptable, the committee then moved into an extended debate over how to structure alternatives for the voters. One council size could go in the main charter, and then other alternatives could be presented to the voters as amendments to the charter. Members of the African American community, and ultimately others, were adamant that the voters be given the choice of keeping the council size the same at fifteen. Their determined stand may have ultimately saved the charter, because we soon discovered that there was a hotbed of opposition among the public and even among some elected officials against increasing the size of the city council. There was little ground ultimately to campaign against a unified charter, but had a larger council been included in the main charter, council size might have become the lightning rod for opposition.

In New York City, the expansion of the city council from thirty-five to fifty-one members generated little significant opposition, and was passed along with the charter itself in 1989. The differing politics of council size reflect vastly different attitudes toward government in the two cities, and perhaps in the two parts of the country. Antipolitician feeling runs very high in Los Angeles, the home of the tax revolt and a hotbed of term-limits sentiment. Measures to expand the county board of supervisors from its five members, now serving ten million people, have regularly gone down to defeat as well.

Included in the package were additional compromises. On the reorganization of departments, the AC approach was largely adopted. The system would remain basically the same, except that the council could not bury mayoral reorganization initiatives; there would be a time limit for council action, after which a mayoral plan would go into effect.

On the control of civil litigation, a very complicated plan was created based on negotiations between city attorney Hahn and the elected commission that increased the mayor's role in litigating and settling civil issues, but still maintained a central role for the city attorney and the council. The EC had won a great deal on that front, but far less than the mayor had initially wanted. Agreements were reached on the LAPD inspector general, providing less job security than the EC had wanted and providing more oversight by the Police Commission.

On the Living Wage, a key issue for labor, there was another compromise. The AC had been silent, and the EC had called for a Living Wage for city employees and for employees of city contractors. The final agreement was to have a Living Wage in the charter, the amount to be set by ordinance, to apply only to employees of city contractors.

The seemingly easy approval of the compromise on general managers hid the deep conflicts that lay ahead. Agreement on this compromise was a make-or-break issue for the unified charter. The appointed commission would never accept unilateral firing authority; the elected commission could not accept the status quo. Kieffer found that he could sell the compromise to the appointed commission, and Chemerinsky found support even among the mayor's strongest allies on his commission. The Los Angeles Chamber of Commerce broke with Riordan to support the compromise, with the chamber's Jerry Jeffe calling it "fair and reasonable" (Newton, 1998e).

The mayor strongly disagreed. According to Chemerinsky, the mayor called four of the five Joint Conference Committee members at home (not including the fifth, Jackie Dupont-Walker). By the next day, the mayor's allies on the Joint Conference Committee had moved from support to opposition on the compromise (interview).

Under the rules of the Joint Conference Committee, a majority of each commission's representatives had to agree to a motion. Two of Riordan's three allies (Weinberger and Widom) voted against sending the package forward. In order to get three elected commissioners (in addition to himself and Dupont-Walker), Chemerinsky made the argument that the compromise had to be forwarded to the full commissions or the whole process would fail. Rob Glushon, one of the "gang of three," as the mayor's allies were known, concurred and made possible a three-to-two vote of elected commissioners to move the measure forward.

On Monday, December 21, 1998, the JCC voted to send the package to the two commissions. Glushon indicated that his vote to move the package constituted neither an endorsement nor a guarantee to vote for it in the elected commission. On that ambiguous note, the first successful phase of the joint process ended. It was time to see if the commissions would endorse the unified charter.

Privately, Chemerinsky and Kieffer had discussed a contingency plan in case the JCC did not agree to forward the package. They would go around the JCC to the full commissions with a chairs' proposal for a unified charter. This agreement showed how far the two chairs had gone in forming their own coalition.

When an agreement was reached on council size (albeit one that was changed again later on), a unified charter was finally in sight. Meanwhile, the appointed commission had already released its draft charter on November 16 in a well-attended press conference that generated substantial positive publicity. The elected commission's draft charter was expected any day, and finally appeared in late December. In effect, there were now three charters on the table: the appointed, the elected, and the unified charters.

It seemed as if the pieces were coming together to have a unified charter. The main problem was that the mayor, whose support would be critical for the passage of a unified charter, openly opposed it. Riordan, Wardlaw, and Theresa Patzakis had breakfast with Chemerinsky at the mayor's restaurant, the Original Pantry, and urged him to go with the elected commission's charter. According to Chemerinsky, they said that they would raise $3 million for the campaign. After that, Wardlaw and Bill Carrick, the mayor's top political advisers, came to Chemerinsky's office at the University of Southern California to repeat the point. As Chemerinsky recalled the conversation, Wardlaw suggested that it would be hard for him to stay on as chair of the elected commission if a majority of the commission voted against the unified charter.

Riordan's forces believed that they had the high ground on reform leadership. Riordan was backing a new charter and a slate of reform candidates for the school board. He was hoping to put a business-tax reform measure on the June 1999 ballot. Riordan's people were confident that they could control the reform debate with this three-pronged approach.

Just before Christmas, Chemerinsky met with the mayor and informed him that he was going to support the unified charter after the elected commission's draft was released on December 28 (and not before, so as not to disrespect the release of the elected commission's draft). The mayor called Chemerinsky on New Year's Eve to ask him to reconsider and called other members of the commission as well.

The Riordan forces began putting significant pressure on the elected commissioners to reject the unified charter. Elected commissioner Richard Macias stated publicly that he had been informed by the East Coast superiors in his law firm that he ought to do whatever Mayor Riordan wanted him to do. Riordan's allies were bolstered. Nick Pacheco, planning to run for the city council, received a promise of the mayor's endorsement and financial support. Woody Fleming reported that the mayor had promised to raise $300,000 for his campaign for the city council in the downtown ninth district (Chemerinsky interview). This endorsement went against Riordan's downtown business allies, who favored Jan Perry for the position.

Throughout this period, Kieffer and Chemerinsky were working jointly on political strategy. Intense pressure focused on the evening of January 5, when the unified charter would be brought up for a vote by the elected commission and the mid-day January 6 meeting when the appointed commission would make its choice. Chemerinsky used forty thousand of his personal frequent flier miles to make sure that one commissioner would make it back for the vote. The long struggle for charter reform seemed likely to be decided all in one night and one day.

CHAPTER THIRTEEN

The Fall and Rise of the Unified Charter

> Today may be the most important day in the future of the City charter
> that governs Los Angeles. . . . We urge the commissioners to give the
> voters a singular compromise plan. Let them decide if the entire
> recommendation is good for the city. The first step is having the elected
> commission support the compromise plan today.
> —KNX Radio

> The unified charter proposal is a sham, an elixir sold by carnival
> barkers. . . . All is not lost. Tonight, the elected panel can reject the
> compromise plan and stand up for a meaningful change.
> —*Los Angeles Daily News*, 1999

ON THE EVENING of January 5, 1999, the auditorium at the Department of Water and Power was packed. A long line of speakers waited to be heard. The unified charter had developed a great constituency by this time, including business, labor, civil rights and other civic organizations.

One by one, members of key interest groups trooped to the microphone to call on the elected commission to approve the unified charter. Only Mayor Riordan spoke against it, and called on the elected commission to hold its ground.

Chemerinsky felt that he had a majority for the unified charter. Under great pressure from Riordan, who had appointed him to fill a vacancy on the commission, Richard Macias had indicated that if he were to be the eighth vote, he would back the unified charter. Otherwise, he would vote no. Riordan's three key allies were sure to vote no. The resignation of Marguerite Archie-Hudson, a Riordan opponent and the mayor's replacement of her with Ken Lombard, guaranteed another vote for Riordan's position. But Chemerinsky figured he had the eight votes he needed.

Chemerinsky then gave each commissioner an opportunity to speak. It was obvious the vote would be very close. Chet Widom, a Riordan ally, said the elected commission's proposal was far better than the unified charter. Janice Hahn, expected to be an ally of the unified charter, disparaged the appointed commission and spoke proudly of the elected commission's mandate. When Riordan allies called on Chemerinsky to push the appointed commission closer to their view, the chair responded that this was completely unrealistic.

Macias turned to Riordan and pointedly said, "We've been told we're the independent charter commission. Unfortunately, a number of us have also been told that our jobs are at risk, that our future in this city is at risk. But I have to vote in the best interests of the city" (Meyerson 1999). (After the charter election, Macias was quietly dropped from a Riordan-appointed commission post.)

Chemerinsky passed a note to Janice Hahn, whom he was counting in his camp: "I think we've got the votes, but I think it's going to be eight to seven." Janice said, "Are you counting on me? You can't count on my vote." And she voted no. With her vote, Macias was released from his pledge, and he voted no, making the vote nine to six. Chemerinsky expressed his extreme disappointment and predicted that charter reform was doomed.

With the mayor's people elated, Rob Glushon made a motion that was quickly adopted. The Glushon motion said that negotiations on a unified charter could resume only if the appointed commission accepted most of the main provisions favored by the elected commission. Chemerinsky told the commissioners that it would have been more honest to reject the unified charter outright than to engage in this "charade." Chemerinsky was devastated, and when the Mayor came up to speak with him, he said, "Not now." I spoke to Chemerinsky in a quiet corner, and the normally ebullient chair was on the verge of giving up on the unified charter.

While the mayor's people were very happy, the reaction of city council staff was equally strong. As I made my way out of the room, and tried to find a spot from which I could call Kieffer to report on the outcome, I was immediately surrounded by a half-dozen top aides from the city council. They were yelling at me, saying, "We told you not to work with these people." "There's no chance." "Give up on them, and dump this thing." I was trying not to show my own disappointment and to keep our own options open. I could tell, though, that the apparent failure of the unified charter might be equally appealing to the mayor and to the city council.

The most unhappy people of all were the civic activists who had been drawn to charter reform by the activities of the two commissions. Marvin Braude, former councilmember and advocate of charter reform, Xandra Kayden of the League of Women Voters, and other members of the public were downcast and disappointed.

Attention turned to the next day's scheduled meeting of the appointed commission in the fifteenth-floor boardroom of the Department of Water and Power. The meeting was scheduled for 1 P.M. When I woke up after a long night, I headed over to Kieffer's law offices, where we met with Mary Strobel and Julie Benson of our staff. Our choices were obvious and stark: go to battle with our November sixteenth draft or agree to a unified charter without a partner on the other side. Kieffer was completely certain, and we all agreed, that the second course was the only way to go.

As we filed into the boardroom, we were surprised to find it packed with members of the public, city officials, and reporters. We were, after all, the boring commission. Sitting in a front row seat was Geoffrey Garfield, executive director of the elected commission. There was excitement in the air. As the meeting began, Kieffer broke from his general practice of not taking a personal position on commission issues and spoke in favor of the unified charter:

> This is not a mayor's charter; this is not a council charter; this is not a business charter; this is not a labor charter. This is a charter for the whole community. A few days ago I said that this unified charter is a better document than either the elected commission draft or our own draft. What was true last week is no less true today simply because of the action taken by the elected commission. Therefore, I urge the appointed commission to adopt the unified charter as its own.

Kieffer expressed his hope that if the appointed commission abandoned its November sixteenth charter and voted for the unified charter, that this action would bring the elected commission to our side.

We then heard from members of the public. Marvin Braude and others expressed their deep sadness about the previous evening's action. They expressed their hope that the commission would follow Kieffer's lead and vote for the unified charter.

KNX Radio had begun its news broadcast:

> Will the appointed Charter Reform Commission accept a proposal that was rejected by the elected counterparts? That's the big question. . . . The appointed charter Reform Commission is well into its discussion on a compromise proposal. (KNX transcript, January 6, 1999)

One by one, the appointed commissioners around the table voiced their views. Several said that they were disturbed by the elected commission's actions, but each indicated support. When it was former councilmember Bob Wilkinson's turn, the prospect of a unanimous vote was most imperiled. Wilkinson would eventually oppose the charter when it was on the ballot. He expressed his concerns about provisions that had been given up to the elected commission in the unified charter, and then came to the word "but." When he said that, it was clear that he was going to make the vote for the unified charter unanimous. He finished, "In the interests of getting this charter completed, I will vote for the unified charter."

At this point, Kieffer called for votes to be cast a member at a time. Going around the horseshoe, each commissioner voted yes, and the chair announced that the motion had passed, nineteen to zero. As he announced the result, there was a spontaneous uproar in the room. The packed audience stood up, cheered and applauded. The moment was so moving that I could not turn around from my seat, situated with my back to the audience. It was the pivotal moment of charter reform in Los Angeles.

I have often thought since then that finding the high ground was the key to making charter reform succeed, but I had never really felt the high ground until that nineteen to zero vote. We had done the right thing, and in so doing had restored the faith of the people in the room, and also outside it, that Los Angeles government could be reformed.

As the moment passed, the commissioners took up the Glushon motion. Kieffer recommended that we refer it back to the Joint Conference Committee, thereby avoiding what would have been an inflammatory debate and a choice between rejecting a hostile motion from the elected commission and abjectly accepting it. With that, the appointed commission adjourned. The whole meeting lasted about an hour and a half.

In less than a full day's time, charter reform had gone from dead to alive, from hopeless to infused with momentum. Chemerinsky remembered that "as soon as the appointed commission's meeting was over, I got phone calls saying that the appointed commission replaced its charter with the unified charter and everyone gave them a standing ovation. Garfield called me from his cell phone. And I thought this was just terrific."

KFI Radio began its story:

> Here's the top story in the Southland today. To compromise or not. The arguing over charter reform in Los Angeles moves a step closer to a vote by the public. . . . Last night, the elected charter Reform Commission rejected a compromise with the appointed commission to put a single charter proposal on the ballot. This afternoon the appointed panel unanimously approved the compromise. Today's approval of the so-called unified proposal means at least one charter proposal will appear on the June ballot. (KFI Transcript, January 6, 1999)

By the next morning, a flurry of activity took place aimed at reversing the elected commission's decision in time for its Monday night meeting. For the first time, the appointed commission had earned full legitimacy. The *Times,* which had become increasingly impatient with Riordan's opposition to the unified charter, spoke editorially (1999a):

> One of the ironies of Los Angeles's adventures in charter form is that the appointed commission, widely expected to be little more than a patsy for a city council hostile to change, has emerged as the class act. Through its quiet discussions over the past two years and sincere efforts to incorporate the broadest perspectives, this group has demonstrated precisely the sort of vision that Mayor Richard Riordan has lacked on this issue.

After all the attacks on the appointed commission by Riordan and his allies, this was sweet praise indeed. The appointed commission's standing was enhanced by the support of a civic coalition. A *Times* reporter noted, "By approving the compromise package, the appointed commission also probably secures the support of such leading civic groups as the Urban League, the League of Women Voters and the Los Angeles Chamber of Commerce" (Newton 1999b).

As he sought to turn his commission around, Chemerinsky's hand was strengthened by the positive reaction to the appointed commission's vote, and by the wide community support it engendered. He was able to move Janice Hahn, with the help of organized labor and her brother, City Attorney James Hahn. Chemerinsky made another move to strengthen his position, which was to reduce the Joint Conference Committee (which would now have to put together the details of the final charter) to three members each, thereby removing the ability of the three Riordan allies to block any referral to the full commissions of JCC proposals.

Meanwhile, elected commissioner Chet Widom took to the airwaves to defend his commission's rejection of the unified charter. In a reply to the KNX editorial of January 5, 1999, he cited the need to allow the mayor to fire general managers unilaterally, and to have an independent redistricting commission.

> Unfortunately, the proposals of the appointed commission and the so-called compromise are in opposition to these principles. . . . if there is more than one proposal on the June ballot, we have great confidence in the ability of our citizens to make the right choice for the future of Los Angeles. (Widom 1999)

In contrast to the *Times,* the *Daily News* (1999b) praised the Elected Commission for rejecting the unified charter:

> They said "nuts" to the blitzkrieg of pressure from the public employee unions, the city council and the influence peddlers who oppose any form of power sharing with the residents and taxpayers of Los Angeles. . . . Perhaps Tuesday's vote was the birth of a new Los Angeles, a more democratic Los Angeles, a more open Los Angeles.

As Chemerinsky met with Riordan's allies, Weinberger, Widom, and Glushon, he heard that they were angry that he was quoted in the *Times* as "deeply disappointed that his colleagues had voted against the compromise package" (Newton 1999a). Chemerinsky was equally angry at what he perceived as his three colleagues' decision to turn away from the compromise on general managers.

Mayor Riordan invited Chemerinsky for lunch that Friday, and as the chair headed into the mayor's office, he was surprised to see Weinberger, Widom, and Glushon coming out. Kelly Martin later commented,

> We knew what he was going to say before he came in because he had told the other members of the committee, and we had actually had a meeting with Rob Glushon and Bill Weinberger and Chet Widom before that meeting. [Erwin was] really taken aback, because again I think he got confused and thought his

model was like the [appointed commission] model. A chair has got to also hold his votes. And coming out of that meeting, it was clear to us that we had those three votes and that those were the three people who understood that while compromise might be necessary, there was a whole bunch of other things on the table.

The deputy mayor gave Chemerinsky a list of items the mayor wanted in the charter, which Chemerinsky immediately said were unacceptable. There is considerable disagreement about what was said at the meeting. Chemerinsky felt that the mayor and his top staff suggested that he step down as chair if he couldn't defend the elected commission's charter. Deputy Mayor Kelly Martin said that she suggested that if Chemerinsky was having difficulty convincing Kieffer of where things were, that maybe someone else could do a better job. Either way, the meeting ended badly and a period of very intense lobbying was underway.

Richard Macias called Chemerinsky to say that he was not ready to support the unified charter, leaving Chemerinsky one vote short of a majority. Chemerinsky then undertook a high-risk strategy of gathering the minority of commissioners who strongly favored the unified charter (himself, Jackie Dupont-Walker, Anne Finn, and Bennett Kayser) and threatening to walk out of the elected commission and join the appointed commission in the unified charter. Dupont-Walker told Chemerinsky, "I'm with you. We'll walk together." Informing Riordan's allies about this plan created a firestorm, but was also effective.

Chemerinsky and Kieffer meanwhile talked about how to get the three Riordan allies on board, and agreed on several concessions, in effect to the mayor. But when Glushon asked to speak directly to Kieffer, the chair of the appointed commission made, in Chemerinsky's view, "another great strategic call: He said he won't deal with them. He will deal only with me, not with them, because I'm the chair." Kieffer said, "I knew his problems and was trying to help him with them. At one moment, Rob Glushon tried to say that he was brokering a deal, and I let it be known that I would not talk to Rob Glushon again. . . . the gang of three were ready to throw him out. They just didn't have the votes to do it."

Meanwhile, a number of key leaders were imploring Riordan to end his opposition to the unified charter. Riordan had already upset some of his business allies in December by seeming to offer to trade support for a living wage in the charter for labor's backing of Riordan's position on mayoral authority (Orlov 1998a; Newton 1998e). The Chamber of Commerce and LABA, the keys to downtown business, were pushing in the direction of compromise, as was Warren Christopher. City hall reporter Marc Haefele (1998) noted the irony:

This obsession has already alienated the mayor from much of his original downtown support: business avatars are marveling at the sight of the mayor allying himself with Big Labor by promoting a charter living-wage provision in return for support for his general-managers firing-authority plank. . . . His intransigence should leave us with a historical imprint of Riordan's character: He breathed life into charter reform on a whim, and on a whim he killed it.

Haefele ridiculed the members of the elected commission for their rejection of the unified charter, and added, "You felt the presence of swollen political egos." He added that "it was also a perfect illustration of why this city must reject increased mayoral power. . . . Riordan gave us a garish illustration of power's abuse. It showed that the city still needs all the protection it can get against a bullying chief executive who sets his own personal agenda against the public will." Referring to the elected commission's charter as the "low-road document," Haefele (1999) concluded that the "unified document, which has the backing of labor, business and countless other civic groups, can be called the 'high-road charter.'"

Riordan's majority on the elected commission soon began to crumble. Even Glushon and Weinberger, two of his key allies, urged Riordan to compromise. Glushon said that he would introduce a measure to reconsider the unified charter at the next scheduled commission meeting, the following Monday (Newton 1999c).

Finally, the mayor relented. In a letter to the elected commission, Riordan offered to support the unified charter if it provided "significant reform," and called for a separate ballot measure on the general manager firing.

In an editorial "Has Riordan Seen the Light?" the *Times* (1999a) commented on Riordan's clause about significant reform: "What that means, only the mayor knows." The editorial concluded: "The elected commission should reconsider its rejection of the compromise package. We urge it to do so when it meets Monday. We expect the mayor to have the courage of his new convictions."

Obviously under considerable pressure, the elected commission met on Monday evening. Chemerinsky pleaded with his commissioners to follow the lead of the appointed commission's nineteen to zero vote and not "marginalize and humiliate ourselves."

The Riordan forces were confused, and Bennett Keyser, a Riordan opponent, managed to make the first motion, to adopt the unified charter unchanged. It passed seven to six but fell one vote short of the eight votes required in the elected commission for a motion to pass.

With the Keyser motion defeated, the commission followed Chemerinsky's lead, and voted thirteen to one to adopt the unified charter, pending several changes that Chemerinsky and Kieffer had already discussed. The commission passed a Glushon-Weinberger motion to agree to the unified charter pending joint drafting, the development of separate ballot measures on general manager and on neighborhood councils, and the acceptance by the appointed commission of the elected commission's view on firing commissioners and on Prop. 5.

On January 13, the appointed commission met to consider the latest elected commission action. Present at the commission meeting was an under-the-weather Mayor Riordan, who spoke to the appointed body about the virtues of its elected counterpart. On the other hand, it was advantageous to have the mayor speaking in favor of a unified charter.

The appointed commissioners were ambivalent about the options proposed by the elected commission, and some called for renewed, tougher negotiations. Kieffer commented, "Everybody has a gun here, and everybody has to check it" (Greene 1999c). In the end, the commission voted twelve to one to simply refer the compromise package to the conference committee, keeping the unified charter alive.

That decision left about seven weeks to draft a charter that reflected the numerous agreements made between the two commissions in these intense negotiations. With the dramatic passage of the unified charter, the chairs now faced the task of creating a finished charter for presentation to the city council. They had to move beyond policy agreements, to actual language. The actual charter had yet to be written, line by line. In addition, there were remaining policy disagreements raised by the EC at its January 11 meeting, and referred to the JCC by the AC on January 13.

On January 18, 1999, the first chairs' memo in more than three weeks to a newly reconstituted JCC addressed these remaining matters. Chemerinsky had outraged the Riordan commissioners by creating a permanent body with only three members from each commission, giving him a way to break their blocking majority.

The press of time was a great advantage for the chairs; the calendar was the most reliable enforcer: "The goal of the Conference Committee meeting on January 20 must be to resolve all remaining areas of disagreement between the two Commissions." There were still reassurances: "As before, we are not presenting charter language, but instead we are recommending the concepts to be reflected in the new charter."

The role of the chairs and the commissions as governors became more and more clear as the level of detail grew. In this memo, the chairs recommended agreements on the timing of the controller's report on the budget, and proposed a compromise of forty-five days for the council to override a mayoral veto, between the AC's sixty days and the EC's thirty days.

Labor issues were taken up and resolved. On the complicated issue of civil service exemptions, compromise emerged again: "Because there were strong feelings and pressures on both sides of this issue, we attempted simply to compromise between the two approaches." In actuality, the changes in exempt positions were significant, and represented the one area in which the commissions took on the civil service question. The commissions provided greater flexibility for the mayor to obtain exempt positions for city departments.

Determined to win the mayor's support once and for all, Kieffer ran into Deputy Mayor Kelly Martin in the hallway and proposed a final deal. The mayor would gain the authority to unilaterally fire most city commissioners. The trade would require the elected commission to drop the two ballot measures on general manager and on neighborhood councils. Kieffer had previously tested this idea with Deaton and council president Ferraro. "I threw it out to Kelly Martin, and her eyes lit up." Kieffer (interview) called Deaton, who said, "Go for it."

Kieffer presented the deal to Chemerinsky moments before the conference committee meeting, and both hoped that this would be the final step to bring the mayor on board. The two chairs agreed to sign on to the deal. Martin reported that the mayor was in agreement. Kieffer announced, "We have a charter" (Newton 1999d).

The deal did not sit well with everybody. Some elected commissioners were upset that the separate ballot measure to authorize elected, decision-making neighborhood councils would be off the ballot. The *Daily News* (1999c) blasted the unified charter again: "What we need is not a better lemon rolling off the charter reform assembly line but a better Los Angeles." The United Chambers of Commerce of the San Fernando Valley came out against the unified charter the next day (Orlov 1999b).

Appointed commissioner Anton Calleia noted, presciently, that not having the option to keep the council at fifteen members would not work: "I think this is a devious way to get this before voters. What if people like the charter reform but want to keep the council at 15 members?" (Orlov 1999a).

As important as the mayor was to the process, there was a deep and abiding concern about organized labor. The early decision to remove civil service from the table had been generally maintained, but there were some important labor issues in the charter. The most important was that substantial changes were being proposed in the system of exempt positions. While labor ended up opposing the unified charter, their opposition was ultimately halfhearted. It would have been much tougher had their opposition been enthusiastic.

Under the collective bargaining agreement, changes to the charter that affected employee provisions must be subject to a meet-and-confer process. This process does not require the government to adopt proposals of labor, but it does require a good faith effort to listen to labor's concern on every such provision. The question became: who would represent the government for the meet-and-confer process?

At this point, the council was distancing itself from the appointed commission, and there was a general sense that since we got ourselves into this, we ought to handle meet-and-confer.

The normal designated representative of the city was the CAO. We received a call notifying us of the impending meet-and-confer and requesting that we send representatives. I went to the first meeting with Mary Strobel, the AC's deputy director and staff counsel. Representing the EC were Jackie Dupont-Walker and Bill Weinberger. Upon our arrival, we were informed by the CAO's representative that the commissions were to act as the government's representatives. We had assumed that our role was to provide background about commission decisions and to report labor's input to the chairs and the JCC. Instead, we were doing the meeting-and-conferring as if we were the government.

Over a period of weeks, representatives of the two commissions met around a large table with several dozen representatives of various bargaining agents for city employees. This new role created some trust between the commissions, and particularly the staffs. Chemerinsky attended most of the meetings, and we worked closely with him to have a common position relative to labor. As the two staffs worked together on meet-and-confer (Marlene Jones of my staff and Steve Presberg of the EC) some of the wariness went away. It was critical to be on the same page in dealing with the unions.

Organized labor clearly knew the charter better than any other interest group in the city. Forty percent of the charter was devoted to employee provisions, and we were speaking in effect about the charter as employee contract. Nobody would have the same level of intensity about the charter.

Over the course of meet-and-confer, the group in a very collegial manner worked through a list of labor concerns until all had been resolved. In most cases, there were small changes that could be made to accommodate labor. In the area of exempt positions, some more significant alterations were made to ensure that the system was not open-ended. By the end of the process, labor could say that they had been heard. This was one reason that the commissions were deeply disappointed by labor's ultimate opposition to the charter at the behest of the city council. As Chemerinsky put it, "We gave them everything they wanted, and then they opposed the charter."

While the new charter met the concerns of labor, the more militant Valley groups were displeased with the product. The Valley Industry and Commerce Association wrote in late January that it had four major objections to the unified charter: the cost of adding new council members; the inclusion of the living wage; the use of an advisory redistricting commission rather than an independent one; and the danger that area planning commissions would delay land use decisions. This view of area planning commissions suggested that the secession forces had done an excellent job of keeping under wraps the inherent battle between Valley business and home-owner associations over land use decisions. Richard Close, one of the principal secession leaders, complained about the absence of decision-making power for neighborhood councils (Orlov 1999c).

The elected commission passed a revised version of the unified charter on January 25, 1999. The vote was ten to four, and this time the mayor's allies, particularly Rob Glushon, were the chief supporters. Those who favored elected decision-making neighborhood councils were in the minority. Janice Hahn complained, "This last horse trade—I think you traded a thoroughbred for a nag" (Newton 1999e).

The appointed commission, in its turn, adopted the document unanimously. An exchange between two appointed commissioners showed how visions of reform differed generationally. Retired councilmember Bob Wilkinson, "alive with the memories of the corruption and nepotism that had sullied city hall" in decades long ago, assailed the "blanket authority" given to the mayor. But Alexandra Glickman, a young businesswoman, retorted, "With all due respect, this is not the Shaw regime. These days people can't even sneeze without everybody hearing about it. I'm going to vote for this charter" (M. Siegel 1999).

The Final Draft

The biggest remaining problem was that the two draft charters prepared by the respective staffs bore no relation whatsoever to each other. They could have been drafted for different cities. The two charters were structured differently; they incorporated different policy decisions; and they were built on completely different assumptions.

The elected commission's draft began as a set of policy changes on a blank template; the appointed commission's draft was a massively rewritten version of the existing charter. The appointed commission's draft had been thoroughly vetted by all of city hall except the mayor, whose staff had chosen to ignore drafts sent over for comment by the appointed commission. The elected commission's draft had not been vetted, except possibly by the mayor's office.

Ron Deaton, the council's chief of staff, had established a committee of senior city officials to review each chapter of the appointed commission draft. This committee met numerous times with the appointed commission's chief drafter, Mary Strobel. I attended several of the meetings. Around the table sat top officials of the CAO's office, the CLA, the city attorney, and various city departments. The committee focused on legal land mines and logical inconsistencies rather than policy issues. Members, including Deaton, had marked up the draft word for word, searching for the sort of problems that could doom a charter. As a result of this vetting process, the appointed commission's charter was essentially "fireproof" to the sort of problem that could undermine its standing.

The issue of whose draft would be used had been a bone of contention between Kieffer and Chemerinsky for months. In October, Kieffer told Chemerinsky that the only way to get it done was to use the appointed draft. Kieffer recalled, "You can't reconcile drafts of documents. You can't interlineate them. You can't compromise on paragraphs. Now, I knew that our draft had been vetted from day one, going back two years earlier. I just knew they hadn't been through all that. Of course, Erwin had to disagree. But I did not take it as a permanent rejection."

The elected commission's draft had not been circulated around city hall, and only the mayor's office seemed to have had input into it. In an interview, Deputy Mayor Kelly Martin indicated that the mayor's staff was looking at it: "I remember reading it, and yes, we were able to have input. We were not shy about expressing our opinion."

Anticipating the draft problem, Kieffer had directed me and Mary Strobel to have our legal staff incorporate into our draft all the policy changes agreed to by the Joint Conference Committee, in case our draft would be used as the template for the unified charter. By the time the dramas of the adoption of the draft charter were completed, the appointed commission had a version that was ready to be considered as the draft of the unified charter reflecting all policy agreements between the two commissions.

With time short, Chemerinsky proposed a solution. He was on his way to a meeting in San Francisco. He would take the version of the charter that the appointed commission staff had produced that incorporated all the changes approved by the commissions, and then propose changes that would incorporate elements of the elected commission's approach.

Chemerinsky said, "I had the sense that the appointed commission had done a much better job with detail work than we had done, and therefore had carried over some things from the existing charter that we left out that really needed to be there, and had done a better job of vetting than we had done." After a close examination, Chemerinsky proposed a relatively small list of changes that were easily incorporated. He switched the table of contents and the order of chapters to reflect the order of the elected commission draft.

There was now a working draft of the unified charter on the table, largely based on the November 16 draft of the appointed commission but incorporating all the policy decisions of the Joint Conference Committee and the two full commissions.

This approach enraged the staff of the elected commission. Steven Presberg (1999), the chief drafter of the elected commission, prepared a scathing twenty-three-page memo to the elected commissioners on the negotiating committee, attacking the draft to which Chemerinsky had agreed. Presberg listed point after point in which the agreed-upon draft did not accord with the elected commission's views. Presberg blamed most of the problems on the appointed commission staff: "The Appointed Staff has, notwithstanding the Conference Committee agreement, replicated their original draft, which in turn is simply a replication of the present charter's provisions." He added, "It would appear that the staff of the Appointed Commission now views your staff, and the entire Elected Commission for that matter, as bystanders in this process."

Presberg's memo had its desired effect on the elected commission, stoking the fires of their resentment. There was a rebellion at their next meeting. Commissioners demanded full and sole custody of the disk on which the charter was written.

Now began the battle of disks. In his occasional column, *Charterama,* Robert Greene (1999d) told how the elected commissioners tried to wrest back control of the charter document:

> Such is the mutual regard of the two commissions that their staffs couldn't even trust each other to type agreed revisions on their computers. There had to be two identical disks—one in the custody of the appointed commission, one under the protection of the elected commission. Nothing was to become valid unless it appeared on both disks.

The agreement on the draft placed the mayor's office at a sudden disadvantage. They had bet their money on the elected commission and its draft charter, and now found that the appointed commission's draft, which they had purposely ignored for what they considered good strategic reasons in the fall, was the basis for the discussion. They had to play catch-up, and play it quickly.

Determined players of the charter game, the mayor's legal staff rapidly went through the new draft charter and highlighted a massive list of detailed changes the mayor wanted made in the final document. They thereupon entered negotiations with the commissions as the final stages of the process unfolded.

They became the source of a *Times* story about a series of "mistakes" they had found in the draft charter (Newton 1999f). The mayor's office took the position that the joint conference committee had agreed to certain things that were not in the draft charter. This position was disputed by Kieffer, who suggested that the real issue was the mayor's desire to reopen issues that had not been resolved to his liking.

Important strategic decisions now had to be made by all parties, and there were misunderstandings and misperceptions on all sides. Both chairs had believed from the very beginning that the mayor had to be at the table at the end, and had to lead the battle to win charter reform. But the process had yielded neither the provisions nor the charter draft sought by the mayor to nearly the extent that he wished.

The chairs had managed a remarkable victory, but if the mayor took a walk at the end, as Sam Yorty had done with the recommendations of the Reining Commission, the charter might be doomed by the opposition of the city council. Kieffer recalled, "We needed to get the mayor back in. That was the only place that money was going to come from for this campaign. The mayor had now gone off, the press had nailed him. He was out there floating. Do we bring him back with his tail between his legs? We couldn't let him hang out there. We had to get a unified charter that had the mayor involved."

The chairs could not give back to the mayor things that had been rejected in open session and with public support. The city council was capable of mounting strong opposition to a unified charter renegotiated to the mayor's liking behind closed doors.

From the mayor's standpoint, he had suffered a significant tactical defeat, but he could still gain critical ground in the battle over the seemingly small details of the charter. The mayor's people were effective and hard-nosed negotiators, who were more committed to their position than were most other participants. The mayor's people were aware that the mayor remained the most politically potent force for charter reform.

When the two chairs presented the charter to the city council on February 7, 1999, it was still actually a work in progress. Most of the elements were in place, but there were negotiations yet to come. In addition, changes recommended by the council, if accepted by the chairs, were still possible. For instance, Councilmember Jackie Goldberg suggested that giving the mayor's executive orders a place in the charter could reduce public accountability. Kieffer immediately agreed that this should be clarified in the charter by simply providing a requirement of public notice.

As Kieffer and I made our presentation to the council, it became obvious that many of the councilmembers were unhappy with the changes to the mayor-council balance of authority. Behind the scenes, Riordan was unhappy with the refusal of the drafting committee to adopt most of his proposals regarding details and language (Newton 1999h).

There were plenty of loose ends. Rob Glushon, one of Riordan's key allies on the elected commission, told the council that the unified charter did not represent the consensus of the two commissions (Greene 1999d). His colleague Janice Hahn said, "I see no reason for this to go to the city council. I think they should pass it on to us and let us as the elected commission finish this up and put it before voters" (Orlov 1999e). Meanwhile, appointed commissioner and former city councilmember Robert Wilkinson announced his opposition to the unified charter, calling it a "power grab" by the mayor's office (Newton 1999g).

Sensitivities between the two commissions were still raw. After Cheme-rinsky praised Kieffer during the joint council testimony, he received some complaints from elected commissioners. He felt compelled to send a memo to his commissioners in which he explained his comments.

With all these factors in the background, weeks of painful negotiations regarding charter language began in January that involved the chairs, the top staffs of the commissions, and several elected commissioners. The ne-gotiations revealed the deep ambivalence that marked the relationship be-tween the mayor and John Ferraro, the council president.

Unlike the open hostility between Riordan and the council as a whole, the Riordan-Ferraro relationship was built on mixed feelings. When I started on the job in 1997, Ferraro told me that despite his conflicts with Riordan, "the mayor has a good heart" and that I should never be reluctant to seek Riordan's input. But Ferraro and the other members of the council also feared that we were going to give away the store behind closed doors. The ideologically and temperamentally moderate Ferraro was just as likely to encourage compromise with the mayor as he was to oppose the mayor, and as outsiders we were often caught in the riptides of their relationship.

The mayor's staff felt supremely affronted at having to negotiate with the commissioners and staff, who were not even elected officials, over de-tails of a charter process they believed themselves to have inspired and led. At times, we were seen by the mayor's office as insulting them by refusing to give them anything important and by the council leadership as having given the mayor the crown jewels—on the same day.

The role of the commissions was one of temporary power and authority, and was far less imposing than the power of elected officials. The commis-sions were buffeted by the moods of these more powerful beings, espe-cially when they careened back and forth from conflict to agreement with each other.

The meetings were held in several locations, and were usually tense. Mary Strobel and I prepared a summary of the mayor's "wish list" on the details of the charter, and found a consistent pattern of seeking to reduce council power (Sonenshein and Strobel 1999). Our restructured version of the mayor's memo made it easier to avoid being nickel-and-dimed by the mayor's staff on items that individually seemed innocuous, but collec-tively represented a major shift of power.

The meetings were grueling negotiating sessions. The mayor's people were relentless, with an absolute belief in mayoral authority. They were no happier with us. On the one hand, Deputy Mayor Kelly Martin enjoyed the opportunity to be negotiating the actual document:

It's so much easier if you're the person there making your own points. And again, knowing when to compromise and when not to, and what to give up on and what not to. But once we were at the table, I just really felt good, because I felt like the momentum was shifting. Because I felt like we were going to get a document that we could live with, and I felt like we were going to get one document, and there was no way then that the council could mess with it, which was always my fear. And they didn't. It wasn't easy. Those were hard-fought negotiations, but that was sort of the nature of the beast. I had done that many hundreds of hours before on many other things. (interview)

Clearly, Chemerinsky was on very poor terms with the mayor's office. At one meeting, Chemerinsky said he had to leave early, and Martin said that was fine because Riordan's ally Bill Weinberger could take over. Irritated, Chemerinsky stayed.

A city hall myth was created when this group of commissioners and mayor's staff conferred several doors down from where a meeting of the Joint Conference Committee would later begin. A top council deputy walked into the room. She looked around and, horrified, spotted the mayor's staff, the chairs, the commission staffs, and a couple of elected commissioners. Kieffer asked her to join us, but she demurred. Within days, the story of the "secret backroom deal with the mayor" had become an article of faith among the members of the council, and helped justify their later opposition to the charter.

At each stage of the process, Kieffer stayed in touch with Ron Deaton, the chief staffer of the city council. Kieffer and Deaton had developed a strong relationship, fueled in part by the appointed commission's respect for the government. With Deaton's input, we were able to keep the negotiations from being a one-sided set of reactions to one constituent, the mayor.

Despite our close contact with Deaton, the perception at city hall outside the mayor's office was that the commissions were giving away the store to Riordan in secret conferences. In mid-February 1999, the pent-up anger at city hall exploded, mostly at the appointed commission. As city leaders became angrier, Riordan began to put out the word that if the deal were to collapse, he would go back to his earlier proposals to appoint the city attorney and to take the council out of the redistricting process.

Meanwhile, negotiations over language continued. At each step of the process, there would be a meeting of the reconstituted and smaller Joint Conference Committee. The gang of three was reduced to one member through Chemerinsky's procedural change, and in any case with the mayor's staff having input into the final changes, there were fewer obstacles to agreement. Witnesses still came forward at this very late date to be heard. The LAPD sent a representative to the very last meeting to unsuccessfully protest the maintenance of the Airport Police in the charter. We were getting closer and closer to completing the unified charter.

In the section on neighborhood councils (article IX of the new charter) the appointed commission gave in to the elected commission on almost every disputed line. With Greg Nelson proposing sections and the two staffs working down to the wire on compromises, the final draft had far more detail to ensure the independence of neighborhood councils than there was in the original appointed commission draft.

The elected commission, whose members were agitated about how the final draft came into being, had the greatest influence by far on the portion of the charter most important to them: the section on neighborhood councils. It was in that section, most vital to the elected commissioners, that the appointed commission gave the most ground in the final editing.

The mayor had one thing he wanted, and that was an early start date for the new charter. The two chairs had selected a start date of July 1, 2001. The logic of this choice was compelling. The National Civic League's *Model City Charter* had recommended that the implementation of a new charter be timed to coincide with new council elections. The Chamber of Commerce and the League of Women Voters strongly favored the two-year date. The city attorney's staff estimated that the work of creating ordinances to implement the new charter would take a full two years. The Coalition of City Unions was adamant about the 2001 start date.

The two chairs appeared together on KNX Radio (1999b) to defend their joint decision on timing. The political and policy logic was that by removing Riordan from the equation, a new charter could have a fresh start without the conflicts of the current office holders. Riordan had contributed to that logic by frequently saying that these new powers would not apply to him, but to the next mayor. He had to reconcile his call for an early implementation date with those earlier statements.

The *Times* (1999b), now increasingly skeptical of Riordan's stance on charter reform, commented:

> Although the mayor just weeks ago disparaged the unified charter as offering little improvement over the status quo, he now can barely hide his eagerness to pull the levers of power than the new charter would give mayors.

After referring to Riordan's "bullying and intransigence," the *Times* called for compromise, noting that "it would be insane to allow the compromise to die over a date." *LA Weekly*'s city hall columnist Marc Haefele (1999b) noted that Riordan's staff members were angry about the date:

> Riordan himself has repeatedly made it clear that it's his successors, not he, who will benefit from charter change. Or so he's allowed the entire city to believe. But now the current gang of mayor's kids want to get their hands on the transition process.

Through his allies on the elected commission, Riordan began to push hard for the earlier date. He argued that the public deserved the benefits of the charter as soon as possible, and should not have to wait. The elected commissioners were already in a mutinous mood over the question of which staff was writing the final charter. At the February 16, 1999, meeting of the EC, Riordan ally Chet Widom made the startling motion that the new charter should take effect thirty days after its passage, except for those portions that required ordinances.

After considerable debate, the EC voted nine to four to adopt an implementation date of January 1, 2000, a full eighteen months earlier than the agreement reached between the two chairs. Chemerinsky voted against the motion (Newton 1999i).

The Chamber of Commerce had been on record calling for a two-year implementation, presumably comfortable that that was also the mayor's position. Organized labor strongly agreed, and made it a key point at the conclusion of the meet-and-confer process. Bob Duncan, head of the Coalition of City Unions, indicated that labor would not support the charter without a two-year implementation. On February 16, the JCC approved all outstanding issues except implementation, as negotiations continued.

The chairs were united on this issue, but were ultimately unable to overcome the united efforts of the city's top elected officials. Going around the commission chairs, Riordan made his own agreement with the city attorney and with the president of the city council.

Riordan promised Hahn that the mayor's budget would include funds for four staff members to do the implementation, and the agreement to seek a compromise date was blessed by John Ferraro. As Hahn described the deal, "I spoke to the mayor the other day and he was very interested in having the charter go into effect sooner. He offered to give me dedicated resources. Everyone got on the same page today, and I think that's great" (Greene 1999e).

For a number of members of the council, the fact that Riordan would exercise authority under the new charter meant that they would not support it. They blamed the commissions for that provision, even though it was put forward by elected officials over the objections of the chairs of the commissions.

The two commissions were created because of irreconcilable differences among elected officials. They managed to create a space within that conflict to generate some authority and power toward the development of a charter that the elected officials could not have created on their own. By the end, the commissions had developed a certain amount of autonomy from the elected officials. But in the final analysis, when the elected officials pulled together and agreed upon something like the implementation date, the power and authority of the commissions were no match.

The mayor, the city attorney, and the council president came together around the compromise of a one-year implementation, with the charter to take effect on July 1, 2000. In a late-night phone call, Kieffer, Chemerinsky, the mayor's office, and the CLA's office came to terms. It meant we were done. On February 24, the JCC approved the final charter unanimously.

With all the mayor's objections dealt with either by rejection or by acceptance, with the implementation date set, the unified charter was finally a real document ready to be presented to the city council. In a final compromise, the new charter would have fifteen councilmembers in it. Two additional measures would give voters the opportunity to increase the council to either twenty-one or twenty-five members.

In our third appearance before the council, Kieffer, Chemerinsky, Strobel, and I presented the final charter as a unified document of the two commissions. We answered questions that ranged throughout the charter. Comments from the floor revealed the emerging opposition from councilmembers. But we had a charter, and since it was unified, the council had no choice but to put it on the ballot.

The proposed charter made significant changes, and also left important features in the charter. A summary of these provisions was prepared by the CLA and made available to the voters in a pamphlet sent out by the city clerk (see appendix 1).

COUNCIL OPPOSITION

As the process of charter reform reached its crescendo in January and February 1999, the council was moving steadily toward an opposition stance. There had been plenty of moments that foreshadowed this outcome. During the battle over the mayor's authority to fire general managers, Chemerinsky (interview) had called Jackie Goldberg to ask for her help in moving labor-oriented elected commissioners. She had responded, "I'm starting to not feel good about this whole thing."

On February 14, 1999, I watched Goldberg on Bill Rosendahl's widely watched cable television program. She said that the new charter created a big shift of power to the mayor, and that there were no checks on this authority; the new charter would, in her view, imperil the city's tradition of good government. It certainly sounded like preparation for opposing the charter, and her opposition could be formidable.

Organized labor had been similarly on the fence. The one consistent position for city employees was opposition to Riordan. The charter looked better to the extent that Riordan disliked it. But when Riordan finally pronounced himself on board, the appeal of the charter to the city employees declined.

Members of the council felt hamstrung and blackmailed by the situation they faced. Yet there was no other way to get charter reform on the ballot. Had there been no elected commission, the council might well have taken the appointed commission's charter under advisement and buried it. Back in 1997, Kieffer met with councilmember Mark Ridley-Thomas. Kieffer recalled: "Mark said he wasn't worried. When we were done with our work, the council would do whatever they wanted with it. I found myself thinking that they simply don't know the level of force we are going to bring to bear on them, as long as we could reach agreement with the elected commission."

It took a long time for the council to understand that their leverage would be much smaller if the elected commission survived and if there was a unified charter. For many months, there had been a hopeful feeling at city hall that the elected commission would just simply explode, run out of money, collapse internally, or fail to even produce a charter. Some felt that, facing collapse, the elected commission would be *forced* to throw in its lot with the appointed commission.

But the elected commission had great staying power. A unified charter, even if built largely around the structure of the appointed commission's draft, gave the elected commission a chance to play its big card. This reality made it easier for the elected commission to swallow the adoption of a charter largely drafted by the appointed commission, especially when it dominated the charter drafting on neighborhood councils.

By the time we came to testify in front of the council, the members were still buzzing over their belief that a secret cabal had conspired to give the mayor everything he wanted. The mayor and his staff were still angry that we had not given them enough. The councilmembers had obvious concerns over individual portions of the charter. Hal Bernson disliked the new neighborhood councils. Rudy Svorinich complained about changes to Proposition 5. Jackie Goldberg and Ruth Galanter complained about the mayor's new authority.

One by one, members of the council joined the opposition. There were reports that some influential members were insisting that Ferraro lead the opposition if he wanted to be reelected as council president. As the council put off its final vote on the charter to Tuesday, March 2, the elected commission scheduled a meeting for the Saturday before, to cast its final votes on the amended charter. The commission vote held the proviso that if the council did not pass the charter on Tuesday, all bets would be off.

The assumption for some weeks had been that if the council wanted changes, and both chairs agreed, then it would still be the unified charter. The difficulty was defining the line that could not be crossed. If the council did not approve the unified charter or made changes that crossed that undefined line, the elected commissioners were prepared to revive their earlier, more radical proposals and push them to the ballot. Kieffer said, "If they did make major changes, or refuse to put it on the ballot, I would have joined in supporting the unified proposal with the elected commission and I think so would most of our commission." The *Times*'s Jim Newton (1999j) described the elaborate end game:

> So deep is the distrust between the elected commission and the council that neither wants to be the first to vote on a charter package, because some members of each group are convinced that the other will then amend the proposal. One result is a convoluted procedure for finalizing the votes: Elected commissioners are expected Saturday to consider approving the unified charter and signing a transmission letter to the city clerk. But they also intend to hold onto that letter until after the council votes, delivering it only if the council joins them in supporting the compromise.

At the Tuesday council meeting, most councilmembers were unhappy. Bernson said it created a mayoral "semi-dictator," while Nate Holden called it "a slick attempt to establish autocratic government in this city." Bernson could be heard muttering, "I'm going to vote to put this on, but this is insanity" (Newton 1999k). But the council had no choice. The compromise between the two commissions meant that the council could not stop the measure from going to the ballot.

On March 2, 1999, the council voted unanimously, but reluctantly, thirteen to zero, to place the charter on the June ballot. Ruth Galanter walked out before the vote, unhappy with the result but unwilling to vote to prevent the measure from going to the ballot. Clearly, few councilmembers favored the new charter. Only Cindy Miscikowski, Joel Wachs, and Mike Feuer spoke out in support of it.

The *Times* (1999c) was much more enthusiastic about an outcome that "only the most wild-eyed optimists" could have envisioned and chided the council to "serve the city by joining, not blocking, this vital journey."

One of the aspects of Riordan's mayoralty that has drawn justified praise has been his ability to make big projects happen, to generate "social capital" so that a downtown cathedral will be built or a reformist slate of candidates will win control of the school board. He clearly moved the charter forward. His relentless desire to push his elected commission's draft charter on the voters, however, had to be blocked by cooler and more responsible heads. It was the two commissions, and especially the chairs, Kieffer and Chemerinsky, who forced Riordan against his will into playing a more responsible role in this critical community project. For a short time of several months, the two chairs played the community leadership role that the mayor would ordinarily be expected to assume.

And then, when it really counted, Riordan took back the leadership role and carried the charter to victory. Unlike Sam Yorty, who walked away from charter reform when his favored policies were not enacted, Riordan enthusiastically and energetically committed himself to carry the charter over the finish line. When he did so, he was handed the civic coalition that had been assembled by the commissions and a unified charter built by the two commission chairs. What might have looked in retrospect like a finely tuned alliance of the Riordan political group and the civic arena was more like a shotgun marriage. But it worked.

CHAPTER FOURTEEN

The Campaign for the Unified Charter

AFTER ALL THEIR battles over charter reform, the mayor, both commissions, and a broad civic coalition ended up in the same camp. The city council ended up in lonely and ineffective opposition, with unenthusiastic backing from labor. The mayor-council conflict that had bedeviled charter reform held its form to the very end. No circumstance, no set of compromises or agreements could bridge the conflict between mayor and council.

By the time the campaign got under way, three councilmembers supported the charter: Feuer, Miscikowski, and Wachs. The council districts of those who supported the charter (five, eleven, two) were precisely the ones represented by those who had voted for the original Feuer motion in 1996 to create a single charter reform commission whose recommendations would go directly to the ballot. Things had come full circle, or perhaps they had not moved at all from where they were in 1996.

It was ironic that the charter that the mayor supported and the council opposed was, in its details, more influenced by the council and the experienced hands of the city government than it was by the mayor. It had been thoroughly vetted by city officials and only briefly, and at the end of the game, by the mayor's staff. It bore the stamp of many years of experience in city government, which the appointed commission had believed essential to preserve. But because of perceptions, it had come to seem an alien document to officials who did not know how great had been their influence on the final document.

As the sides formed for the upcoming battle over the June election, new alliances fell into place. Now the appointed commission was completely allied with the elected commission and the mayor. This was unfamiliar territory, as the mayor had treated us, for strategic reasons, as irrelevant for two years. It was easier to join hands with the elected commissioners who, like the appointed commissioners, had taken bold steps away from their patron.

The campaign was organized financially and strategically by the mayor. Riordan was not going to repeat Yorty's decision to abandon the charter reform he had started three decades before. Riordan had already shown his political potency in the April 13 municipal elections, in which his endorsed council candidates did very well, and in which his endorsed school board candidates defeated three incumbents.

Bill Carrick, one of the nation's top Democratic political consultants, was put in charge of the campaign, and the mayor raised the money personally. Carrick had run the Riordan slate for the elected charter commission in 1997.

Carrick had been prepared to run the campaign for the elected commission's charter if no agreement on a unified charter had been reached, but he knew it would be difficult. He told Riordan "that it would cost a lot of money, as much as $3 million. We would have to confront the possibility that the *Times* would be opposed. The campaign would have had to focus on mayoral power to the exclusion of everything else, and Riordan would have been on his own without a broad coalition."

The creation of the unified charter, over Riordan's objections, made the chances of passage much greater. The commission process of developing the unified charter had generated a broad civic coalition, a parade that Riordan could now march to the front of instead of battling against. According to Carrick, "Now once it became a single measure, our strategy was to dominate the communications environment, free media, paid media, endorsements, everything. My goal throughout was to push the council into a corner, so that they would only be fighting for themselves."

With his fund-raising and political leadership, Riordan made the success of the campaign possible. However, the process of building the unified charter also brought the broad coalition required for victory. As Carrick noted, "It's always easier to vote no than yes." Before Riordan signed on to the new charter, the two commissions had recruited much of the city's business and civic leadership to the side of the unified charter.

The *Times* was an enthusiastic backer of the unified charter, as was the influential League of Women Voters. The Urban League and the leaders of the African American–Jewish Leadership Connection helped draw minority and progressive support despite the suspicion of Riordan held in the black community. Further media endorsements came from the skeptical *Daily News,* the *Sentinel* in the African American community, *La Opinion,* the *LA Weekly,* and KNX Radio.

The broad coalition in favor of the charter included bitter enemies, many of whom would not have joined Riordan on his envisioned charter. Riordan shared billing with city attorney James K. Hahn, whom Riordan had recently tried to run out of office by supporting an electoral opponent. The great advantage of having both Hahn and Riordan, an outcome that would have been impossible behind only one commission's charter, was that Riordan drew from a center-right constituency and Hahn from a center-left base. Hahn could reach African American voters in a way that Riordan could not hope to match.

Also high on the list of supporters was Keith Comrie, whom Riordan's staff had referred to as a village idiot during the battles over the role of the CAO in the new charter. Riordan's support made it easier for his close ally, Police Chief Bernard C. Parks, to bring his popular name to the yes side. Speaker of the Assembly Antonio Villaraigosa added his endorsement.

Finally, the charter won the support of the principal organizers of the secession movement—Richard Close, David Fleming, and Bert Boeckmann. All three signed the ballot argument for the charter, despite their expressed reservations that the neighborhood council system did not grant enough authority to the neighborhoods (Greene 1999f).

Polling specialists found that some names were more valuable than others in moving voters on the charter. Riordan's name stood out, with the highest approval rating of any leader in the city. Hahn, Riordan's nemesis, was also very well regarded, along with Chief Parks and County Supervisor Zev Yaroslavsky (who remained neutral). The League of Women Voters was an influential voice in charter matters with the public. Carrick found that

> the council, by contrast, is tremendously unpopular. As a result, the council in LA is not good at being the opposition to the mayor. In creating an opposition, they lost a lot of credibility by having seemed to negotiate in good faith for a unified charter, after a lot of pressure was brought on the mayor not to be the skunk at the picnic. They completely lost elite opinion, who uniformly found the council's behavior strange and irresponsible.

The councilmembers did become the main opposition. They raised the money, with a number of councilmembers making $50,000 donations from their campaign war chests. They signed ballot arguments and spoke against the new charter. Understanding the difficulty of being the sole organized opposition, they put their main effort into winning the support of organized labor.

Organized labor was placed in a difficult position. Labor had elected candidates to the elected commission. They had come to the meetings of both commissions, and had seen their concerns addressed. The new charter included a living wage for city contractors. There were positive changes that emerged from an extended meet-and-confer process. But the council signed the collective bargaining agreements that were the lifeblood of employee organizations, and the leaders of the council demanded that labor join the opposition to the charter.

At a dramatic meeting to decide its endorsement, the County Federation of Labor heard the lions of the council—Richard Alatorre, Jackie Goldberg, and Ruth Galanter—speak passionately to the membership. After years of devoted service to labor, they demanded a favor of labor: to oppose the charter. The union members responded with a strong majority in opposition. Labor's position was expressed by one of the key labor political advisers, Mark Siegel:

> Labor did all it could to get the unified charter, and did all it could to tinker with the unified charter to make it better, but let's not forget that they were very happy with the current charter. There were no real policy objections. At first,

the political decision was we should come out in favor of it. How can we position ourselves in the public eyes as agents of change and not agents of the status quo? And then basically Jackie Goldberg, John Ferraro, Ruth Galanter came around and said: "We've protected you all these years from the mayor. We're calling in our chits and we want you to oppose it. This is a race. This is a contest, a test of wills between the city council and the mayor."

According to Siegel, the mayor worked hard with Miguel Contreras, the head of the AFL-CIO, to keep the big union network neutral. At the endorsement meeting, Kieffer and Chemerinsky spoke, as did Hahn. But the councilmembers carried the day.

Chemerinsky (KCRW, 1999b) said on the eve of the charter election:

We worked carefully with labor throughout the entire process. We would never have approved this charter unless we believed that labor was on board and so I was shocked and distressed when labor decided to oppose the charter. We met with labor as part of the meet-and-confer process and they gave us a list of 12 things they wanted changed in the charter. We were able to do 11 of the 12; the 12th was quite minor. We thought we'd met all of the demands.

While the council had labor in its camp, there was no enthusiasm from labor, and very little money and activity. Julie Butcher recalled, "We didn't fight very hard." It was essentially a payback to the solons of the council.

Despite the tremendous personal stakes felt by the opposed councilmembers, it was difficult for the no side to gain traction, and to find people with great stature in the community to lead the opposition. While individual members retained their popularity, the council as a body generated little affection. The only councilmember who could move voters citywide, according to Carrick, was Joel Wachs, who was a staunch supporter of the charter.

There were more popular provisions than unpopular ones in the charter, and the potentially unpopular ones were difficult to run against. The idea of a new charter, the provision of neighborhood councils, and the new authority for the controller to conduct performance audits were very popular with the voters. Civil service was largely intact, so there was little incentive for organized labor to mobilize on the no side.

Even with labor only mildly opposing the charter, the opposition could have made substantial gains on the issue of council size. But the two commissions had been unable to agree on the size of the city council. More and more, it was clear that no increase could possibly win voter support, and that any increase could set off a voter revolt. As far back as 1997, Carrick's polling on charter reform found "absolutely no support whatsoever for increasing the size of the council. As to council size, there was simply no discussion. When we raised the question with voters, they simply ended the discussion" (interview). Pollster Richard Maullin found the same thing in his surveys, adding to the sense that the commissions dodged a bullet when their own pride and racial and ethnic competition prevented a reasonable compromise.

Council size might have been the very issue that enabled the council to defeat the charter. In fact, the council did try to take advantage of the existence of the separate measures to increase the size of the council by lumping the costs of council expansion in with the much more modest cost of the new charter. Thus, their literature cited the presumed $26 million annual cost of the new charter.

The council had a very tough row to hoe, with far less money to back it up. But they did have some good shots. One was to draw on the long Los Angeles tradition of opposition to corruption and to executive authority.

On June 2, 1999, Rudy Svoronich argued against the new charter on public radio's *Which Way LA?* (KCRW radio 1999b). Svoronich's summary of the arguments for the no side began with the cost, "up to 26 million dollars a year for more paper pushers at City Hall. This new charter proposal sets us back 75 years, which we believe could open Los Angeles up again to a time of crime, cronies, and corruption." And "the other thing that this charter does, which is very, very scary, is it tips the balance of power to a mayor's office in lieu of a check and balance. City commissioners can be removed without council approval."

One of the most telling arguments related to services. Svoronich asked, "If you needed to have a pothole filled, who would you call? The Mayor's office? Of course not. You call your local council office."

His final point was complexity: "If the voters of the city of Los Angeles have not read this entire document, this multi-page pamphlet that was sent to every voter, then they shouldn't vote for it. And if they have read it from cover to cover, I'm certain that they wouldn't want to vote for it."

The striking thing about the ballot arguments, pro and con, in the charter debate was that both sides were grounded in the reform principles of Los Angeles government. The con side emphasized the threat of corruption and the inefficiency of new participatory mechanisms, while the pro side emphasized opportunities for participation and accountability.

The con side was seriously hampered by the stature of the endorsements of the charter, the mayor's ability to finance the campaign, and the eclectic objections to the charter that brought the opposition together. They had multiple, often conflicting lines of attack. Some opponents complained that the new charter gave too much power to the council by reducing charter provisions to ordinance, while others said it gave too much to the mayor (Orlov 1999g). Yet the real problem for the opponents was that the civic coalition had gained complete control of the high ground of reform, and the council's arguments seemed only to veil self-protection and self-interest.

The ballot argument for the new charter (City Clerk 1999, 34) was signed by the two charter reform commissions, Riordan, City Attorney

Hahn, Controller Rick Tuttle, three councilmembers, and Police Chief Parks. The list included Warren Christopher, three leaders of the secession movement, and the heads of the Chamber of Commerce and the League of Women Voters. The argument noted, "Two charter Reform Commissions have worked together to develop a unified, comprehensive new charter that has the support of . . . a broad coalition of civic and non-profit organizations."

In response, the opposition was eclectic in membership and in arguments. Most of the councilmembers signed the argument against the new charter, along with County Supervisor Gloria Molina, leaders of some home-owner groups and several well-known progressives like Tom Hayden. The key argument (City Clerk, 1999, 37) was that "this charter abolishes the checks and balances in our city government and **opens our city up to a level of corruption** that has not been seen since the Big Boss days of the 1920's on the East Coast" (emphasis in original).

The ballot arguments for the measures to increase the size of the city council revealed how dangerous the issue might have been to the new charter. Cost estimates of adding council members made charter reform look very expensive, and opponents now added Chicago to the mix of cities not to emulate (City Clerk 1999, 72):

> The charter reformers are saying that 15 members each representing 230,000 people is too many. The example they give is that Chicago has 50 councilmembers each representing 60,000 residents. What the reformers are really saying is that CHICAGO-STYLE POLITICS should be brought to Los Angeles. The nerve of the charter reformers to speak of CHICAGO-STYLE POLITICS and Los Angeles politics in the same breath, **that is ludicrous!** (emphasis in original)

These arguments against council size would have been far more serious had the larger council been embedded in the charter proposal. Standing on their own, separate from the charter proposal, they were much less challenging to the charter itself—even though charter opponents sought to import the cost of the larger city council into their cost estimates of the new charter.

PREELECTION POLLING

Even after all the attacks on the new charter, its prospects for passage looked good. The SEIU, in unenthusiastic opposition to the charter, sponsored a private poll by Fairbank, Maslin, Maullin and Associates (220-806W) of city voters in April. Surprisingly, the council's rating was reasonably high, except in the area of efficiency. On the other hand, voters endorsed the notion presented by Riordan that the council "has too much power over the day-to-day operations of city departments." Nearly 50 percent agreed.

Three main provisions of the new charter won majority support: performance audits of city departments by the elected controller (82 percent), neighborhood councils (78 percents), and enhancing the mayor's authority over city departments (71 percent). In stark contrast to earlier polls, 55 percent of the voters had either seen or heard about the charter reform process. Nearly 40 percent were definitely or probably ready to vote for the new charter, with only 13 percent opposed, and a third undecided. When voters were read the exact ballot wording, support went up to 46 percent, opposition increased to 25 percent, and undecided declined to 21 percent.

Different readings of arguments for the charter changed the votes. When the performance audits were included, support increased considerably, with strong support going from 18 percent to 27 percent, and with strong opposition declining from 26 percent to 19 percent. On council size, 28 percent strongly opposed increasing the council's membership. Another 19 percent were somewhat opposed.

The SEIU poll also assessed which leaders would be most credible on the charter vote. Riordan headed the list with 24 percent rating him the most believable, and 46 percent somewhat believable. Ironically, "your local council member" (generally in opposition to the charter) was not far behind, at 19 percent very believable and 43 percent somewhat believable. The other two most believable politicians were City Attorney James Hahn (24 percent very and 41 percent somewhat believable) and County Supervisor Zev Yaroslavsky (25 percent very and 38 percent somewhat believable).

Based on these polling results, said union leader Julie Butcher (interview), "We knew the charter was going to pass."

ANALYSIS OF THE ELECTION RESULTS

On June 8, 1999, the new city charter was approved by a margin of 60 percent to 40 percent. On first reading, the charter vote looked like Riordan's 1997 reelection with strong white, Jewish, and Latino support and African American opposition. But a closer look indicates that the charter vote joined together overlapping coalitions: the conservative alliance behind Riordan and a reform coalition of Jews and educated white voters.

Data and Methods

Mark Drayse and I analyzed the votes on charter reform, the 2001 mayoral race, and secession (Sonenshein and Drayse 2003). Map 7 shows the geography of support for the new charter (measure 1); maps 8 and 9 display votes for increased council size (measures 3 and 4); maps 10 and 11 show the vote for the 2001 mayoral race, and maps 12 and 13 the vote for San Fernando Valley secession (measure F).

Census data were linked with precinct voting data in order to allow the analysis of demographic, social, and economic variables as factors in voting. We then tabulated the results of the vote by groups of precincts. The precinct groups were based on (1) location in the San Fernando Valley or the rest of the city of Los Angeles, and (2) four ethnic political constituencies: Jewish precincts, white Republican precincts, black precincts, and Latino precincts. These precinct groups were constructed from census data as well as voter data compiled by the Statewide Database (the State of California's redistricting database maintained by the Institute for Governmental Studies at the University of California, Berkeley).

Jewish precincts were those precincts in which at least 20 percent of registered voters were Jewish. White Republican precincts had a population at least 70 percent white, as well as 35 percent or more registered voters stating Republican party affiliation (excluding Jewish precincts). Black precincts had a population at least 50 percent African American. Latino precincts were those in which at least 50 percent of registered voters were Latino. Designating Latino precincts in this way provided a smaller set of precincts than if we had used a 50 percent Latino population, due to the lag between Latino population and voting eligibility.

To further evaluate voting patterns, we analyzed the results using a regression analysis. Independent variables in the models included indicators of *ethnic and immigrant populations* (percentage Jewish, percentage Latino, percentage white, percentage black, percentage foreign born); *education and income* (percentage with college degree, median household income), and *place* (Valley). For each of the four votes, models were constructed for all precincts, white Republican precincts, Jewish precincts, and Latino precincts.

We also created separate models for white Republican, Jewish, and Hispanic precincts, using the same variables. For example, to more fully understand the support of Jewish voters for charter reform, we looked for a relationship *within Jewish precincts* between the percentage of Jewish voters and the vote for charter reform. A significant relationship between the concentration of Jewish voters and the charter reform vote would lead to a preliminary conclusion that Jewish voters tended to favor (or oppose) charter reform.

An important caveat about the regression analysis needs to be addressed at the outset. We certainly face the problem of ecological fallacy if we assume that the votes of individuals with particular social and economic characteristics can be understood using aggregate data. Our results should be treated with caution. We attempt to understand the voting behavior of individuals representing different ethnic groups by incorporating ethnic indicators as independent variables in the regression models. In appendix 2, Gary King's (1997) methodology to address ecological problems is applied to this data.

Ultimately, to gain a firmer understanding of the vote by group, we would need to conduct or analyze voter surveys providing individual data, rather than data aggregated by precinct. We are confident, however, that our analysis suggests important connections between ethnicity and support for charter reform and secession, and the reform coalitions that emerged in each election. And our approach emphasizes the role of *place*.

A second caveat is that these data represent those who came to the polls, rather than all voters. In Los Angeles city elections, absentee ballots are counted in a separate group and are not attached to geographical precincts. However, in most cases (with the possible exception of the 2001 mayoral race in which Hahn did better in the absentee vote than in the vote at the polls) the exclusion of absentees does not dramatically alter the structure of the data.

As an additional method of analysis, we looked at the vote by city council district. These districts follow certain historical patterns of race, ethnicity, and ideology, and it is therefore possible to make tentative comparisons of the charter votes to earlier elections.

On the surface, the vote for the new city charter was carried by white voters over minorities, an outcome that would be consistent with the conservative coalition model of multiethnic politics. But the coalition for charter reform does not easily fit into the model of the Riordan/Giuliani conservative alliance. The map of the charter reform vote, precinct analysis, and council district data show a somewhat different creature from any of the normal models of coalition.

In Riordan's 1997 reelection, the Valley carried him and provided his highest average percentage, with the Westside areas coming in second. In the charter race, by contrast, there was greater support on the Westside than in the Valley. In fact, of the 45,168-vote margin by which the new charter passed, nearly half (48.9 percent) came from the two Westside/Valley liberal/moderate districts, the fifth and the eleventh. These two districts provided an edge of over 22,000 votes. All four of the Valley districts (two, three, seven, twelve) together delivered a margin of only 11,572 votes.

The single largest bloc of support for the new charter came not from the conservative northwest Valley where secession sentiment was strongest, but from the white liberal, educated, Jewish Westside and near San Fernando Valley (map 7; table 9). The regression analysis shows that the best predictors of support for charter reform were the percentage of Jewish voters and the percentage of persons with a college education (table 10). This result is consistent with the votes cast in council districts 5 and 11.

In other words, the long-standing reform constituency that had backed reform in the Bradley years led the charge for charter reform. Whether in the San Fernando Valley or in the rest of city, precincts with significant Jewish populations gave 82 percent of their votes to the new charter. These were the same precincts that had provided overwhelming support in 1992 to a liberal police reform measure championed by liberals and the African American community. With no clear interest dimension for this community, it appears that this support for charter reform was based on a long-standing belief in governmental reform.

White conservative areas, relatively new to the reform coalition, were in favor of charter reform, but to a lesser degree than educated liberal voters. Voters in white Republican precincts supported charter reform by a two-to-one ratio, with stronger support outside the San Fernando Valley. Some of these Valley voters may have been too skeptical of government to become enthusiastic about reform; or may have had secession in their minds as an alternative. Voting for reform measures was a new thing for these conservative voters, whereas it was the normal pattern for liberal educated whites.

Thus, within the white vote for charter reform were two considerably different perspectives on reform. These differences would become more pronounced when the city voted on secession three years later.

The minority vote was split on charter reform. African American voters were the most opposed to the new charter, reflecting their community's strong distrust of Riordan and the high proportion of government employees in the black community. In African American precincts, only 35 percent of voters supported charter reform. The regression analysis indicates that percentage black population was negatively associated with support for charter reform. With his philosophy of privatizing government services and his support from the white-led police union, Riordan was perceived by many African Americans as a serious threat to their interests. A charter that sought to increase Riordan's authority and that was opposed by most of organized labor would have a difficult time with black voters.

Latino voters seemed to favor the new charter. The position of the Latino community was one of the big unknowns going into the race. Both Latino councilmembers (Mike Hernandez and Richard Alatorre) had opposed the charter, although Assembly Speaker Antonio Villaraigosa supported it. In both council districts with large Latino populations (one and fourteen), the charter passed.

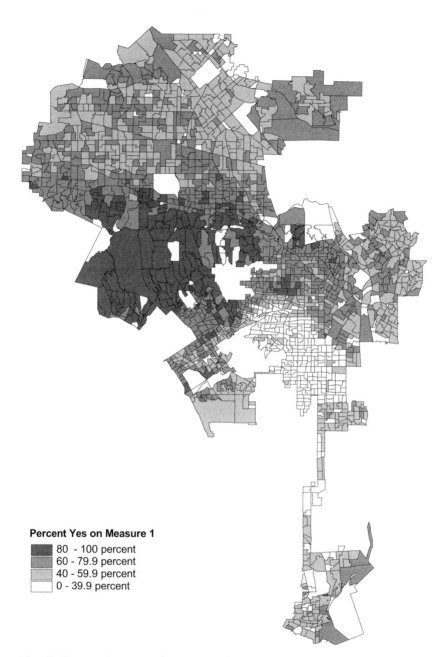

Percent Yes on Measure 1

80 - 100 percent
60 - 79.9 percent
40 - 59.9 percent
0 - 39.9 percent

Map 7. Vote on Measure 1 for new city charter

TABLE 9
Vote by Groups, Measure 1

Precinct Groups	Number of Precincts	Total Votes	Vote for Measure 1	
			Percentage Yes	Percentage No
All City of Los Angeles Precincts*	**1,755**	**186,945**	**60.3**	**39.7**
Jewish Precincts	154	15,271	81.8	18.2
White Republican Precincts	100	13,098	66.2	33.8
Black Precincts	145	18,283	35.1	64.9
Latino Precincts	175	24,073	59.0	41.0
All Other Precincts	1,181	116,220	61.1	38.9
All Valley Precincts	**651**	**71,966**	**63.9**	**36.1**
Jewish Precincts	57	6,129	80.3	19.7
White Republican Precincts	71	9,094	64.9	35.1
Latino Precincts	48	7,678	57.0	43.0
All Other Precincts	475	49,065	62.8	37.2
All Non-Valley Precincts	**1,104**	**114,979**	**58.1**	**41.9**
Jewish Precincts	97	9,142	82.8	17.2
White Republican Precincts	29	4,004	69.4	30.6
Black Precincts	145	18,283	35.1	64.9
Latino Precincts	127	16,395	59.9	40.1
All Other Precincts	706	67,155	59.9	40.1

Source of voting data: City of Los Angeles, Office of the City Clerk
*Excludes votes by mail. Votes by mail were 59.7% in favor of charter reform. The overall vote in favor of charter reform was 60.0%.

Latinos were considerably more likely than African Americans to back the charter, even though most Latino elected officials backed organized labor's call to oppose the charter. While the geographical analysis of the charter vote is not the best vehicle to measure Latino voting, it does indicate that Latino precincts were much more favorable to the charter than were African American precincts. Latino precincts voted 59 percent in favor of charter reform.

In the regression models, the variable for the percentage of Latino population was not statistically significant. To some degree, this lack of associ-

TABLE 10
Regression Analysis of Measure 1

Predictors	Standardized Coefficients (Beta)			
	All Precincts (n = 1,684)	White Republican Precincts (n = 100)	Jewish Precincts (n = 154)	Latino Precincts (n = 175)
Percentage Jewish	0.292***	0.159	0.185**	—
Percentage Latino	0.041	—	—	0.022
Percentage White	−0.051	0.139	—	—
Percentage Black	−0.342***	—	—	—
Percentage Foreign Born	0.135***	−0.012	−0.065	0.548***
Percentage with College Degree	0.501***	0.492**	0.593***	0.242**
Median Household Income	−0.017	0.094	0.139	−0.095
Valley	0.028	0.135	0.169*	−0.063
Adjusted R Square =	0.709	0.452	0.464	0.353

Significance levels:***(.001 level), **(.01 level), *(.05 level)

ation may be due to the relatively strong white vote for the charter. However, the percentage of foreign-born persons was strongly associated with the vote for charter reform. While this seems to indicate support for charter reform among immigrants, this result should be considered with caution, given the low voter turnout among recent immigrants and the ethnic diversity of immigrants in Los Angeles.

The voting patterns on Measure 1 look like an overlapping of two coalitions: the Riordan conservative alliance and the white liberal reform movement without African Americans. Had Riordan (and some of his opponents at city hall) had their way and fostered two competing measures on the ballot, the key blocs would likely have split apart. Riordan would have held his antigovernment conservatives, but his opponents might well have won the liberal Westside and much of the good-government crowd. This split, which did later occur in secession, might have doomed both proposals and thereby would have helped the secessionists to argue that reform was a farce.

The map of the charter vote is grist for the political imagination. If secession were to pass in Los Angeles, it would have had to look something like the coalition for Measure 1. White conservatives, rather than white liberals, would have led the way, but secession would have had to seize the high ground of reform so that the good-government constituency would favor it. It would draw support from Latinos and Asian Americans and isolate African Americans in opposition. To win citywide, secession would have had to be a forward-looking reform proposal like the charter reform itself.

The Vote for a Larger City Council

On the issue of council size, yet another type of coalition emerged. Overall, only one in three voters favored increasing council size. The single largest group in support of a larger city council was the same reform-minded Westside and near Valley bloc that favored the charter (maps 8–9; tables 11–14). On the Westside, a majority wanted a larger council, even though there was no conceivable way that this change would improve the standing of the Westside at city hall. Westside precincts with significant numbers of Jewish voters were 51 percent in favor of Measure 3 and 55 percent in favor of Measure 4. The regression analyses for Measures 3 and 4 show that the percentage of Jewish voters and the percentage of college-educated persons were positively related to the vote for a larger council.

The strongest blocs against the larger council were white Republicans and African Americans, albeit for different reasons. White conservatives consistently opposed larger elected bodies out of opposition to higher taxation, an ideological antigovernment position. In white Republican precincts, only 33 percent voted for Measure 3 and 32 percent voted for Measure 4. African Americans apparently feared that their stable share of council seats (three out of fifteen seats since 1963) would be reduced if the council were enlarged. They gave little support to increased council size, voting 26 percent in favor of Measure 3 and 22 percent for Measure 4. The regression models indicate that the percentage white population was negatively associated with the vote for Measure 4. The percentage black population was negatively associated with the vote for both measures.

Other minorities might have found, however, that a larger council would help their prospects for representation. A secondary bloc of support for the council size measures could be found on the Eastside, where it is difficult to tell if these supporters were Latinos, Asian Americans, or white liberals. In Latino precincts, 42 percent voted for Measure 3 and 40 percent for Measure 4. The percentage of foreign-born residents was the best predictor of support for a larger council in these precincts. We believe that this is intriguing, if preliminary evidence that for Latinos and Asian Americans the larger council placed their interests at odds with those of African Americans.

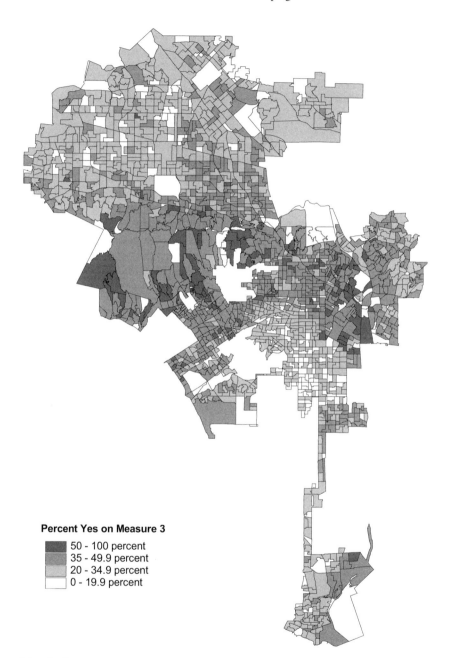

Percent Yes on Measure 3

- 50 - 100 percent
- 35 - 49.9 percent
- 20 - 34.9 percent
- 0 - 19.9 percent

Map 8. Vote on Measure 3 to increase council to 21 members

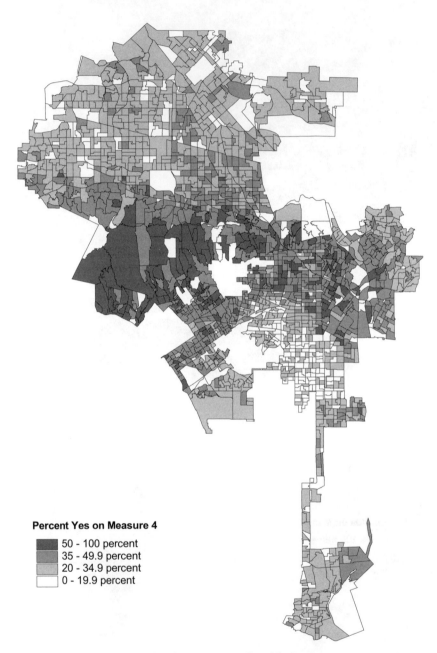

Percent Yes on Measure 4

50 - 100 percent
35 - 49.9 percent
20 - 34.9 percent
0 - 19.9 percent

Map 9. Vote on Measure 4 to increase council to 25 members

TABLE 11

Vote by Groups, Measure 3, to Increase Council to Twenty-One Members

			Vote for Measure 3	
Precinct Groups	*Number of Precincts*	*Total Votes*	*Percentage Yes*	*Percentage No*
All City of Los Angeles Precincts*	**1,755**	**175,198**	**37.1**	**62.9**
Jewish Precincts	154	13,632	48.1	51.9
White Republican Precincts	100	12,295	32.6	67.4
Black Precincts	145	17,369	25.9	74.1
Latino Precincts	175	22,733	41.6	58.4
All Other Precincts	1,181	109,169	37.0	63.0
All Valley Precincts	**651**	**68,038**	**33.8**	**66.2**
Jewish Precincts	57	5,565	44.1	55.9
White Republican Precincts	71	8,623	29.7	70.3
Latino Precincts	48	7,301	37.7	62.3
All Other Precincts	475	46,549	32.7	67.3
All Non-Valley Precincts	**1,104**	**107,160**	**39.1**	**60.9**
Jewish Precincts	97	8,067	50.9	49.1
White Republican Precincts	29	3,672	39.3	60.7
Black Precincts	145	17,369	25.9	74.1
Latino Precincts	127	15,432	43.4	56.6
All Other Precincts	706	62,620	40.2	59.8

Source of voting data: City of Los Angeles, Office of the City Clerk

*Excludes votes by mail. Votes by mail were 34.7% in favor of Proposition 3. The overall vote in favor of Proposition 3 was 36.5%.

TABLE 12
Regression Analysis of Measure 3

Predictors	Standardized Coefficients (Beta)			
	All Precincts (n = 1,684)	White Republican Precincts (n = 100)	Jewish Precincts (n = 154)	Latino Precincts (n = 175)
Percentage Jewish	0.263***	0.159	0.032	—
Percentage Latino	0.232***	—	—	−0.027
Percentage White	−0.079	0.200*	—	—
Percentage Black	−0.141**	—	—	—
Percentage Foreign-Born	0.227***	−0.036	−0.009	0.394***
Percentage with College Degree	0.607***	0.544***	0.629***	0.125
Median Household Income	−0.183***	−0.031	−0.341**	−0.175
Valley	−0.235***	−0.062	−0.043	−0.160
Adjusted R Square =	0.410	0.593	0.184	0.296

Significance levels: ***(.001 level), ** (.01 level), *(.05 level)

TABLE 13
Vote by Groups, Measure 4, to Increase Council to Twenty-Five Members

Precinct Groups	Number of Precincts	Vote for Measure 4		
		Total Votes	Percentage Yes	Percentage No
All City of Los Angeles Precincts*	1,755	177,417	36.2	63.8
Jewish Precincts	154	14,037	51.1	48.9
White Republican Precincts	100	12,400	32.1	67.9
Black Precincts	145	17,409	22.2	77.8
Latino Precincts	175	23,015	39.5	60.5
All Other Precincts	1,181	110,556	36.3	63.7
All Valley Precincts	651	68,690	32.8	67.2
Jewish Precincts	57	5,704	46.0	54.0
White Republican Precincts	71	8,630	28.5	71.5

TABLE 13 (continued)

Precinct Groups	Number of Precincts	Vote for Measure 4		
		Total Votes	Percentage Yes	Percentage No
Latino Precincts	48	7,373	34.9	65.1
All Other Precincts	475	46,983	31.6	68.4
All Non-Valley Precincts	**1,104**	**108,727**	**38.4**	**61.6**
Jewish Precincts	97	8,333	54.6	45.4
White Republican Precincts	29	3,770	40.1	59.9
Black Precincts	145	17,409	22.2	77.8
Latino Precincts	127	15,642	41.7	58.3
All Other Precincts	706	63,573	39.8	60.2

Source of voting data: City of Los Angeles, Office of the City Clerk
*Excludes votes by mail, Votes by mail were 29.1% in favor of Proposition 4. The overall vote in favor of Proposition 4 was 34.6%.

TABLE 14
Regression Analysis of Measure 4

Predictors	Standardized Coefficients (Beta)			
	All Precincts (n = 1,684)	White Republican Precincts (n = 100)	Jewish Precincts (n = 154)	Latino Precincts (n = 175)
Percentage Jewish	0.308***	0.203*	0.121	—
Percentage Latino	0.171***	—	—	0.019
Percentage White	−0.180**	0.101	—	—
Percentage Black	−0.235***	—	—	—
Percentage Foreign-Born	0.179***	−0.032	−0.067	0.404***
Percentage with College Degree	0.658***	0.272	0.570***	0.210*
Median Household Income	−0.133***	0.145	−0.135	−0.204*
Valley	−0.258***	−0.281**	−0.120	−0.195*
Adjusted R Square =	0.531	0.572	0.317	0.359

Significance levels: ***(.001 level), **(.01 level), *(.05 level)

Compared to the coalition for the new charter, the coalition for a larger city council was more urban, less suburban; more Jewish and definitely not white conservative, and certainly not African American. The possibility of some sort of alliance between Jewish voters and some Latino (Sonenshein 2001) and Asian American voters is intriguing, particularly given the results of the 2001 mayoral election. There, the James K. Hahn coalition resembles the anti-larger-council alliance of white conservatives and African Americans, and the Antonio Villaraigosa coalition looks a bit like the pro–larger council alliance of white liberals and Eastside minorities.

While the new charter was designed to respond to the Valley, and the increase in the council size was aimed at Latinos and Asian Americans, both proposals received their strongest support from Westside Jewish voters, whose interests had little relevance to the charter process. The white liberal group represented a reform constituency, as it did in the vote for police reform in 1992.

While reform was completed in order to placate the Valley, its greatest appeal was to a part of the city that was least alienated. Polls had shown that the Westside was the only area of the city that did not feel short-changed in power at city hall (*Los Angeles Times* Poll 2002).

The main reason that these liberal voters endorsed the city charter can only be guessed, but at its root it seems to be ideological. No clear interest argument was made to liberal voters, particularly on the Westside. However, the notion of a citywide reform process obviously had an appeal, and the good-government approach won support as well. Unlike Valley conservatives alienated from city government, white liberal voters might have given more credence to the possibility of reform.

In their study of the dynamics of institutional reform, Bowler, Donovan, and Karp (2002) argue that beliefs among political elites, not simply political self-interest, help to explain their actions on reform. Voting analysis of the Los Angeles charter reform election adds another dimension to this view. We see *at the mass level* the impact of philosophy and belief. Clearly, reform had a resonance for many voters that was not explainable in terms of self-interest alone.

Riordan justifiably received the major credit for the passage of the new charter, for initiating and pursuing the effort, for bankrolling and organizing the campaign, and for helping to shape the winning coalition. The charter victory was the centerpiece of Riordan's most dominant showing at the polls. In addition to the winning campaign for the charter, which was entirely a Riordan financial operation, Riordan's candidates for the school board all won. Riordan endorsees defeated three school board incumbents.

One of Riordan's severest critics, *LA Weekly* columnist Marc Haefele, commented: "I don't think the Mayor has looked this good since the immediate aftermath of the 1994 earthquake when he was the guy who took charge. It's a very solid sense that when the Mayor finally figures out how to step in and be effective in any area where his presence is definitely needed, he can figure out the right thing to do and be effective" (KCRW radio 1999b).

Yet even though Riordan was the key figure in the passage of charter reform, it was the creation of the civic coalition and its ability to effectively support a unified charter that may have saved the situation. The voting coalition for charter reform was ultimately a mixture of two coalitions: the conservative alliance behind Richard Riordan and a civic coalition for municipal reform. In a pattern identified by Finegold (1995a, b), an ideological coalition was transformed into a majority coalition by its linkage to a set of ideas that together comprise reform.

The creation of the unified charter put in place the conditions for a strong coalition that could head off secession. It also showed the obstacles facing secession. In order to win a citywide vote, secessionists would need to forge an alliance between their conservative base and the civic coalition. This was to prove a most daunting task.

The charter coalition provided a real political alternative to secession. Charter reform in essence took the coalition that might have carried secession and turned it on to reform. Had there been two charters on the ballot competing against each other, the function of providing a political alternative to secession would have been far less meaningful.

The coalition for charter reform was an unusual, and perhaps unstable, one. It brought together white liberals and white conservatives, but did not close the ideological distance between them. It was a statement of the inclusion of conservatives in the long-standing liberal reform tradition, but was unlikely to foster permanent alliances for reform. It built intriguing linkages to immigrant communities. Most of all, it was enough to win the critical battle to demonstrate that under great duress Los Angeles government could change.

PART FIVE

The Battle over Secession

CHAPTER FIFTEEN

Implementation

> America's most fragmented urban government is getting a charter. It has to work—or the city itself may not have much of a future.
> —William Fulton and Paul Shigley, "Putting Los Angeles Together"

> Giving this mayor this charter is like giving a teenager a Testerosa.
> —Anonymous source, *Los Angeles Times*

WITH THE PASSAGE of charter reform, Los Angeles had developed a coherent civic response to the fundamental challenge represented by secession. But would it be enough? Would Riordan's success in winning charter reform reduce his battles with the city council? Would the focus on mayoral authority overshadow the new participatory structures essential to making the case for keeping the city together? And would the implementation phase, as has so often happened with reforms, be the burial ground of reform and the seedbed of frustration that might energize secessionists?

Just as the creation of the charter reflected warring views of reform, so did the implementation. While Riordan was the clear winner in the charter battle, his victory was by no means complete. One key victory he did win was the implementation date. In the final compromise, Riordan won an early start date of July 1, 2000, giving him one full year to exercise the powers he had long sought. As a result, there would be inevitable conflict with the angry and defeated majority of the city council.

Over the course of the year of implementation that Riordan fought for and won, Riordan was to learn that formal power was no guarantee of getting his way. In fact, pushing mayoral authority only strengthened countervailing forces.

As soon as the ink was dry on the date of implementation, Riordan began issuing executive directives to city departments indicating that his office was now in charge. Riordan took the opportunity to appoint a successor to his nemesis, CAO Keith Comrie, even before the implementation date. Comrie had announced his retirement after the development of the unified charter. Riordan chose William Fujioka, the general manager of the Personnel Department, a generally well received choice that seemed to augur a CAO's office more closely tied to the mayor.

However, things worked out poorly. Riordan took the position that emergency personnel in the CAO's office should be transferred to the mayor's office. Fujioka correctly noted that the new charter specifically prohibited such a transfer. I could testify that after extremely intense and difficult negotiations with the mayor's office at the end of charter reform, a line was added to the charter precisely to prevent the mayor from moving these officials into his office. Section 231(i) gives the mayor authority to "supervise emergency procedure preparedness activities in the various departments and offices, including the Mayor's office, in a manner consistent with city policy." This language was meant to ensure that while the mayor ran emergency management, he or she could not transfer city staff from other departments and agencies into the mayor's office.

The mayor was angry at Fujioka's stance, and it was not long before this and other disagreements led to a decision to fire Fujioka. Riordan asked Fujioka to resign and accept reassignment to the Personnel Department. Fujioka refused. Under the old charter, then still in effect, firing the CAO would require a majority vote of the council.

Riordan chose to back off, intending to fire Fujioka under the new charter, under which the CAO would be able to appeal to the council, which by a two-thirds majority could overturn the removal. Once again, Riordan's war with a CAO would push the CAO into the orbit of the city council. Fujioka managed to survive for the rest of the Riordan administration and into the Hahn mayoralty.

The new charter also promised to have an effect on the relationship between the LAPD and civilian authorities. Shortly after the charter passed, the Rampart scandal emerged. The testimony of a police officer, Rafael Perez, that he and colleagues had manufactured evidence, framed people, and shot them, created a devastating state of affairs in the department. It also placed the mayor and the police chief in a weaker position than they had been during charter reform. The legal cost to the city was likely to be in the tens or hundreds of millions of dollars.

The budgetary and liability questions were huge, and inevitably involved the council. When Riordan proposed that the city use its funds from a tobacco settlement to pay Rampart costs, he ran into the CAO (now temporarily renamed OARS under the new charter) once again. Fujioka wrote a memo to the city council disagreeing with the mayor's plan, and suggesting that the council set up a separate fund for liability costs. The council agreed, further alienating the mayor from the CAO.

Meanwhile, the LAPD inspector general had been given greater authority by the new charter, and this placed the chief on the defensive. With the Rampart scandal raising questions about Parks's leadership, a shift in the Police Commission created more cross-currents.

The appointment of Gerald Chaleff as president of the police commission to replace Edith Perez marked yet another unforeseen development that eroded Riordan's power. While a Riordan ally, Chaleff was far more critical of the chief than Perez had been, and began to stake out independent territory for the police commission.

The first case came when Parks released the department's internal report on the Rampart scandal. The report, which largely acquitted the top brass and blamed middle management, was acclaimed by Riordan, with vast overstatement, as "the greatest document of its kind in the history of the world." Riordan called a press conference to announce the report, even before it was formally presented to the police commission. He then had to admit that he had not read the whole report.

In calling the press conference, Riordan undermined his own commission and suggested that it lacked any independent credibility. The report should have been presented by the chief to his governing board, the police commission. In a bad comedy of errors or intention, Riordan excluded the members of the city council from the press conference. When several councilmembers appeared, they were rebuffed by city hall security, and Councilmember Rita Walters had her hand painfully caught in a door.

Chaleff, the president of the police commission, boycotted the press conference. Other commissioners attended. Chaleff said he thought it would be improper to attend, since the commission alone was empowered to evaluate the chief's report. Even though the unified charter, in a little-noticed change, had made it easier for the mayor to fire police commissioners, the mayor found it politically impossible to do what he told intimates he most wanted to do: fire Chaleff.

As the months continued, Riordan maintained his effusive backing of Parks, even as Parks made clear his distaste for civilian oversight. Parks came into serious conflict with the council over his interpretation of the new charter. He withheld material from the inspector general, despite the clear language of the charter giving the inspector general access to all such information. Parks disputed this interpretation. When councilmembers verged on ordering Parks to follow the new charter, he did so with great and obvious reluctance.

With Parks and Riordan struggling with the council over police reform in the context of Rampart, the federal government entered the picture with a threat to sue the city to force full implementation of police reform. Once again, this confrontation placed Riordan and Parks against a majority of the council. As had happened before, the forces of police reform came from the progressive side.

The federal government insisted that the city implement a series of measures, particularly the creation of a computerized system to monitor police misconduct. In addition, there were proposals to study racial profiling and issues regarding the independence of the inspector general.

In a footnote to charter reform, the police union, alienated from Parks, hired civil libertarian Erwin Chemerinsky to write a report. The former elected commission's chair and nemesis of Riordan at the end of the charter process proposed a series of charter changes that went well beyond the new charter. Parks blasted Chemerinsky for being in cahoots with the union, and dismissed his proposals.

In tough negotiations with the federal authorities, the city's position divided as Riordan and Parks resisted a federal consent decree, while the city attorney and the council leadership were in favor of it.

As federal officials continued to threaten a lawsuit, the action moved to the city council. Under the new charter, a legal crisis was possible. The council no longer controlled litigation, but neither did the mayor. The new charter gave the mayor a veto of litigation settlements. If a majority, but not two-thirds of the council, favored a consent decree, and the mayor vetoed it, the city would essentially have no policy. The question would be whether under the complicated arrangements that city attorney Hahn had negotiated with the elected commission, the mayor would be the "client" in dealings with the federal government. Alternatively, the city itself would be the client, and authority would pass to the city attorney.

Despite furious lobbying, the council steadily moved toward support for the consent decree over the mayor's objections. Finally, the council mustered a two-thirds vote, when a seriously ill council president John Ferraro dramatically added his vote to that of the youngest member of the council, Alex Padilla. Once again, Riordan had been defeated in a rear-guard action to protect Parks from civilian oversight.

Evidence was accumulating that despite the council's protestations of defeat in charter reform, and Riordan's claims of victory, greater mayoral authority in the charter was not what people had imagined it to be. Riordan, as a lame-duck mayor in continuing battles with the city council, was weaker after charter reform passed than he had been before.

Riordan's authority in city government before and after the charter had less to do with his formal charter authority than with his ability to frame issues, hold the high ground, marshal political resources, and dominate the debate. He had managed, through battles over charter reform and school governance, to become the most important and energetic advocate of reform in the city. Failing those attributes, even a divided, dispirited, and unpopular city council could exercise significant authority. Without the high ground, without his closest political ally in Bill Wardlaw, with whom he had split over Wardlaw's endorsement of Hahn for mayor in 2001, Riordan found that his formal powers rang hollow.

Riordan used the last month of his mayoralty to distribute millions of dollars out of his mayoral budget to pet causes and in bonuses to staff members. In order to complete these transfers, Riordan used his new charter authority to transfer funds up to $50,000 between departments (a power formerly held by the CAO) to move much larger blocs of money in increments of just less than $50,000.

While many of the causes were praiseworthy and represented some of what was best about Riordan (such as his interest in parks, libraries, and zoos), his violation of the very rules he had insisted be included in the charter was troubling. As Chemerinsky (2001) noted in a blistering column in the *Times*

> What is particularly disturbing about Riordan's conduct is that his aides, in urging that this authority be created during the charter reform process, denied that the power would ever be used in such a manner. Those aides, including those who received bonuses from Riordan's largesse with city funds, said that this provision was necessary to deal with emergencies and contingencies too urgent or too minor to warrant going to the city council for a specific expenditure.

NEIGHBORHOOD COUNCILS

Riordan's preoccupation with formal authority limited his ability to use the charter for the purpose of deflating sentiment for secession by exploring new participatory mechanisms.

The most lively and exciting part of the charter was the provision for neighborhood democracy. Article IX of the new charter was likely to have an impact on whether secession would dominate the debate or whether the city would reinvent its democracy.

Riordan passed over Wachs's deputy Greg Nelson for general manager of the Department of Neighborhood Empowerment, to select Rosalind Stewart, a deputy to Councilmember Cindy Miscikowski. Riordan appointed commissioners to the Board of Neighborhood Commissioners who reflected his ongoing loyalty to his allies on the elected commission. He placed both Rob Glushon and Bill Weinberger on the board, with the latter becoming president.

As general manager, Stewart's job was to follow the steps set forth in the charter to implement neighborhood councils. She was, however, caught at times in continuing mayor-council conflicts. The intentionally vague provisions that emerged as a successful compromise between the two commissions were unclear. The intent of self-selected, participatory neighborhood councils was difficult to implement. The commissions had decided not to tie the hands of future city leaders by spelling out every step of implementation; it would be up to elected and appointed officials to do that.

The department held a series of hearings on neighborhood councils, and enjoyed a strong turnout. But for a number of reasons, the hearings generated considerable unease among many grass-roots organizations. The Riordan people had not invested the kind of energy and interest in neighborhood councils that they had in mayoral power.

In September 2000, the department issued its draft report for public comment. In response to the plan, a counterplan began to develop, spear-headed by Xandra Kayden and others, including Greg Nelson. The counterplan was intended to provide a basis for the council to create its own plan, which would be allowed under the charter if it was not inconsistent with article IX.

Without much fanfare, the area planning commissions emerged as one of the success stories of the new charter. The council ordinance implementing the new charter provisions created seven APCs, and the planning department proposed a map based around existing planning areas. There were two in the Valley (oddly, they were north and south, instead of the more natural political lines of east and west), and the Harbor had its own. The mayor made his appointments, the council confirmed them, and they were up and running in the summer of 2000. Map 5 represents the seven area planning commissions, with a dividing line to separate the North and South Valley areas.

The great significance of area planning commissions was that they actually had authority over some aspects of land use. This was the first example of decentralized authority in Los Angeles. Even further, area planning commissions provided the template on which further reforms were proposed (see chapter 19).

Meanwhile, as the government struggled to make the new charter work, secession kept moving along. Riordan had made a tremendous contribution by driving the charter against great resistance and bringing a victory home. But his ongoing battle with the city government and his lack of attention to the neighborhood empowerment process weakened the city's case against secession. If the government is that bad, a voter might ask, why should I stay with it? It would be up to the new mayor elected in 2001 to fight and win that battle.

CHAPTER SIXTEEN

The 2001 Municipal Elections

THE 2001 municipal elections once again reshuffled the deck of secession. City attorney James K. Hahn, supported by African Americans and white moderate and conservative voters, won the mayoralty against a strong Latino challenger, Antonio Villaraigosa. Hahn would have to fight the climactic battle of secession in November 2002 with a shaky, new coalition that was untested and raw. Like the charter coalition, it would be yet another ad hoc alliance that might not live to fight another day.

After a decade of political reform in Los Angeles, the terrain of Los Angeles politics had changed. Secession would soon be decided by a democratic vote. The chief of police could be removed by civilian authorities outside the civil service process. General managers of city departments were exempt from civil service. A new city charter dramatically reshaped the power of the mayor and created a new level of citizen participation. Police reform made great progress in 1992, 1995, and 1999 ballot measures. Elected officials were now term limited.

The political terrain had changed in another way: the coalition lines that had defined Los Angeles politics in the Bradley era were eroding, and it was unknown what would take their place. Between 1964 and 1993, it was clear what defined liberal and conservative in Los Angeles. Blacks were liberal, often joined by Jews and Latinos. They backed police reform and Tom Bradley. White Republicans were conservative along with some Jews and Latinos, and they opposed police reform and Tom Bradley. Riordan's election and reelection in 1993 and 1997 did not change the basic pattern, but merely moved the chess pieces onto other parts of the board. More and more, post-Bradley Los Angeles politics was marked by shifting lines of group alliance.

At the very moment that elected officials were finding their powers enhanced through political reform, the coalition structure of local politics had changed profoundly. The battle over charter reform showed that the pieces of a stable coalition structure had been detached from each other, and were floating free, looking for other attachments. In the vote on charter reform, for example, African Americans and Jews were the two poles of opposition and support. Latinos were closer to Jews and other whites than to African Americans.

A similar pattern had developed in Riordan's 1997 reelection, but with white conservatives on the opposite end from African Americans. Yet other alliances were possible. In 1994, the immigration issue found Latinos and Jews in strong opposition to Prop. 187, the measure to deny public services to undocumented residents, while conservative whites supported it and African Americans were split.

In that context, a term-limited Richard Riordan prepared to give up his office, as did the city attorney, the city controller, and a bloc of city councilmembers. With so many offices up for grabs, the accelerating political changes of Los Angeles democracy would be led by largely different people.

The election marked the sudden coming of age of Latinos. In the secession election of 2002, Latinos would be a critical constituency (even more than they were in the passage of charter reform in 1999.)

By 1997, the Latino share of those who voted rose strongly over 1993, and the white share declined. The signs of mobilization had appeared in the 1997 municipal elections, and seemed to suggest a new progressive alliance between Jews and Latinos in Proposition BB for new school bonds (Sonenshein 2001).

What was most startling was the transformation in the Los Angeles electorate between 1993 and 2001. In brief, non-Jewish whites were being replaced by Latinos, with important political consequences.

The *Los Angeles Times* exit polls of 1993 and 2001 revealed a dramatic shift in the proportion of the vote cast by whites and by Latinos. In 1993, whites cast 72 percent of all votes in the runoff; in 2001, they cast 52 percent. Latinos cast 8 percent of the votes in 1993, and 22 percent in 2001.

The biggest decline was among *non-Jewish* whites. Remarkably, the Jewish share of the vote remained stable between 1993 and 2001, with a temporary drop in 1997.

While Jews represented one-fourth of all white voters in 1993, they represented a third of white voters in 2001. The first consequence of these changes was a partisan one. Since Los Angeles Jews are twice as likely as non-Jewish whites to be registered Democrats, and Latinos are also heavily Democratic, the Republican base of Los Angeles voters had clearly declined. In 2001, the smallest proportion of Republicans (18 percent) in modern times came to the polls. That decline was to affect the upcoming secession vote as well.

Los Angeles was becoming more Democratic as it became more Latino and less non-Jewish white. But was it necessarily becoming more liberal? And how would this affect the dynamics of secession and reform?

A wave of candidates ran for mayor, including two Latinos, the city attorney backed heavily by African Americans, a city councilman, and the state controller. As a result of term limits and the higher visibility of Los Angeles city hall, there was a greater array of statewide power brokers running than at any election in memory. Riordan had a favorite candidate, Republican businessman Steven Soboroff.

Riordan had lost his principal political ally, William Wardlaw, who rebelled when Riordan asked him to support Soboroff. Wardlaw not only left Riordan's side, where he had loyally served for years, but went over to the camp of Riordan's rival, James Hahn. Along with Wardlaw, Hahn obtained the help of Riordan's favorite political consultant, Bill Carrick. With Wardlaw and Carrick, along with Hahn's longtime ally George Kieffer, Hahn had a formidable organization that matched anything Riordan could bring against him. Hahn was on the A list of city name recognition, a list that was led by Riordan, and also included Yaroslavsky and Parks. Hahn even recruited his 1997 foe, Riordan ally Ted Stein, to endorse his campaign.

Riordan was still a powerful force. He endorsed several candidates for the council, including Nick Pacheco in the fourteenth district. Pacheco had been a loyal voice for Riordan on the elected commission. Riordan also endorsed Woody Fleming, another Riordan backer on the elected commission, in the ninth district.

Other races showed the impact of term limits for the first time. Councilmember Mike Feuer announced his candidacy for city attorney, in which he would be opposed by a Riordan deputy, Rocky Delgadillo. Councilmember Laura Chick ran for city controller, also facing a Riordan ally, Laurette Healey. State officials headed to Los Angeles, and vice versa. Jackie Goldberg won election to the state assembly, and her brother sought her council seat, as did former councilmember Mike Woo and elected charter commissioner Bennett Keyser. Tom Hayden left the state senate to seek Mike Feuer's fifth district council seat. No matter who won, there would be a major turnover at city hall to complement the new city charter.

The main candidates for mayor included five Democrats and one Republican. Four were white, two Latino. Two were Jewish. The general belief among political insiders was that two white candidates would make the runoff, and that a Latino mayoral victory was still an election away. Two strong Latino candidates, Congressman Xavier Beccerra and former Assembly Speaker Antonio Villaraigosa, seemed likely to cancel each other out.

With his strong base in the African American community, Hahn seemed a shoo-in for the runoff, joined by another white candidate who would presumably have the support of the white voters who had backed Riordan. Thus, the speculation was that Hahn would face one of the two Jewish moderate candidates, either Steven Soboroff or Councilmember Joel Wachs. In that case, Hahn would be the moderate liberal and his opponent would be the moderate conservative.

This scenario was dramatically altered, however, by the steady rise of Villaraigosa from the pack and into a serious threat to Hahn. The significance of Villaraigosa's rise was the possibility that he could construct a liberal coalition, to the left of Hahn, without African Americans but with the support of Latinos and Jews. In essence, the hope was that he could become the Latino Tom Bradley.

Villaraigosa's campaign became an unexpected test of Latino political power in Los Angeles, the increasing role of organized labor, and the possibility of the city shifting to the left. Would Los Angeles's emerging democracy be a social democracy, and move more toward the San Francisco model? Was Los Angeles about to repeat the Tom Bradley saga, but around ethnicity rather than race?

Villaraigosa's emergence was aided by state campaign finance reforms that allowed the state parties to put money into Los Angeles's nonpartisan elections. As recently as 1993, Democrat Michael Woo had to go to court to accept the *endorsement* of the state Democratic party. Based on a voter initiative passed in November, 2000, state parties could spend unlimited funds to contact their party members about particular elections, including local elections. Such activities did not have to be reported, nor the donors identified, even under the city's strict campaign-finance laws.

Soboroff also benefited from this legal change, as the state Republican party poured resources into his race. Hahn's lead began to evaporate as both Villaraigosa and Soboroff pulled ahead of the remainder of the pack.

The County Federation of Labor, led by Miguel Contreras, gave its endorsement to Villaraigosa, placing its massive ground forces in the former Speaker's camp. Hahn had the backing of city employee unions, and thus the labor movement was split between the two Democrats.

As Villaraigosa's campaign gained steam, he campaigned effectively in white neighborhoods, and especially among Jewish voters. Neck-in-neck with Beccerra for Latino voters in early polls, Villaraigosa pulled ahead and Beccerra's campaign soon withered on the vine. Meanwhile, Hahn was stuck in the mid twenties, avoiding many of the candidate debates and hoping to hold his position in the runoff. He seemed to be running the risk of falling behind both Villaraigosa and Soboroff and not even making the runoff.

On the night of the primary, Villaraigosa continued his surge, and moved well past Hahn, with 30 percent of the vote. Hahn was second with 25 percent, and not far behind was Soboroff at 21 percent. The breakdown of the vote seemed to indicate more good news for Villaraigosa than for Hahn.

Villaraigosa had won two-thirds of Latino votes, but it seemed inevitable that he would improve that showing in the highly publicized general election. He had done exceptionally well among white voters, among Jewish voters, and in the San Fernando Valley. He finished ahead of Hahn in all these areas, and was nearly even there with the two moderate Jewish candidates, Soboroff and Wachs.

If Villaraigosa could increase his Latino support base, and continue to do well among white voters, he would defeat Hahn. With Villaraigosa's primary victory, there was a massive surge of interest locally, nationally, and even internationally because of the possibility of a Latino mayor in Los Angeles.

On the surface, the runoff pitted two liberal Democrats against each other in a city that had just had an eight-year reign by a business-oriented Republican. But with white voters constituting the balance of electoral power between an African American–supported Democrat and a Latino-supported Democrat, the white vote would be critical to either candidate's success. For the first time in memory, white conservatives in the Valley did not have an obvious favorite in the finals, but they could help choose the winner.

For Hahn, the strategic calculation was that the excitement surrounding Villaraigosa's campaign could be punctured by a focus on the issue of crime, and by casting Villaraigosa as too liberal and untrustworthy. His strategy would be to conceptualize Los Angeles voters as Democratic, but not necessarily liberal. He would lock up the conservative wing of the San Fernando Valley as quickly as possible.

The Villaraigosa calculation was that a strong labor and Latino mobilization would put victory within reach, and that a "high road" appeal to white voters, especially Jews, and a progressive appeal to younger African Americans would provide the margin of victory. A hoped-for endorsement by popular outgoing Mayor Richard Riordan would help insulate Villaraigosa among white voters in the Valley from the charge of being excessively liberal.

Not long after the primary, the previously lethargic and nearly fatally complacent Hahn campaign took on new life, and control of the campaign. Hahn won the endorsement of the Police Protective League (PPL), after endorsing the three-day workweek sought by the police union and by promising to take a critical stance toward the rehiring of Police Chief Bernard Parks. Villaraigosa blasted Hahn for changing his positions to win the endorsement. Hahn gathered endorsements from several secession leaders in the Valley.

Hahn accused Villaraigosa of being too liberal on the crime issue, a contrast emphasized by Hahn's history of gang injunctions as city attorney and Villaraigosa's position in favor of prevention as a response to gangs. The PPL helped Hahn make the case by running radio ads sharply contrasting the records of the two candidates on crime.

Meanwhile, Riordan withheld his endorsement, and reduced its ultimate value by initially downgrading both candidates as lacking managerial skills. While Riordan finally endorsed Villaraigosa, after a long delay, he never made a case on radio or television for why Hahn had been an inadequate city attorney and Villaraigosa would be a better mayor. Compared to the PPL's tightly focused and harsh campaigning, Riordan's endorsement seemed to do Villaraigosa almost no good at all.

Within several weeks, Hahn had placed Villaraigosa on the defensive on the crime issue. A *Times* poll conducted two weeks before the election held troubling news for Villaraigosa. Hahn was leading him by seven points overall, but even more seriously, he had opened up a vast lead on the question of crime. Fewer than one in five voters thought that Villaraigosa was better at fighting crime than Hahn. With Riordan's endorsement carrying little force, Villaraigosa was left unarmed for the main assault from the Hahn forces, a harsh commercial that castigated Villaraigosa for writing a letter to President Bill Clinton in the case of a convicted drug trafficker.

For the rest of the campaign, Villaraigosa tried to make an issue out of the Hahn commercial, which had disturbing images combining a black-and-white picture of Villaraigosa, a drug pipe, and other visuals that created a connection between the candidate and drugs. Villaraigosa soon found himself in the impossible position of trying to fight a negative ad without further publicizing it.

Villaraigosa's sole remaining hope was a massive mobilization effort by organized labor and by the Latino community. However, an examination of the city's voting records shows that the climb was dauntingly high. Registration had been reopened between the primary and the general election, making possible a major mobilization of Latino voters energized by Villaraigosa's campaign. However, a comparison of the number of registered voters in the fifteen council districts in the primary and the general election indicated that there was no dramatic reshaping of the electorate. Each district gained roughly a thousand voters, and there was no pattern of comparatively larger voter registration in Latino districts.

Even with the very energetic mobilization campaign conducted by the Villaraigosa forces, they were climbing a bigger hill than even they realized. When the absentee ballots were counted in the first round of reported voting, Hahn had nearly a two-to-one lead among those voters who had already cast ballots before any last-minute mobilization could reach them. Even though Villaraigosa held his own on election day, the gap in absentee voting (nearly a quarter of all voters) spelled defeat.

In the voting totals, Hahn held his African American support and won substantial majorities among conservative and moderate whites. Villaraigosa won only 48 percent of Jewish voters, although he won nearly 60 percent of Westside Jews. Villaraigosa won the great majority of Latinos, more than 80 percent, and won a quarter of African Americans according to *Times* exit polling. He won majorities of those who considered education the top issue, which was the most mentioned issue, but lost on the crime issue.

Villaraigosa had a coalition of Latinos, young African Americans, and liberal whites. It was a younger, more liberal coalition than Hahn's. Hahn's winning coalition was more surprising, combining the most his-

TABLE 15
Vote by Groups, Mayoral Election

Precinct Groups	Number of Precincts	Total Votes	Percentage Hahn	Percentage Villaraigosa
All City of Los Angeles Precincts*	**1,763**	**461,693**	**51.0**	**49.0**
Jewish Precincts	154	38,412	58.0	42.0
White Republican Precincts	99	27,516	68.9	31.1
Black Precincts	145	39,694	78.0	22.0
Latino Precincts	189	63,518	21.2	78.8
All Other Precincts	1,176	292,553	51.3	48.7
All Valley Precincts	**660**	**172,976**	**55.5**	**44.5**
Jewish Precincts	57	15,482	63.3	36.7
White Republican Precincts	71	19,291	71.4	28.6
Latino Precincts	52	16,444	25.7	74.3
All Other Precincts	480	121,759	56.0	44.0
All Non-Valley Precincts	**1,103**	**288,717**	**48.4**	**51.6**
Jewish Precincts	97	22,930	54.3	45.7
White Republican Precincts	28	8,225	62.9	37.1
Black Precincts	145	39,694	78.0	22.0
Latino Precincts	137	47,074	19.7	80.3
All Other Precincts	696	170,794	47.9	52.1

*Excludes votes by mail. James Hahn received 64.2% of votes by mail. Overall, Hahn received 53.5% of the vote.

torically liberal voting group, African Americans, with conservative and moderate whites. No one had put that coalition together since Sam Yorty in 1961, and then it was highly unstable and short-lived. It did, however, remind people of the Proposition 187 coalition (Meyerson 2001), suggesting that the Latino surge in Los Angeles had changed the meaning of liberalism, and had created a sense of threat to historically liberal groups.

While immigration had made Los Angeles a more Democratic city, it had not necessarily made it a more liberal city. And the white areas of the Valley continued to be more conservative than the rest of the city (maps 10 and 11).

TABLE 16
Regression Analysis of Vote for Villaraigosa

	Standardized Coefficients (Beta)			
Predictors	All Precincts (n = 1,763)	White Republican Precincts (n = 99)	Jewish Precincts (n = 154)	Latino Precincts (n = 189)
Percentage Jewish	0.046*	–0.078	–0.180**	
Percentage Latino	0.854***			0.764***
Percentage White	0.104*	0.124		
Percentage Black	–0.251***			
Percentage Foreign-Born	0.081***	0.124	–0.170*	0.037
Percentage with College Degree	0.451***	0.626***	0.086	0.030
Median Household Income	–0.25***	–0.333**	–0.342**	0.172*
Valley	–0.192***	–0.393***	–0.522***	–0.114*
Adjusted R Square =	0.794	0.528	0.340	0.684

Significance levels: ***(.001 level), **(.01 level), *(.05 level)

TABLE 17
Regression Analysis of Vote for Hahn

	Standardized Coefficients (Beta)			
Predictors	All Precincts (n = 1,763)	White Republican Precincts (n = 99)	Jewish Precincts (n = 154)	Latino Precincts (n = 189)
Percentage Jewish	-0.054**	0.091	0.176**	
Percentage Latino	–0.853***			–0.763***
Percentage White	–0.103*	–0.127		
Percentage Black	0.250***			
Percentage Foreign-Bron	–0.803***	–0.135	0.159	–0.028
Percentage with College Degree	–0.437***	–0.609***	–0.073	–0.037

TABLE 17 (continued)

Predictors	Standardized Coefficients (Beta)			
	All Precincts (n = 1,763)	White Republican Precincts (n = 99)	Jewish Precincts (n = 154)	Latino Precincts (n = 189)
Median Household Income	0.327***	0.351**	0.341**	0.197**
Valley	0.193***	0.397***	0.534***	0.117*
Adjusted R Square =	0.798	0.498	0.345	0.695

Significance levels: ***(.001 level), **(.01 level), *(.05 level)

The pair of Democrats in the runoff clarified what has been implicit in the changes in Los Angeles: that there was a two-headed minority movement of African Americans and Latinos, and that their roles were both complementary and competitive. African Americans are established and older, and depend to a greater degree on government jobs than do Latinos. They hold political positions they consider imperiled by changing demographics and political demands. Their support of Hahn was founded on familiarity with the Hahn family, but also had an element of defense against an uncertain future.

Also Democrats, Latinos are younger and more insurgent. Less dependent on government jobs, they draw their union base from the County Federation of Labor and private employers.

The two-headed minority movement both strengthens the Democratic base in Los Angeles and fractures the progressive movement, reducing the inevitability of a shift to the left. A similar dynamic in New York City hurt liberalism when insurgent minorities came up against former insurgents, Jewish voters.

An implication of the 2001 election for secession and reform was that Latinos were going to play a pivotal role in the outcome. Despite Villaraigosa's loss, Latinos showed major strength in the election and a high degree of voting unity.

The demographic shift of Latinos to the Valley was also likely to change the dynamics of the secession story. Between 1990 and 2000, the Eastside council districts lost considerable population, while the East Valley was the fastest growing portion of the city. Latinos in the East Valley might hold the key to the secession vote. With their support, secession might carry enough votes in the Valley to hold off expected opposition in the rest of the city. Valley Latinos could provide a way to redefine the Valley secession movement as more than white flight.

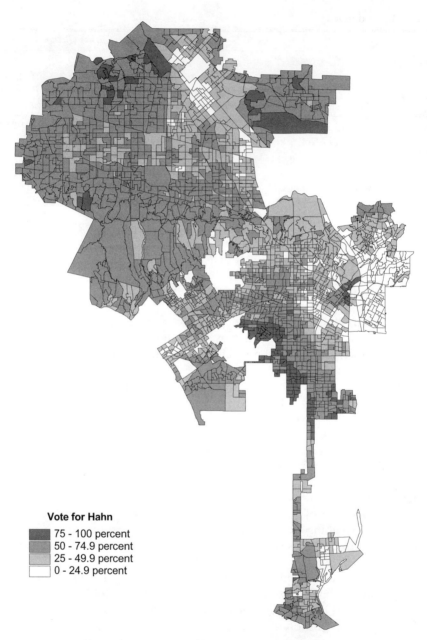

Vote for Hahn

▓	75 - 100 percent
▒	50 - 74.9 percent
░	25 - 49.9 percent
□	0 - 24.9 percent

Map 10. Vote for James K. Hahn, 2001 Mayoral Runoff Election

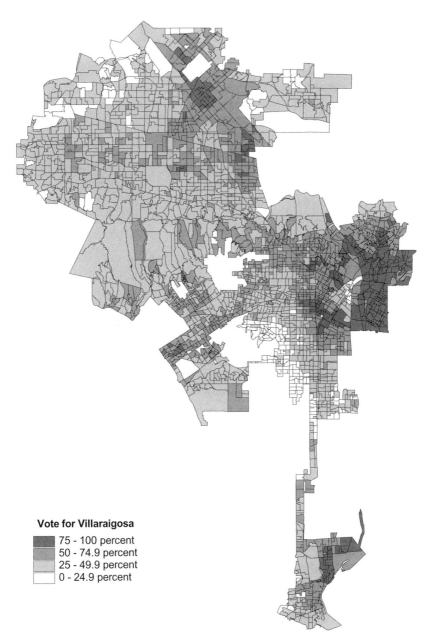

Vote for Villaraigosa
- 75 - 100 percent
- 50 - 74.9 percent
- 25 - 49.9 percent
- 0 - 24.9 percent

Map 11. Vote for Antonio Villaraigosa, 2001 Mayoral Runoff Election

Valley secessionists could also take heart in the temporary alliance between African Americans and conservative whites. They could imagine a
scenario in which African Americans would support secession with the
knowledge that in a broken-up city, they would be more powerful in the
remaining city.

The election of Hahn as mayor and of elected charter commissioners
Janice Hahn, Nick Pacheco, and Dennis Zine to the city council suggested
that city leaders would be more adept than Riordan at implementing the
neighborhood-council provisions of the new charter. Throughout the
campaign, candidates for citywide offices and for city council expressed
their strong support for the new charter, with special emphasis on neighborhood councils. They pledged to do their best to enhance the strength
of neighborhood democracy. They were binding themselves to a process
of reform implementation in way that had not happened before. The commitment to reform could help the city defeat secession.

A new set of councilmembers and a new mayor might also escape the
mayor-council conflicts of the Riordan years, allowing the new provisions
for mayoral authority to be effectively implemented.

But Hahn was coming to the secession campaign with an odd coalition
of former and future enemies, with little to tie them together. It would be
difficult to hold his coalition together, and to forge a strong enough alliance to fight off the challenge of secession.

The Vote on Secession

IN THE AFTERMATH of the charter reform election of 1999 and the mayoral race of 2001, the city faced secession head-on. An election was set for November 2002 that would determine whether the city would be carved into at least two pieces.

With the adoption of charter reform and the popular idea of neighborhood councils, city leaders had a major tool in building their antisecession coalition. City leaders now had the high ground of reform. The new mayor, James K. Hahn, could and did argue that the city was already reforming and that secession would be unnecessary and indeed dangerous.

Secessionists, most of whom had signed the ballot argument for the new charter, had the difficult task of arguing that the new charter did not go far enough to decentralize authority. Had charter reform failed, secessionists might have been able to argue that the city could not reform itself, and that only a breakup would move the ossified institutional structure. That would have given them a long-shot chance at the high ground of reform.

As the coalitions emerged on both sides of the secession question, the charter reform that had been opposed by some progressive groups such as unions and African Americans became a valuable vehicle in a much bigger battle over urban equity. The consequences for working-class and minority neighborhoods of a city breakup would have been profound. While these groups had not all seen the value of charter reform in isolation, they were quick to see its importance in the battle over secession.

Between Hahn's election and the secession campaign, a series of events intervened to hasten the momentum of secession. The most important was the continuing impact of the state's facilitation of secession (McHenry 2002). Beginning with the state's elimination of the city council veto in 1997, the state under bipartisan leadership eased the path further. The state gave the Local Agency Formation Commission (LAFCO), a body made up of county and city officials, control of the process, and its sympathies were not with the city.

As Los Angeles headed toward its historic vote on secession, the coalition lines of the city's politics, so fixed for decades, were in considerable flux. The pro-secession areas as well as their longtime adversaries, African Americans, were both behind Mayor Hahn. The new mayor had to balance the two and try to hold the city together. The shakiness of electoral coalitions at the citywide level provided yet another opening for an insurgent secession campaign. It seemed possible that a civic coalition might not be forged to block it. Los Angeles might break up simply out of disinterest and disorganization.

Charter reform helped city leaders devise a strategy to take on secession. In particular, the neighborhood-council movement provided the basis for a positive alternative to secession. Hahn moved quickly to restore the momentum of neighborhood councils. He appointed Greg Nelson as general manager of the department and provided vigorous support for the formation of neighborhood councils. With a revamped effort on neighborhood councils, Hahn was in a position to take the high ground of reform against the secessionists—to focus on the roll-up-your-sleeves work of implementing reform in contrast to the breakup proposal of the secessionists. The bulk of the campaign would be negative, highlighting the risks of breakup, but the positive image of reform could only help the city's case.

Hahn would need a strong political base in order to fend off secession. It was, after all, Riordan's political base, resources, and organization combined with a civic coalition that had carried charter reform to victory. The fundamental political problem that Hahn faced was that the odd coalition that propelled him into the mayor's office was inherently unstable.

The last time Los Angeles had seen such a mayoral coalition of white conservatives in the Valley and inner-city African Americans was in Sam Yorty's upset election in 1961. As in the Hahn election, Yorty's coalition was not built on elite trust between the two groups, but rather on separate appeals that paid off on election day. Within weeks, Yorty had chosen to orient himself to white conservatives, and abandoned African Americans on holding the LAPD accountable (Sonenshein 1993).

THE PARKS REAPPOINTMENT

Hahn was never to have Yorty's opportunity to choose one coalition leg over another, because policy choices had to be made early on that caused him to lose support from both groups. The reappointment of controversial African American police chief Bernard C. Parks was due within months after Hahn's inauguration. The police union, another Hahn ally, strongly opposed Parks's reappointment, and in an odd alliance, so did such civil libertarians as Erwin Chemerinsky. In the mix-and-match coalition world of early-twenty-first-century Los Angeles, the police union was now at least temporarily in favor of police reform.

The African American community, especially its political leadership, was deeply committed to Parks. They viewed him as the leading African American public official in the city and, while some were privately cognizant of Parks's personal rigidity, believed that Hahn had promised implicitly to reappoint the chief. Black leaders believed that they could bring Parks and Hahn together, and help the chief save his job.

Once again, the shifting coalition lines of Los Angeles were emerging. Blacks had been the leading edge of support for police reform in association with white liberals. Now, a police chief unfriendly to civilian oversight found his greatest support among African Americans. As Parks's great city-wide popularity eroded, African Americans became his remaining base of support. African American affinity for Parks was not only based on protecting an African American in a key post, and did not indicate that they no longer favored police reform. They also were extremely suspicious of the police union with its long history of conflict with minority communities. Many blacks came to believe that Parks was being targeted because he was too tough on brutal officers.

The formal decision on the chief's reappointment was in the hands of the civilian police commission. Believing that Parks would not support the new mayor's positions on police issues, Hahn moved on his own to announce his opposition to Parks's reappointment. The reaction among African Americans was fast and furious. The black leadership told Hahn that he was out of the "family" for good. As a result, Hahn went into the secession campaign without the principal base of his political support for his entire career and without the community most likely to oppose secession. Secessionists were hopeful that the Parks battle might even bring African Americans into the secession camp.

LAFCO, SECESSIONISTS, AND HAHN

The city found itself in a continuing battle with the state agency that would qualify secession for the ballot, the Local Agency Formation Commission. LAFCO's nine members included two from the city, two from the county, and the remainder from small cities and special districts. The executive director, Larry Calemine, was an early founder of the Valley secession movement.

LAFCO was unsympathetic to the city's arguments that secession would cause serious damage to the city and that a Valley city would not be financially viable. At the early stages of the process, the city had done little to endear itself to LAFCO, resisting calls for information and cooperation. Near the end of the process, one LAFCO member compared secession to the Boston Tea Party with the secessionists as the heroes.

While the city eventually took a less imperious attitude toward LAFCO, Hahn continued to argue that secession's impact would be much more deleterious than LAFCO was assuming. In addition, he raised the level of rhetoric against secession in the public arena, attacking it as a dangerous and hare-brained notion.

Hahn was now committed to the removal of Parks and the complete rejection of secession, potentially alienating two pillars of his support. His third, often overlooked, pillar was the city government itself, its employee unions, city contractors and other businesses, and well-connected city commissioners. Mollenkopf (1992) called these groups "public sector producer interests." That group now became Hahn's core base of support in the battle against secession. It had limitations as an electoral base, and by itself would not be sufficient for Hahn's reelection in 2005. But it did provide a considerable institutional foundation.

The broad coalition against secession developed slowly, and had to surmount considerable alienation among its leaders. The three principal vote getters in recent Los Angeles elections—Hahn, Riordan, and Villaraigosa—all strongly opposed secession. But neither Riordan nor Villaraigosa, past and present rivals of Hahn, were likely to join easily with him. Hahn's key black supporters, such as businessman and former Laker star Earvin "Magic" Johnson, were equally alienated from the mayor because of the Parks controversy. Little by little, each emerged to oppose secession, but without a formally coordinated effort. Few black leaders, for example, wanted to be seen as helping Hahn in the fight against secession.

Hahn did have considerable assets going into the race. He would be well funded by business and labor, and he had key political strategists William Wardlaw and Bill Carrick. He would have the money and the talent to make the city's case against secession. He also had the benefit of the citywide vote requirement. Secessionists would have to convince Valley residents that they would be better off without the city while arguing to city residents that they would be fine without the Valley. Hahn, by contrast, merely had to convince a citywide majority that the whole enterprise of secession was just too risky.

The unity of organized labor would be a principal factor in the campaign. There was no disagreement about labor's ultimate position opposing secession. But, according to city employee leader Julie Butcher (interview), there were furious internal debates between her group and the County Federation of Labor about whether to run a slate of labor-endorsed candidates for seats in the new Valley council or for Valley mayor. In an interview with Rick Orlov of the *Daily News,* Miguel Contreras had mused that "we might be in the position of opposing secession while running a slate of candidates for the new Valley council and mayor." Contreras cited the successful effort in 1997 to elect labor candidates to the charter commission that labor opposed (Orlov 2002).

Butcher (interview) argued that unlike 1997's measure to create an elected commission, secession was eminently beatable if labor opposed it wholeheartedly. Her argument was adopted, and the labor movement not only chose not to run a slate of candidates, but issued strong demands to labor-supported candidates that they not run at all.

The city's campaign against secession was built on several pillars. Heavily outspending the secessionists, Hahn's team raised the fear level of voters about the consequences of secession. City services were applied with great force to Valley neighborhoods. Hahn promoted the reforms in the new charter as evidence of the city's readiness to respond to neighborhood concerns. The citizens advisory commission on redistricting that was established by the new charter designed new council district lines that addressed long-standing concerns among Valley activists. Council lines were redrawn so that the Valley had five districts wholly within the Valley.

The most important strategic question would be decided on August 9, when the deadline for candidates filing for Valley and Hollywood seats would occur. The key to secession was to expand beyond its base in the West Valley and build support among Latino and Jewish Democrats in the Valley. The strategy was not as far-fetched as it might have appeared. State support of the secession process indicated interest among state Democrats in at least considering a new Valley City.

The first key moment occurred on July 11, 2002, when Democratic State Senator Richard Alarcon, a leading potential candidate for Valley mayor, announced that he would not run and would publicly oppose secession. Rumors had been spreading that organized labor was putting great pressure on Alarcon not to run.

The confidence of city officials was reinforced by a major poll reported by the *Los Angeles Times* on July 2, 2002. The *Times* survey found that support has declined for secession both within the Valley and citywide from its March poll. In addition to the overall figures, what was most striking about the results was the reemergence of a phenomenon that had seemed gone forever: the liberal biracial coalition.

As in the heyday of the Bradley coalition, sentiment on Valley secession was divided along racial, ideological, and geographical lines. Those in favor were concentrated in the West Valley, among whites, conservatives, moderates, and Republicans. The opposition consisted of African Americans, Jews, and white liberals. Latinos were in the middle, breaking along geographical lines. Valley Latinos were supporting secession; Latinos on the Eastside were opposed. Even without the elite ties that had held the Bradley coalition together, the various strands of the coalition were coming together to defeat secession.

In another sign of the declining prospects of secession, secession leader Richard Close announced that he might sue the city to challenge the dual voting system if the Valley lost (Sheppard, 2002). More momentum came to the city leadership with Hahn's appointment of former New York City police commissioner William Bratton as the new police chief.

On November 5, 2002, the voters of Los Angeles rejected Valley secession by a two-to-one majority. In the Valley itself, the vote was very close, with 51 percent in favor. Of the fifteen council districts, secession passssed

in only two, the Valley's third and twelfth. Huge majorities went against secession in the black community and in the white liberal Westside and South
Valley areas (table 18). Latinos voted against it in large numbers. The vote
against secession might have been greater had not Republicans so much
outmobilized Democrats in the off-year election (Meyerson, 2002).

The secession campaign re-created the old Bradley coalition of African
Americans, liberal whites, especially Jews, and Latinos against white con-

TABLE 18
Vote by Groups, Valley Secession

Precinct Groups	Number of Precincts	Total Votes	Yes	Percent Yes	Percent No
			Vote for Valley Secession		
All City of Los Angeles Precincts*	1,471	419,797	139,214	33.2	66.8
Jewish Precincts	133	39,262	12,308	31.3	68.7
White Republican Precincts	88	31,955	16,775	52.5	47.5
Black Precincts	134	33,618	3,745	11.1	88.9
Latino Precincts	148	43,876	10,051	22.9	77.1
All Other Precincts	1,320	346,184	120,684	34.9	65.1
All Valley Precincts*	553	181,060	93,393	51.6	48.4
Jewish Precincts	51	16,917	8,188	48.4	51.6
White Republican Precincts	62	23,317	14,491	62.1	37.9
Latino Precincts	41	13,058	4,899	37.5	62.5
All Other Precincts	399	127,768	65,815	51.5	48.5
All Non-Valley Precincts*	918	238,737	45,821	19.2	80.8
Jewish Precincts	82	22,345	4,120	18.4	81.6
White Republican Precincts	26	8,638	2,284	26.4	73.6
Black Precincts	134	33,618	3,745	11.1	88.9
Latino Precincts	107	30,818	5,152	16.7	83.3
All Other Precincts	569	143,318	30,520	21.3	78.7

Source of voting data: Los Angeles County, Registrar-Recorder/County Clerk
*Includes mapped precincts. The overall vote in favor of secession, including all 1,823 precincts, was
33.1%. The overall vote for secession in the San Fernando Valley was 51.1%, and the overall vote for
secession in the rest of Los Angeles was 19.2%.

servatives in the northwest San Fernando Valley. Clearly, the defeat of secession was a major progressive project that united even those progressive forces that had opposed charter reform.

The base of the secession vote was among whites and in the San Fernando Valley (map 12). In white Republican precincts in the Valley, secession received 62 percent of the vote. No other group registered a majority for secession. In the regression model for the secession vote, variables for percentage white and Valley are the strongest predictors of secession support. Precincts most likely to oppose secession were those with high percentages of African American, Jewish, Hispanic, and Democratic voters, and a high percentage of college-educated persons (table 19). Having already voted for a successful reform, the good-government constituency was not drawn to secession.

And yet . . . there is a politics of place in these numbers. Regression analysis of white Republican precincts indicates that while percentage white is a strong predictor, Valley is an even stronger predictor than in the citywide analysis. In other words, even within white Republican areas, the more white the precinct and the more likely it is to be in the Valley, the stronger the secession vote (table 20).

While secessionists were not close to a majority citywide, they narrowly won the Valley. To achieve that, they won the votes of more than white Republicans alone. They obtained a solid minority of the vote in precincts with large populations of Jews and Latinos in the Valley compared to how these groups voted over the hill.

Place (as defined by Valley versus non-Valley) was of great significance for whites, Jews, and Latinos. In all three areas, the Valley variable is extremely significant, most powerful in Jewish precincts, but still very strong in white Republican precincts and Latino precincts. The potential for a cross-racial, cross-ideology coalition of place in the San Fernando Valley can be seen in the numbers and on the map. For these reasons, the city of Los Angeles is not yet out of the woods.

The rise of place in Los Angeles politics and the growing Democratic base in the Valley suggest that there was a road not taken that might have led to the success of secession. It might yet do so in the future. According to Hogen-Esch and Saiz (2003) it would have involved an ideology of "multiracial suburbia."

According to Hogen-Esch and Saiz, the secession campaign could not overcome the impression that it reflected an underlying fear of the Valley becoming an urban nonwhite community. In this view, had secession embraced its future as a multiethnic metropolis, an urban center with a suburban, home-owning vision, it might have generated an entirely different response outside the conservative precincts of the Valley. Had secession ultimately been a Democratic, rather than a Republican, project, it would

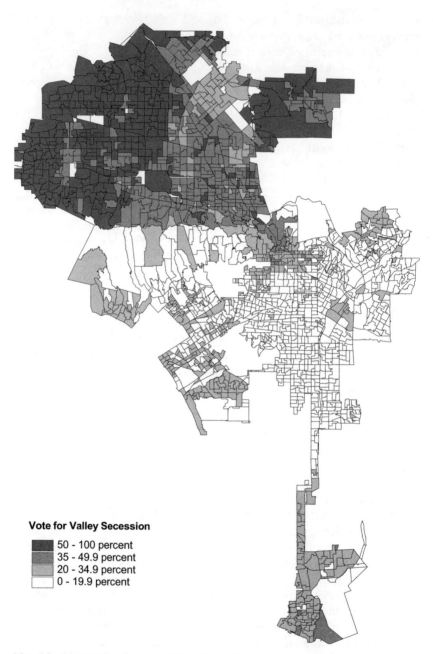

Vote for Valley Secession

- 50 - 100 percent
- 35 - 49.9 percent
- 20 - 34.9 percent
- 0 - 19.9 percent

Map 12. 2002 Valley Secession Vote (Prop. F)

TABLE 19
Regression Analysis of Secession Vote

Predictors	Standardized Coefficients (Beta)			
	All Precincts (n = 1,471)	White Republican Precincts (n = 88)	Jewish Precincts (n = 133)	Latino Precincts (n = 148)
Percentage Jewish	−0.260***	0.066	−0.097**	
Percentage Latino	−0.240***			−0.297***
Percentage White	0.231***	−0.158**		
Percentage Black	−0.312***			
Percentage Foreign-Born	−0.062**	−0.117*	0.036	−0.239***
Percentage with College Degree	−0.181***	−0.030	−0.064	−0.237***
Median Household Income	0.074***	0.056	0.095	0.152*
Valley	0.713***	0.913***	0.906***	0.649***
Adjusted R Square	0.849	0.863	0.864	0.778

Significance levels: ***(.001 level), **(.01 level), *(.05 level)

have been able to split the anti-secession forces in the city that so effectively monopolized the political resources against secession.

The secession campaign ultimately failed to expand beyond its base among white conservative voters in the San Fernando Valley. While it earned a beachhead among a solid minority of Valley Latinos and Jews, it did poorly everywhere else. The right-wing roots of the secession project doomed it in a citywide vote, and activated a revived version of the Bradley coalition.

New alliances and coalitions were forming, as the old ones either held a marginal position or evaporated. Table 20 presents a correlation matrix of votes on the various issues surrounding charter reform and secession.

The patterns are inconsistent, but offer evidence of some similar voting between Latinos and Westside liberal whites, and also surprising levels of similar voting between African Americans and conservative whites. As diversity continues to reshape Los Angeles politics, the path to reform will consist of linking reform constituencies to these and other changing group patterns.

At the end of the day, charter reform had done its job. A liberal coalition marked by diversity had monopolized the contested symbol of

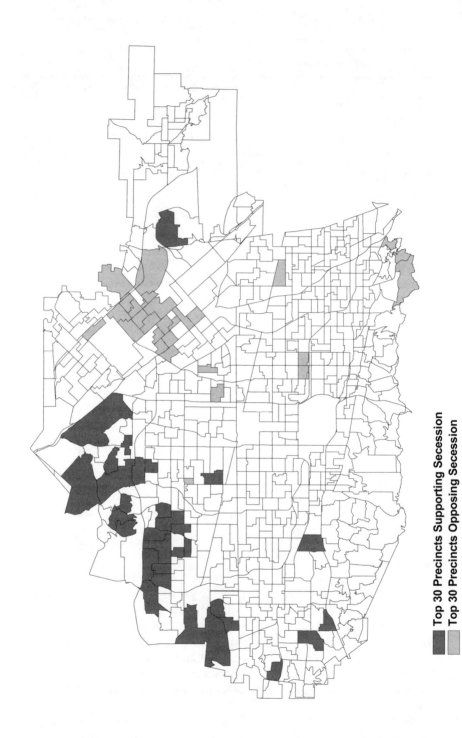

■ **Top 30 Precincts Supporting Secession**

■ **Top 30 Precincts Opposing Secession**

Map 13. 30 Top Precincts for and against Secession, Valley Only

TABLE 20
Correlation Matrix: Measures 1, 3, 4; Mayor's Race; and Secession

	Vote for Measure 1	Vote for Measure 3	Vote for Measure 4	Vote for Hahn	Vote for Villaraigosa	Vote for Valley Secession
Vote for Measure 1	1	0.658	0.748	−0.202	0.209	0.298
n	1,755	1,755	1,755	1,671	1,672	1,498
Vote for Measure 3	0.658	1	0.806	−0.440	0.439	−0.145
n	1,755	1,755	1,755	1,671	1,672	1,498
Vote for Measure 4	0.748	0.806	1	−0.403	0.407	−0.126
n	1,755	1,755	1,755	1,671	1,672	1,498
Vote for Hahn	−0.202	−0.440	−0.403	1	−0.998	0.186
n	1,671	1,671	1,671	1,671	1,666	1,459
Vote for Villaraigosa	0.209	0.439	0.407	−0.998	1	−0.183
n	1,672	1,672	1,672	1,666	1,699	1,471
Vote for Valley Secession	0.298	−0.145	−0.126	0.186	−0.183	1
n	1.498	1,498	1,498	1,459	1,471	1,515

Note: All correlations significant at the 0.001 level.

reform, so that secessionists could not portray themselves as the sole vehicle for restructuring the institutions of government. Reform had given the city's leaders a tool with which to defeat the notion of a city breakup, and to argue that reform was already under way. It would remain an open question whether, with secession beaten, reform would develop the institutional strength to continue to reshape the city's political institutions.

PART SIX

The Future of Urban Reform

CHAPTER EIGHTEEN

Toward a Reform Regime

GOVERNING POSTSECESSION LOS ANGELES

A CITY WITH great diversity but relatively little social capital met a mortal
threat of secession and vanquished it. In a two-pronged effort, city leaders
generated a significant set of governmental reforms and won approval
from the voters. Then under a different mayor, with a new and shaky coalition, city leaders ran a unified, dominant effort to defeat secession in a
citywide vote. Leadership unity was a key variable in the construction of
both coalitions, as mayors found ways to surmount their own conflicts
with other key power brokers in the city. Those who sought to keep the
city together found in charter reform the path to the high ground.

In his study of school reform, Clarence Stone (1998) describes the difference between winning temporary victories and developing a long-term
"performance regime." The question for Los Angeles is whether, with secession in retreat, there will develop the inside-outside pressure to maintain a long-term "reform regime" dedicated to improving the operational
effectiveness and responsiveness of the city government.

The study of secession and reform in Los Angeles indicates that the fate
of the city was partly decided by the struggle to reform its governance. In
a city with no party organizations, with a weak institutional structure, with
few mediating institutions between neighborhoods and city hall, both
those who challenged the structure of the city and those who tried to keep
the city together were drawn into a battle to define good government in
Los Angeles in the context of the secession threat.

The major reforms that emerged in the charter process included neighborhood councils and area planning commissions. They are underway, and
we will know more about their effectiveness in time. While these reforms
hold great promise for increasing the levels of participation of Los Angeles
residents, two types of proposals for reform were not implemented. One
was a larger city council and the other was creating some intermediate
level of government that would be elected and have some decision-making
authority.

There may come a time when increasing the size of the city council will
have more electoral appeal. The composition of the electorate is changing.
The proportion of white Republicans, hostile to government spending, is
declining. The share of Latinos is steadily increasing, and they may find a
larger council appealing. But these changes are still off in the distance.

The new charter gave city officials a strong argument to make, in the face of secession sentiment, that reform was on the way. Secessionists, who claimed that the charter did not go far enough to decentralize political authority, continued to press on. While the participation changes were very significant, the absence of an elected institution with some formal authority left an opening for further reform.

During and after the election, two sets of broader reform proposals emerged. One was administrative decentralization, championed by the mayor and allies on the council; the other was the devolution of authority, led by the secessionists and advocates of boroughs. Once again, the decision whether to adopt an idea associated with New York City government is on the table in Los Angeles.

BOROUGHS AND ADMINISTRATIVE DECENTRALIZATION

The concept of boroughs is highly elastic, but in general refers to a sub-government within a larger urban political system. As commonly conceived, a borough system is to a city government what a state government is to a national government. It is a *federal* relationship between the city and the borough in which power and authority overlap between city and borough. If the borough is designed to have ultimate power over the city, then it is almost a *confederal* system. If the borough has virtually no power or autonomy, it is barely a federal system; it is closer to a *unitary* government.

Tokyo, Berlin, Toronto, and London have systems in which delivery of services is highly decentralized. The problem for comparative purposes is that these major cities lack the home rule that even small American cities take for granted. While boroughs provide neighborhood input into decisions, the greater role is held by the national government. After returning from a trip to Paris, *LA Weekly* columnist Marc Haefele (2002) was enthusiastic about Paris *arrondissements,* but also noted a particular natural advantage for Parisians: "its other decisive life-style advantage may be that it has three times as many (15,000) cooks as lawyers."

The greatest contemporary innovation in London government is not the borough system; it is the creation by the Labour Government of the Greater London Authority in 1999. In other words, the energetic reform in Great Britain is to build a *bigger* local government so as to augment citizen power. When Conservatives were in power, they had removed much of London's home rule authority and were delighted to deal with a weaker series of borough governments with limited powers (Pimlott and Rao 2002).

The New York City case is the most obvious potential model for Los Angeles. No American city has had such powerful boroughs as New York City. Gerald Benjamin and Richard Nathan (2001) trace the creation of the Greater New York City out of the raw materials of two major cities, New York (Manhattan) and Brooklyn, along with several independent jurisdictions. The result was the five-borough system.

The five boroughs soon enough became key parts of New York City government. Led by elected borough presidents, the boroughs flexed their muscles in the citywide Board of Estimate, the mighty body that controlled land use and city contracts. While a majority of board members were citywide elected officials, the borough presidents still had considerable power.

The problem for borough designers in Los Angeles is that what works for New York City's highly political culture may be disastrous in Los Angeles. The depth and richness of the New York City political system is indicated by its large city council, its five boroughs, its hugely powerful mayor, and its strong party organizations. And there is considerable debate about how well boroughs have worked in New York City. Fred Siegel, a New Yorker interested in Los Angeles, has argued that while boroughs failed in New York City, they could succeed in Los Angeles (Planning Report 2002).

New York itself has turned away from the main aspects of borough power. The Board of Estimate was declared unconstitutional in 1986 by a federal judge, leading the city to undertake a comprehensive charter reform (Mauro and Benjamin 1989). The charter commission (only one at a time, in New York City) decided that the representational problems of the board could not be solved, and voted to eliminate it. At this point, they had to devise a role for the borough presidents.

Even without formidable powers, the elected borough presidents clearly fulfilled a representational role that was valued by New Yorkers. As the commission's chair said at the time, in language reminiscent of the challenge of Los Angeles,

> If [the borough presidents] didn't exist, we would want to invent something akin to them, because what they provide is an intermediate role between those who are elected in the smallest constituencies and those who are elected in the city as a whole. And with [a] government as big as ours, covering as large a physical area, covering as many people, we need that intermediate voice. (Schwartz and Lane 1998)

BOROUGHS IN LOS ANGELES

Borough proposals in Los Angeles have had both a substantive and a symbolic function. The symbolic function has been to make a big Los Angeles palatable to smaller communities that might join and choose to remain with Los Angeles. Their substantive purpose has been to solve the problem of a growing city too big to govern with a small, nonpartisan corps of elected officials. A far less recognized function, both substantive and symbolic, has been to support the development of *regional* government.

Local lore has it that the first borough proposal in Los Angeles was a bait-and-switch plan to annex San Pedro and Wilmington so that a growing Los Angeles could have the harbor. Actually, the first borough proposal had to do with building regional government as well as gaining the harbor.

In 1903, the city council appointed a citizens' commission to explore the consolidation of the city and county of Los Angeles. (For a thorough account of borough proposals in Los Angeles in the first half of the twentieth century, see Maccoby 1950, which is the source for most of the material below on that period of time.). This bold and radical plan was completed by the commission in 1906. The commission's long-term goal was to build a city-county consolidated government. Of California's fifty-eight counties, only San Francisco has such a system.

The commissioners believed that this very large government should be governed by a borough system, consisting of nine units of government: San Fernando, Pasadena, Monrovia, Whittier, Long Beach, San Pedro, Redondo, Santa Monica, and Los Angeles. In other words, the borough plan was intended to support a much broader expansion of the local government.

Under the commission proposal, there would be an elected mayor and other citywide officials; the sheriff would be the chief of police. Each borough would elect a president and a borough board; their duties would be local in nature.

The commission proposed a two-chamber city council: one branch made up of borough presidents and one of borough commissioners. According to Maccoby, the commissioners were extremely impressed by the new borough system of New York City adopted between 1898 and 1901. The commissioners believed that competition among Long Beach, San Pedro, Wilmington, and Los Angeles for control of the harbor would be eliminated with a unified city-county government (Maccoby 1950).

The commission's proposals were never adopted, and boroughs next appeared in a more limited form in 1909. As Los Angeles prepared to consolidate with Wilmington and San Pedro, an agreement was reached to insert into the city charter of Los Angeles a provision for a borough system for the harbor area only. The borough alternative was not available to other portions of the city.

The provision called for the gathering of signatures of at least 50 percent of the qualified voters to make a proposal for a borough. Upon the submission of valid signatures, the city council would be *required* to place a measure on the ballot. If successful, a borough would be established that would be governed by an elected five-member board. Opponents of consolidation argued, presciently, that Los Angeles would not keep its word (Maccoby 1950, 62).

When, four years later, a Wilmington borough petition was presented to the city council, the council refused to place it on the ballot. The case made it all the way to the California Supreme Court, where Wilmington's lawyers accused the city of using boroughs as "bait." The Los Angeles city attorney argued that the charter provision was itself unconstitutional because it applied to only one area of the city.

The California Supreme Court ruled that the provision was indeed unconstitutional, but only because the state constitution had undergone a change. In 1911, the constitution authorized the creation of boroughs in all or part of a city, but in 1914 was amended to protect home rule for charter cities by limiting borough plans to those that would divide the whole city into sections. However, later amendments to the state constitution removed language that precluded cities from establishing boroughs in only one part of a city.

The 1925 charter of Los Angeles included a section on boroughs. However, these borough provisions were somewhat weaker than the earlier proposals. Article 30 of the charter (City of Los Angeles 1925, 116–18) allowed any portion of the city to apply for borough status with a petition of 25 percent of registered voters if the territory included four thousand acres or forty thousand persons. The council was not required to place the measure for borough status on the ballot, but was permitted to do so "at its discretion."

If a borough proposal passed, a five-member Advisory Borough Board would be created and appointed. After a period of time, voters could petition to have the board elected. The borough board could ask the council to levy a tax on property above and beyond existing city taxes that could be appropriated by the board for borough purposes. However, the borough board would not be able to administer services.

In 1932, the state constitution was amended once again to ban the creation of boroughs in one portion of a city. The next case of boroughs was brought forward by Mayor Fletcher Bowron in 1947. Bowron was deeply frustrated by the lack of mayoral authority, and envisioned a three-part reform: ensuring that department heads reported to the mayor; developing a New York–style borough plan; and consolidating city-county services. Again, the regional governance agenda of a borough plan emerged. Apparently, Bowron saw the borough plan as a method to entice smaller communities to consolidate with Los Angeles in order to take advantage of the broader services Los Angeles could deliver (Maccoby 1950, 68).

Bowron proposed the creation of five boroughs: San Pedro/Harbor, Western Los Angeles, including Venice; Central Los Angeles; the San

Fernando Valley; and the area east of the Los Angeles River. Under Bowron's plan, the borough presidents would serve full-time, while borough councilors would be part-time. The borough presidents would also serve on the citywide council. Bowron was sympathetic to the Board of Estimate plan used at the time in New York City (Maccoby 1950).

Bowron's plan, which went through several formulations, would have divided services into those that are citywide (police, fire, airport, water and power) and those that are local in nature. Boroughs would have considerable taxing authority for these local services.

After Bowron's proposals failed to win council support, the boroughs idea faded until the 1960s. On three occasions, councilmembers or council committees made proposals for boroughs, but none received council support to go to the ballot until the Reining Commission took it up in 1969. The Reining Commission was in the process of developing a completely new city charter. While the commission reviewed borough proposals in Los Angeles history (Los Angeles City Charter Commission 1969, 24–25) it chose instead to recommend elected neighborhood councils with advisory authority. Each council would appoint a Neighborman to represent neighborhood interests (27).

The city council made major changes to the Reining Commission proposal, and eliminated neighborhood councils in the measure that went to the ballot, and twice failed. However, councilmember Ed Edelman (later a member of the appointed charter reform commission, 1997–99) rewrote the boroughs provisions from the 1925 charter (section 30) to include in the proposed new charter.

The Edelman proposal created "community service districts" with some resemblance to boroughs. Under the Edelman plan, local community districts would be established in a proposed article 25 of the charter. As in the 1925 charter, a petition signed by 25 percent of registered voters in an area of at least four thousand acres or forty thousand persons would trigger council review. The council could at its discretion place a measure for a community service district on the ballot.

If passed by the voters of the district, five candidates would be elected at the same election to be the first advisory board. The board would have powers comparable to those of managing commissions of proprietary departments, and could also authorize the council to levy a tax of ten cents per hundred dollars of assessed value as a surcharge for district purposes. The board could allocate those funds and also represent the needs of the district before the council and other government bodies.

In 1973, the city council placed a measure on the ballot to remove the boroughs section from the charter as part of a general charter cleanup. It was passed by the voters.

Boroughs made a brief appearance in the latest charter reform. However, boroughs were overshadowed by the vigorous debate over neighborhood councils and whether they should be elected or appointed, decision-making or advisory.

By 2001, secessionists were looking hopefully at polls showing that secession might pass citywide, and by 2002, LAFCO had decided to place measures on the November ballot for Valley and Hollywood secession. There were increasing calls to create some middle ground between secession and the newly reformed city government.

As city leaders increasingly feared that secession might win, the concept of boroughs reemerged in the local debate. Based on local impressions of the New York City governance model, boroughs seemed to respond to the perceived need to create intermediate institutions between neighborhoods and city hall.

In July 2002 newly elected city councilmembers Wendy Greuel and Janice Hahn presented a proposal to implement a borough system in Los Angeles. The original Greuel-Hahn plan was to place on the November 2002 ballot a measure that would commit the city to establishing a borough system. The measure would simultaneously create and elect a fifteen-member borough implementing commission to develop a plan. The borough plan would then be brought back to the voters within two years. The boroughs would have some decision-making authority and would be built around the new area planning commissions incorporated into the 1999 city charter.

In the original version of the Greuel-Hahn plan, borough boards would have "authority over issues of local concern and delivery of local services," including the following specific powers:

- community borough budget through an amount of the city budget to be established by the borough implementing commission
- community borough land use through an appointed body to have the powers of area planning commissions
- coordinate delivery of services, including police and fire
- exercise broad authority, where law permits, over local schools

Shortly after the Greuel-Hahn proposal surfaced, former Assembly Speaker Bob Hertzberg, like Greuel a Democrat from the San Fernando Valley, offered a different borough plan. The Hertzberg proposal would place on the ballot the immediate implementation of a borough structure that would eliminate the city council and replace it with a nine-member board of borough presidents. These presidents would be elected within their boroughs by their fellow, elected borough board members.

Under the Hertzberg plan, the city would be divided into nine equal boroughs. Borough boards would be elected by subdistrict; the borough president would be elected by the other members. The borough boards, which would meet in a designated borough hall, would have authority over a range of local activities. In addition, the presidents of the borough boards would become the city council, meet every two weeks and be "vested with the legislative power of the city." Because the Hertzberg proposal called for borough presidents to serve on a citywide legislative body, the boroughs had to be equal in population in order to comply with the constitutional principle of one person, one vote.

The borough board would coordinate the delivery of services within the borough. The number of area planning commissions would be increased from seven to nine to match the number of boroughs.

Hertzberg's plan was immediately hailed by Valley secessionists and the *Los Angeles Daily News*. As secessionists found themselves trailing in the polls in August, several made a private proposal (that obviously did not remain private) to Mayor Hahn to remove secession from the November ballot if the city would adopt the Hertzberg plan. Hertzberg's proposal also received considerable local and even national media attention when Neal Pierce endorsed it wholeheartedly in a national column.

While the Hertzberg plan was bold and dramatic, and had much in common with earlier proposals by Bowron and others, it had some serious disadvantages. It was inconsistent with the direction of the recent charter reform which had intended to strengthen the council's oversight and legislative roles. Council members would be incidental to city business, meeting every two weeks, and the mayor's power would expand to a degree perhaps matched only in New York City. The council size issue would get worse, not better, with fewer than fifteen districts.

The Hertzberg plan also bore an uncomfortable resemblance to the New York City Board of Estimate, eliminated in the 1989 charter reform. The council would be a collection of borough presidents, rather than a legislating and overseeing city council. In New York City, such a board not only overshadowed the city council but became a site both of mayoral domination and of deal-making between mayors and borough presidents.

The problem for both proposals was that in the absence of a secession threat, it would be difficult in the short run to generate political support to place either measure on the ballot. Following the model of charter reform, the advocates of borough proposals made an effort to multiply their political resources by developing a joint proposal.

Efforts to reconcile the two borough proposals seemed promising at first, but were ultimately fruitless. On virtually every point compromise was easy. No compromise could be found, however, on the basic premise of whether the city council should be abolished.

The city council held the power to place any measure on the ballot in the late summer of 2002; it was too late for a petition drive to place a ballot measure on the November ballot. Just before the council moved to take up borough proposals, the *Los Angeles Times* published a poll on Valley secession that seemed to take the wind out of secessionists' sails, and therefore made the prospects for boroughs quite a bit fainter. The poll showed citywide voters coalescing against secession, and a strong surge of African Americans against it (*Los Angeles Times* Poll 2002).

The council did not take up the Hertzberg proposal, for which little support appeared on the council. The Greuel-Hahn plan was brought up for a vote, and failed.

The president of the council, Alex Padilla, had already announced his opposition to placing boroughs on the November ballot. He did not favor the Greuel-Hahn measure or a backup proposal to create an appointed commission on boroughs with a timeline for the ballot. He instead offered a proposal for a Commission on Governance of Los Angeles that would consider boroughs among other alternatives. It would have no due date for reporting its recommendations, nor would it be targeted toward a particular election. Padilla made clear that he preferred changes by ordinance to changes requiring amendments to the city charter. Padilla's proposal to create a broad commission on governance with no specific timeline was defeated on a tie vote. Mayor James K. Hahn was reported to be confident enough about the secession election to not feel the need for a borough alternative.

At city hall, boroughs were dead in the water, victims of the declining fortunes of the secession campaign. While borough proposals seemed to have died, they continued to be discussed and promoted outside city hall. The *Los Angeles Times* endorsed continued exploration of boroughs, but time had run out before the November election.

After the defeat of the Greuel-Hahn plan, councilmember Tom LaBonge (fourth district) offered a proposal for administrative decentralization. The LaBonge plan, which quickly garnered substantial support in the council, called for a program to decentralize service delivery by department. LaBonge would create regions equivalent to area planning commissions, increased from seven to nine. The existing Board of Public Works, a five-member appointed board, would be expanded to as many members as there were service areas. Each Board member would have authority to supervise delivery of services within one area. Unlike the borough proposals, which focused on political decentralization, the LaBonge proposal conceptualized the issue as largely involving the delivery of services. Greater reliance for representation was placed on the council, through the creation of regional committees of council members.

The LaBonge plan was overshadowed after the election by the release of Mayor Hahn's program for decentralization of city service delivery, known as TeamWork LA. Under the Hahn plan, neighborhood city halls were established in the seven area planning commission regions. A service cabinet of top department officials met regularly to coordinate services. The Hahn plan also seemed to envision a much greater role in constituent service for the mayor's office than had been the practice in the past.

On June 20, 2003, Mayor Hahn announced the opening of neighborhood city halls in six areas of the city (McGreevy 2003). The plan would place city employees into these local buildings, where they would coordinate services under the direction of a regional cabinet of city officials.

Thus, the city was most likely to experiment with decentralized service delivery without, in the short term, decentralizing political authority. As the new charter and its participatory mechanisms kicked in, the debate might change to push city leaders toward borough proposals. But the pressure to consolidate reforms first was likely to prevent their immediate implementation.

Conclusions

Under the pressure of a powerful secession movement, Los Angeles has made considerable progress in enhancing its own democratic institutions. However, calls continue for the decentralization of political authority through boroughs. With no borough proposal on the ballot in November 2002 to compete with the vote for secession, borough designers examined long-term plans to implement their vision of locally elected people with authority over some aspects of city services.

Regardless of the fate of new decentralizing proposals, the area planning commissions have created a new physical model for the city. In time, the seven areas may evolve naturally into self-conscious communities, making new forms of representation both inevitable and natural.

With the defeat of secession in 2002, the reform impulse in Los Angeles may soften. But secession will not go away. It is too entrenched, with too much institutional support at the state level to disappear completely. Los Angeles residents will still have to consider what kind of city they want to have and how best to redesign their political institutions. The experiment in administrative decentralization that emerged postsecession will be evaluated carefully to assess whether greater devolution of authority to the local level will be the next frontier of Los Angeles reform.

CHAPTER NINETEEN

Conclusions and Implications

REFORM, TWENTY-FIRST-CENTURY STYLE

UNDER SEVERE stress, the city of Los Angeles undertook a major institutional reform. Studies of institutional structure and social capital would have suggested great difficulty for Los Angeles in carrying this enterprise through. A fragmented institutional framework, a low visibility political culture, high levels of demographic diversity, and relatively few grass-roots political organizations characterize Los Angeles. The combination should present major obstacles to the development of "civic capacity."

And yet, despite these obstacles, Los Angeles succeeded in a complete overhaul of its governing charter and, even more significantly, in creating a wholly new framework for resident participation. How did it happen?

Los Angeles reform could not have been accomplished without the creation of a civic coalition of reform-minded activists. But success was not solely the result of the long-standing efforts of citizen activists to reform city government. After all, that pressure had been operating since the early years of the 1925 charter, and had never been able to achieve what was accomplished in 1999.

Bowler, Donovan, and Karp (2002) refer to the impact of "exogenous" and "endogenous" factors in institutional change. Two "exogenous" factors played a critical role. The first was the movement for secession in the San Fernando Valley. By itself, secession was not enough to force governmental reform, but it was a major contributor to the sense that something needed to be done at city hall.

In the mid-1990s, secession became a major force, as the state government eased the way to the ballot. With this state help, secessionists moved forward a step at a time, through petitions for a feasibility study, to testimony before a local government commission, and then to a ballot measure. Secession was a formidable exogenous threat that seemed to grow stronger over time.

The second exogenous threat came from a political figure who, technically, might be seen as endogenous to the government, since he received a city paycheck (of only $1, by his choice) as mayor. Mayor Richard Riordan, however, was such an outsider to the city government that his critique of government practically defined his mayoralty. With his private resources committed to the fray, Riordan became a major threat to the institutional structure of city hall and to such interests as organized labor that were closely tied to city hall. He was able, in fact, to create a semiexogenous body—an elected charter reform commission—through the application of his private funds in the political arena.

Without Riordan's push for greater mayoral authority and for a complete overhaul of the city government, many powerful actors might have felt that they could beat secession with only minimal concessions. Riordan's challenge, when combined with the hard-to-measure threat of secession, became impossible to ignore. Riordan acted as a political entrepreneur (Steinacker 2001).

With secession and Riordan pushing for reform, the good-government forces that had long been unable to achieve comprehensive reform could get a better hearing for long-pursued ideas, such as greater mayoral authority, a better organized charter, and citizen participation.

At the endogenous level, for those leaders within the institutional structure that was being targeted for change, fear of secession and of Riordan's search for authority drove them to take a more active role in charter reform than they would have ever envisioned without those exogenous factors. The city council had long served as the burial ground of institutional reform proposals. Organized labor had resisted reforms in the operations of city government that would affect the working conditions of its members.

Yet under exogenous pressures, the city council moved to create an appointed charter reform commission, never envisioning that two years later that commission would be in a position to stand before it expecting its document to be adopted wholesale. Organized labor entered the battle over the elected charter reform commission, and surprised itself by winning control of that body when labor had only intended to get in Riordan's way. The city council and organized labor were now inevitably in the middle of the charter reform struggle, which Riordan and secession had put on the agenda. The city government was forced to pay close attention to the evolution of the new charter. Indeed, the final charter bore the stamp of the experienced hands at city hall.

For the next two years, these exogenous and endogenous forces carried on a political struggle along several dimensions. One was the inside game of power at city hall. Another was the outside game of designing methods of increasing participation. The challenge was to create a winning reform coalition in an environment with little consensus about which reforms were the best ones to adopt.

At the height of the charter reform struggle, the two charter reform commissions became central actors. Whether the commissions should be characterized as exogenous or endogenous is hard to answer. They were city commissions, paid for from city funds. Yet they were also outsiders. The elected commission was much more the outsider than the appointed commission, but even the city council-created body had an identity separate from city hall.

With the mayor and council in severe conflict with each other, the commissions themselves competed like siblings over resources, recognition, and policy. When matters reached their lowest point between the commissions, the chairs of the two commissions forged a two-person alliance and resolved all the outstanding substantive issues that divided the commissions. They sold this agreement first to a joint conference committee of the two commissions, and then in a dramatic series of votes after New Year's Day in 1999, to both commissions. Along the way, the commissions created a powerful exogenous force—a civic coalition that became a communitywide advocate for the unified charter.

At the mass level, which is rarely considered in the emerging studies of institutional reform, charter reform cultivated and enhanced a *constituency for reform*. This is the ultimate exogenous factor. Pushed by major newspapers and by politicians and civic activists, charter reform became an issue that had meaning for many members of voting public. A voting constituency had emerged for reforms such as the ballot measures to create an ethics commission in 1990; to increase civilian authority over the Los Angeles Police Department in 1992; to provide greater mayoral authority over the appointment of department general managers in 1995; and then to pass the charter in 1999.

This voting constituency was not the same on each issue, although there are subtle associations across coalitions. Those who supported the charter tended to support Riordan. Those who voted to increase the size of the city council tended to support Villaraigosa's mayoral campaign in 2001 (table 20).

Reform is a contested symbol that can belong to liberals or conservatives, whites or minorities. LAPD reform was a classic liberal/minority issue, while Riordan's charter proposal drew significant support from conservative whites and was least popular with African Americans.

However, a common member of these reform coalitions was the educated white voter on the Westside of Los Angeles, in precincts with a large Jewish voting population. Normally drawn to liberal propositions, these voters were pulled into the charter reform debate and provided the single largest percentage of the vote not only for the charter but also for measures to increase the size of the city council.

Clearly, secession was a profound exogenous force that motivated charter reform from the outset, but ultimately the main constituent for reform was the liberal reform voter. "Good-government" arguments were compelling to these voters, and the design of the charter was more a response to the need to maintain the support of this constituency than it was fear of downtown business.

There was also an intriguing level of support for reform in some minority communities. Latinos supported the new charter more than African Americans, even though there were few direct benefits for them in it. Latinos and Asian Americans were less hostile to expanding the size of the city council (from which they would have gained benefits) than white conservatives and African Americans. The politics of diversity was not incompatible with the politics of reform. Latinos and Asian Americans were to some degree drawn into the charter process, even if it was in support of the one element of the charter that failed to win voter support.

The assertion that cities with large immigrant populations are low in social capital may underestimate the potential for civic capacity in diverse cities. While the lives of new immigrants and their children may be filled with struggle and challenge, they may also represent hopeful communities ready to take their position of civic participation and leadership. Certainly in Los Angeles, they were open to reform and against breaking up the city.

Charter reform happened in Los Angeles because exogenous forces set off a process of institutional consideration of reform—a process that eventually spun out of the control of the political figures who had set it in motion. Once the best laid plans of political leaders to control charter reform began to erode, there was no certainty that charter reform would succeed. Citizen leadership in the charter reform commissions and among members of a civic coalition played critical roles in preventing the collapse of the process and in developing a successful charter. From that point on, Riordan took charge and directed the campaign to win voter approval.

The important role of civic activists in charter reform might lead to further questions about assertions of low social capital in Los Angeles. Social capital is what social capital does. In a city without a dense network of civic organizations, the *unity* and *mobilization* of those civic forces that do exist may create an immense amount of civic capacity. In fact, the very lack of dense social and political organization may have prevented the kind of factional struggle that could have greatly impeded the ability of the commissions to challenge even a popular and powerful mayor.

Once the charter had passed, however, political leadership reasserted itself. The elected officials of the city may not have been able to create a new charter on their own, but they unquestionably knew how to get it passed and utilize it to head off the threat of secession. The city had shown that it could reform itself, and that fact became an important thread of the argument for keeping the city together.

The energy and symbolism of reform had now been invested in the very institutional structure that had for so long resisted change. Those who wanted to break up the city could not gain access to the great power of the reform symbol because the city already had it. The argument for secession was reduced to "fair share," a demand to get more resources and attention to the Valley at the cost of attention to the rest of the city. And when the votes were counted in November 2002, the reform constituency on the Westside and in other portions of the city had joined with African American voters who had opposed the new charter to overwhelmingly defeat secession.

New York City is often characterized as more politically developed than Los Angeles. Its partisan elections generate voter participation, frame choices, and make government relevant. But there are virtues to the less connected nonpartisan system in Los Angeles. One is that despite furious battles among political leaders, there are pathways to agreement and even consensus when the interests of the city are at stake. In the charter reform and secession campaigns, the main political leaders of the city—often competitors and even personal foes—pulled together into a cohesive leadership alliance that was difficult to challenge.

New York City and Chicago offer very large city councils, and Los Angeles's is relatively small. Los Angeles cannot offer the microrepresentation of these very political cities with their large councils, but the reform-constructed L.A. council provides a greater power base than the larger councils. A Los Angeles councilmember is a mayoral contender to a far greater degree than his or her peer in New York City and Chicago. Each Los Angeles councilmember is very important and powerful, and if a somewhat larger city council can be achieved, the gains will accrue to new immigrant communities which can thereby obtain some real power.

THE COURSE OF SECESSION AND REFORM IN NEW YORK CITY COMPARED TO LOS ANGELES

In both New York City and Los Angeles there was a long history of secessionist agitation. Both secession movements arose in largely middle-class, suburban communities that reacted to rapid demographic change in the cities during the 1980s. Both secession efforts emerged in areas that perceived themselves as culturally, geographically, and politically alienated from city life, and as little more than "tax colonies" of a distant and unaccountable city government.

Situated south and west of New York's other boroughs of Manhattan, Queens, Brooklyn and the Bronx, and connected above ground by only the Verazzano-Narrows Bridge and by the Staten Island Ferry, residents of Staten Island have long considered themselves a "forgotten" (Kurtz 1988) and "rebellious" (Briffault 1992) borough.

In 1898, residents of the City of Richmond (later to be named Staten Island) and other outlying independent jurisdictions of Brooklyn, the Bronx, and Queens voted to join Manhattan to create North America's first megacity. Residents hoped that consolidation would bring improved infrastructure and an economic windfall for the island. Richmond registered the highest voter support for the consolidation. Surprisingly, the consolidation vote came in the face of the objections of the original New York City itself (New York State Senate Finance Committee 1983, 5–6).

Residents of Richmond began to question the decision to abdicate home rule when the city announced plans to relocate garbage facilities to the Island in 1916, 1921, and 1938. Efforts to secede from New York City surged, only to be quelled when the city agreed to shelve the landfill proposals. The decision was finally made to open Fresh Kills landfill in 1947.

Fresh Kills became the largest landfill in the world by the 1980s; by the 1990s it was the only one of the city's landfills still in operation. Until officials agreed to close the dump in 2001, the landfill served as a symbol of the island's powerlessness and its frustration with city government (State of New York Charter Commission for Staten Island 1993, 5–6).

In 1989, Staten Island lost a U.S. Supreme Court decision in *Morris v. Board of Estimate* that resulted in the abolition of the city's Board of Estimate, which had historically functioned as a key force in land use, contracts, and budgeting. Among the Board of Estimate's eleven members, each of the five borough presidents held one spot. The Board of Estimate gave Staten Island a seat at the head table despite its relatively small size. For Staten Island, abolishing the Board of Estimate resulted in a major dilution of the borough's political strength. Staten Island has since accounted for only three of the fifty-one City Council seats.

The court decision on the Board of Estimate led Staten Island's chief advocate, Republican state senator John J. Marchi, to the alternative of secession. Marchi's senate committee on finance had issued a report in 1983 that drew a straight line between the pending court case and secession. Marchi's report argued that the court would be wrong to abolish the Board, but that if it did, a secession process should begin immediately (New York State Senate Finance Committee 1983).

A fiscal analysis by Marchi's committee noted that the key issues in any breakup were water and waste. Staten Island was totally dependent on New York City for its water through a pipeline across the river. The Fresh Kills landfill was the last remaining open landfill in New York City. The resolution of these two issues would be critical to the future viability of an Island city, and would have a dramatic impact on New York City. Marchi argued, however, that there was no legal need for a "home rule message" (a city veto) from New York City on the question of Island secession.

On the last day of the 1989 state legislative session, Marchi helped pass a bill—over the objections of New York City officials—that paved the way for a referendum asking Staten Island residents to create a state commission to study the feasibility of independence. In the wake of local outrage following the abolition of the Board of Estimate, 83 percent of the island's voters approved the referendum in 1990.

New York City leaders complained about the process, arguing that an Island-only referendum violated the rights of city residents. Furthermore, they contended that the state was unjustly overriding home rule. Both claims were rejected by the State Court of Appeals (State of New York Charter Commission for Staten Island 1993:8).

In compliance with the new state law, Governor Mario Cuomo appointed a thirteen-member State of New York Charter Commission to study city-hood for Staten Island. The commission was stacked with secession advocates. It was composed of the Island's state legislators and their appointees and one appointee each from the governor, the Speaker of the Assembly, and the president pro tem of the State Senate. Marchi, the strongest advocate of secession in New York, was named chairman. New York City had no voice whatever in the appointment or operations of the commission. The commission conducted a poll on secession but surveyed only Staten Island residents.

The Charter Commission released a report in early 1993 that found, not surprisingly, that the Island could sustain itself financially as an independent city. The commission did its own analysis of the fiscal impact of secession on the Island, and on the city. Despite city complaints that city workers would be severely harmed by secession (Mayor's Task Force on Staten Island Secession 1993), the commission argued that the impact would not be so severe as to make secession unwise.

An analysis commissioned by Marchi's Senate Finance Committee in 1990 had found, however, that without the revenue from the Fresh Kills landfill, a Staten Island city could not generate revenues equal to its projected expenditures (New York State Senate 1990). The study had an important implication: someday, Islanders might have to choose between getting rid of the landfill and having their own city.

While the city of New York was unable to stop the steamroller of secession in the face of strong interest by the state government, it initially avoided assisting with the data gathering process. Over time, however, the city leadership decided to take a more cooperative role. The charter commission reported that for the first time, the City of New York provided data on budget and services to bodies undertaking the study of secession. Mayor David Dinkins created a Mayor's Task Force on Staten Island Secession in December 1991 to interface with the commission, but also to help shape the data on the impacts of secession. The Task Force issued a report challenging the "rosy picture" being painted by secession adocates (Mayor's Task Force on Staten Island Secession 1993).

The Marchi commission, backed by a strong and respected academic staff, actually wrote a new charter for a proposed City of Staten Island (which would immediately become the state's second largest city). The new charter called for a strong mayor, strong council system quite similar to that of New York City, and for protections for civil service workers. The Mayor's

Task Force on Staten Island Secession argued that these assurances were un-realistic, and that city workers living and/or working in Staten Island would be at very high risk of losing their benefits and even their employment.

Buoyed by the results of the commission report, secession supporters pushed a second bill through the state legislature that led to a November 1993 referendum. In voting for the measure, residents would not only be approving secession but would be creating a new government. After an in-tense political campaign, Proposal 5, which created a city charter for the new city of Staten Island, passed with 65 percent approval.

Legislation enabling secession then passed the Republican controlled State Senate by a vote of thirty-six to seventeen (Finnegan 1995, 4). However, State Assembly Speaker Sheldon Silver, a Manhattan Democrat, blocked the secession effort by demanding a home rule message from New York City before the proposal to create a new city could proceed in the legislature (Campanile and Schneider 1996).

In January of 1995 a New York State Court of Appeals ruling effectively ended the effort by refusing to force the State Legislature to vote on leg-islation enabling secession over the objections of Assembly Speaker Silver. A lower court ruling had previously upheld secession opponents' argu-ments that authorizing the detachment without the approval of the New York City Council and mayor violated home rule provisions of the State Constitution (Spencer 1996:1). These last-minute decisions saved New York City from what had seemed to be a losing battle.

The result was a very close call for New York City, because Cuomo's suc-cessor as governor, Republican George Pataki, would have been very likely to sign the bill if it came to his desk. Staten Island came within a judge's decision of a secession victory.

With the end of the formal secession movement, New York City's polit-ical leadership had another opportunity to bind Staten Island closer. Newly elected Mayor Rudolph Giuliani, heavily supported by conservative Staten Island voters, announced that he would close Fresh Kills. By 1997, polls reported a significant decline in support for Island secession. In 2002, Michael Bloomberg, Giuliani's fellow Republican and mayoral successor, closed the facility for good in favor of an alternative landfill plan.

The 1990 report that suggested the incompatibility between Island inde-pendence and the closing of the landfill had turned out to be prescient. If the Island would not get independence, it would instead get rid of the landfill.

Given that Los Angeles and New York City could not be more different in institutional structure and political culture, do we find more similarities or differences in the way that secession played out in each case? We might expect that Los Angeles, as a fragmented, decentralized city with weak and divided leadership structures, would be vulnerable to a secession move-ment. On the other hand, we might expect that New York City, as a vital, politically connected community of alert residents and top-down mayoral leadership would have a strong idea of itself as a city, and would never let a secessionist movement out of the starting gate.

In reality, both cities nearly lost their battles to keep their city boundaries whole. Contrary to expectations, New York came even closer to defeat than Los Angeles, saved only by a Manhattan-based state legislator's procedural maneuver blocking legislation certain to pass and likely to win the governor's signature. In the end, the city was bailed out by an appeals court ruling that easily could have gone the other way. Yet Los Angeles was also in serious jeopardy. Had the state legislature agreed to secessionists' demands that there be no citywide vote on secession when the rules were made in 1997, it is quite likely that the Valley would have won independence in 2002.

In each city, political reform played an important role, although in opposite directions. In New York, reform *advanced* secession in two different ways. First, charter reform's elimination of the Board of Estimate in 1989 became a clarion call for secessionists who rallied borough residents behind calls for self-determination. Second, the energy of reform was channeled into the development of a Staten Island city charter, with the assistance of some scholars and lawyers. The reform initiatives of secession leaders forced the City of New York into a reactive, defensive mode as a charter commission dominated by secessionists made finding after finding that supported the fiscal viability of the proposed new city.

In Los Angeles, political reform became the city's *solution* to the challenge of secession. Two charter commissions, made up almost entirely of secession opponents, crafted a new city charter that addressed some of the concerns of alienated residents by increasing citizen participation and improving service delivery. Unlike in New York, the scholarly and legal communities of Los Angeles were overwhelmingly on the side of keeping the city together. Not only did this allow opponents of secession to assume the moral high ground—"the city is better united than divided" became a common rallying cry—but their participation deprived secessionists of intellectual resources to advance their cause. When progressive alliances forge coalitions with "experts", their power is multiplied (Finegold 1995a, b). In New York City, some key experts were with the secessionists; in Los Angeles, most were with the city.

Los Angeles leaders made up for their lack of formal political power and for the relative weakness of public attachment to government by their undeniable unity, even across lines of political competition and personal hostility. Riordan and Hahn, who did not much like each other and whose constituencies were opposed to each other's, joined forces with police chief Bernard Parks to back charter reform. Hahn and Riordan joined with Parks, whom Hahn had fired in a contentious decision not long before, to oppose secession. Even Democratic state officials who had facilitated the study of secession's feasibility opposed secession once it was on the ballot.

New York City's leaders were more divided on secession. Key state leaders seemed unreceptive to New York City's complaints about the process, and were content to make secession a question of interest only to the state and the Staten Islanders.

But New York City's leaders, even if divided, could draw upon assets found in the arsenal of traditional political cities, which were largely absent in Los Angeles. The ability of a mayor to impose his or her own will on events is much greater in New York City than in Los Angeles. Aside from its dream of independence, the one thing most desired by Staten Islanders had been the closing of Fresh Kills landfill. Two consecutive Republican mayors, Rudolph Giuliani and Michael Bloomberg, had the authority and political will to respond directly to the public clamor. Giuliani suspended the operations of the landfill and Bloomberg killed it for good, in two fell swoops that only a New York City mayor could manage. The closing of the landfill made independence seem less attractive.

No Los Angeles mayor could as easily, or directly, impose such a solution. Power is far more divided in Los Angeles government, and such a move would have involved complicated regional negotiations with a number of other jurisdictions (not to mention the powerful city council). Los Angeles poltical culture looks much less fondly on the raw exercise of behind-the-scenes power. As a result, Los Angeles leaders had to operate indirectly through the arduous process of reform and consensus-building in order to defeat secession. It was the long way around, but it was the only way Los Angeles knew, and it worked.

A surprising finding is the degree to which both cities, although especially New York City, were at the mercy of state government during the secession process. As McHenry (2002) has argued, a determining factor in the success of secession movements is the set of rules developed at the state level. Time and again the City of New York was on the outside looking in on secession negotiations taking place in Albany. In fact there is a long history of New York State intervention into the city's governmental structure and affairs through state-mandated charter reform commission (Viteritti 1989). While the City of Los Angeles successfully shaped both state law governing secession and had at least some impact on the state commission charged with studying the fiscal viability of secession, New York was a virtual nonplayer in the creation and composition of state commissions that studied secession.

Yet the state of California was no great friend to Los Angeles during the secession struggle. Without the state's intervention to eliminate the city council's veto, the secession movement could not have taken place. Handing the fiscal assessment to LAFCO, dominated by county government and smaller cities hostile to Los Angeles, was not the only possible alternative, but it was one that placed Los Angeles in a disadvantaged position. The county of Los Angeles, which makes substantial money by contracting with cities for services under the "Lakewood Plan," could hardly hide its glee at the thought of winning the contract for public safety services in a new Valley city. (Los Angeles, however, undoubtedly was better off than New York watching a fiscal assessment being conducted by the very commission that would write a charter for the independent city.)

These cases reveal that even large, global cities such as New York and Los Angeles remain at the mercy of state legislatures on matters as fundamental as their territorial integrity. While secession movements revolve around self-determination, home rule was also supposed to allow cities to determine their own destinies.

Los Angeles asserted its autonomy partly by the energy it invested in one critical aspect of home rule—the provisions for governance in a city charter. Political reform became a vehicle for power by a city buffeted by many external and internal challenges.

IMPLICATIONS

The success of charter reform in Los Angeles was not predictable, nor was it inevitable. Human choices were critical factors, and those choices might have been made differently. Reform was not the result of the slow, steady, decades-long coalition building process that underlay the rise of the biracial coalition behind Tom Bradley. This story therefore does not provide a convenient way to identify the conditions under which reform can take place in all circumstances. However, there are some more general conclusions that may be drawn that can lead to further study of the process of reform, so that someday we can more reliably understand how government can be made more flexible and responsive through citizen action.

The Valley secession movement and the response of charter reform in Los Angeles will not be isolated events in urban politics. The transition from municipal incorporation as a way to escape the urban setting to seceding from the city without moving a step may emerge as the next challenge to cities. New York City has already faced substantial sentiment for secession in Staten Island. Suburban, middle-class voters may have the political clout to change rules at the state level so that the road to secession is eased. Such a development would challenge the entire definition of cities as we know them. Cities will have to devise new ways to cope with these pressures, and reform is likely to be one element of that effort.

Are cities good for individual voters? Do they provide social and equity functions that must be maintained even if many individual voters are unhappy? If cities are to remain, how can they govern themselves to keep the attachment of their residents? What role can reform play in that process?

The movement to reform government will likely arouse considerable expectations in the twenty-first century. Many of these hopes will be unrealizable, because it is extremely difficult to reform government. There are numerous barriers, and those with the political skills to create coalitions for enduring reforms may be all too rare.

This study is based on the premise that reform is a process of coalition building in the competitive political arena. It draws on the interests and beliefs of key elites and constituencies, and can be destroyed by such interests and beliefs as well. It is, in that sense, much like most of the politics with which we are familiar.

But this study also suggests that there is another element to reform that is more difficult to measure, but nonetheless is significant. I propose that there is a reform constituency in the electorate that supports political leaders in the building of coalitions for reform. Furthermore, reform is not the property of conservatives, nor of liberals, but rather is a contested value of great importance.

The relationship between ideas and beliefs, on the one hand, and interests, on the other, has long been a source of debate. Politics can certainly be reduced to a struggle over who gets what, when, and how. Calculations must be made of self-interest, however defined, and these can be shown to influence political behavior.

Yet, much of political life is difficult to reconcile with a simple struggle of interests. The area of racial politics is an instructive case. Certainly racial conflict is influenced by realistic conflicts of interests. Yet it would be impossible to explain much of the dynamic of interracial conflict and coalition building without reference to different belief systems about race (Browning, Marshall, and Tabb 1984; Sonenshein 1993). In fact, the way in which an individual or group perceives self-interest may be in turn shaped by preexisting beliefs about such deeply embedded issues as race.

Reform can be seen as a cover for self-interest, but it can also be seen as a set of beliefs about government and civic life. Unlike racial ideology, which tends to have a consistent constituency over time and even over cities, reform is a more malleable philosophy that can take different forms even in the same city.

Urban reform has long had a bad name in the scholarly realm. Much of the urban literature has treated reform as a phenomenon of importance to small cities and as a vehicle to reduce the access of government for low-income people and minorities. This study suggests that both in the minority struggle for political incorporation and then in battles to define the direction of city government, reform is a valuable, contested symbol. It can be wielded by conservatives, by moderates, and by liberals; by whites, by blacks, and by Latinos. Reform ultimately symbolizes the ability of potential leadership groups to govern effectively and responsively, and thereby to be entitled to rule.

The struggle to implement reform both activates old coalition lines and shapes newer ones. It is supremely political, especially where there are no party organizations to play the role of "regulars." It overlays additional issue battles over the racial and ideological competition that has structured much of local politics beginning in the 1960s.

In the era of minority incorporation, the connection among these three elements was significant. African Americans and Latinos rose up to political incorporation through mobilization and then alliance with liberal whites. Often opposed by party regulars, these minority movements generated a substantial degree of reform. In Finegold's terms, progressive coalitions were not only cross-racial but tapped into "experts," a euphemism for reform.

In the twenty-first century, the setting for these three elements has changed. At least in the largest American cities, nonliberals, not supported by African Americans, captured the flag of urban reform. While these large cities may seem anomalous as other cities continue to elect minority, progressive mayors, their impact is great. And, the experience of these cities does not challenge the notion of the persistence of race. What it does challenge is the belief that minority coalitions are agents of change, rather than agents of the status quo, and that such coalitions can rely on the support of white liberals. It also indicates the disturbing possibility that the isolation of African Americans may increase as Latinos rise up.

The "new mayors," Republicans in New York City and Los Angeles and a moderate Democrat in Chicago, can be partially explained with reference to the notion of reform as a contested value. To the extent that each mayor was seen as challenging the structure of urban government, they each found a way to capture the flag of urban reform. It will be important for urban progressives to take a second look at reform, and to consider the right design of political institutions to be an important progressive activity.

In the twenty-first century, government must become more agile, more flexible, and more responsive. It will always be government, and to expect it to dance the tango on command is a pipe dream. But government need not be hidebound and totally resistant to institutional change. Progressives will need to pay closer attention than they have to the value of institutional reform. When government is criticized and unable to respond, it is far harder to achieve a progressive public agenda.

DIRECTIONS FOR FUTURE RESEARCH

The theory and practice of urban reform is in need of reexamination. We need to ask: Is structure destiny? Is social capital predictive of civic capacity? Do cities accomplish great purposes or achieve major reforms because of institutional structure and social capital? This study of a city with weak political institutions and low levels of social capital suggests that these variables are the ingredients rather than the recipe. Institutional structure in particular provides constraints and opportunities, but human choices and political skill widen the available courses of action.

The fields of political science and public policy need to reconnect with each other. The art of reform is a proper subject for political science, especially if one is willing to see reform as itself a political behavior variable. One does not have to share the view that reform is about a set of beliefs to agree that these beliefs can have a significant political impact. Public policy needs to address the *political* requirements of successful reform, or suffer the fate of generations of reformers watching marvelous policy documents gather dust on the bookshelf. Public policy needs to be informed by politics; political science needs to take reform seriously once again. Bert Swanson (2000) suggests that social scientists examine proposed and enacted reforms in the role of "clarifiers." If reform proposals compete in a marketplace of ideas, we should bring social science to bear in explaining their likely consequences and beneficiaries.

These research directions will profitably link both political science and public policy to the emerging global search for methods of democratic governance. In areas as far apart as the working-class Latino city of South Gate in California, to emerging democracies worldwide, people are finding in the reality and symbolism of reform the hope of achieving democratic goals. All confront the demoralizing resistance of political institutions to reform, even when there would be great political benefits to change. All need to consider the impact of political coalition-building on the process of successful reform.

Finally, we need to reconsider the role of ideas and beliefs in political action. Political philosophers have long searched for the best, the most ideal government. While that search may now seem naïve to the behavioral social scientist, it is quite serious for citizens and for many leaders in government.

The focus on self-interest as the motivator for all political action has been immensely valuable. It would be impossible to undertake serious political analysis without it. Nothing would be more unrealistic than to assert that politics is really a struggle of ideas and beliefs, or to accept at face value the self-styled principled statements of each and every politician.

Yet in reducing all political action to self-interest we risk missing something important about civic capacity and civic participation. To many ordinary people, who are not political actors except as voters and observers, what is right and wrong in government is quite important. They may cast votes not only on their self-interest (although this is highly relevant to their decision) but also on what they consider right and wrong.

Pierson has noted (2000, 478) that sociologists have challenged the new institutionalism to take into account that "in structuring institutional arrangements, actors may be motivated more by conceptions of what is appropriate than by conceptions of what would be effective." We must therefore be alert to "the sensitivity of actors to the need to legitimate their activities."

It is not that reform coalitions have no form or durability. It is, rather, that reform is neither the property of conservatives nor of liberals, neither minorities nor whites. It is a contested symbol that is critical to urban leadership because it indicates the capacity to adapt to changing circumstances. Reform has many nuances and identities, from the antigovernment reform of white conservatives, to police reform for progressives and minorities, to a more progovernment stance still being shaped by Latinos. Reform clearly has a place in the new and complex politics and government of diversity.

Reform is an important symbol of the allocation of power and authority, but it is also a symbol of good government conducted in the right way. That symbolism matters to the community, and it even matters to people who are less active in politics than the average voter. As we expand our political analysis to build on self-interest but to understand the value of ideas and beliefs, we will come closer to a true understanding not only of politics but of the enterprise of democratic governance.

On January 28, 2003, in South Gate, California, a city of Latinos, many of whom are immigrants, a bloc of Latino officeholders accused of corruption was recalled from office by 80 percent of the voters, most of whom were also Latino. Reform had come to an immigrant community, not as a secondary effect of good-government efforts by whites, but simply by the urge for good government in a blue-collar immigrant community. Perhaps there is in the South Gate story a reminder that reform knows no ethnicity and no social class. In an age of diversity, reform is too important to be relegated to the history books.

Summary of the Charter Proposal

GENERAL PROVISIONS

(Article 1)

Organization of the charter

- *Replaces* the current one-volume charter with two volumes. Volume one contains the provisions on how the city is governed. Volume two contains the rules on civil service, pensions, and retirement.
- *Removes* many details on the structure of city departments and governmental procedures, leaving these details to be set by ordinance. (An ordinance is a city law that can be changed without the vote of the people.)

Nondiscrimination

- *Retains* the charter prohibition against discrimination in city employment based on sex, but *adds* a prohibition against discrimination based on race, religion, national origin, ancestry, sexual orientation, age, disability, or marital status.

POWERS AND DUTIES OF ELECTED OFFICIALS

(Article II)

Code of Conduct

- *Adds* a provision stating that the behavior of all elected officials is expected to meet the highest personal and professional standards.
- *Adds* a provision authorizing the city council to censure any of its members whose behavior falls far below the highest personal and professional standards.

Term Limits

- *Retains* current term limits for elected city officials.

Redistricting

- *Retains* the city council's duty to draw district boundary lines for election of city council and Los Angeles Board of Education members, but *adds* a requirement for the appointment of citizen commissions to advise the council on where to draw boundaries. *Adds* a requirement that district boundaries be drawn as much as possible to keep neighborhoods and communities together.

Mayor

- *Adds* mayoral duty to represent the city before the state and federal government in accordance with city policy, and to supervise the city's intergovernmental relations activities.
- *Adds* a provision authorizing the mayor to declare a local emergency, to supervise the city's efforts to prepare for emergencies, and to coordinate the city's emergency response.
- *Adds* a provision authorizing the mayor to issue executive orders to city departments if those orders do not conflict with the charter or ordinance.
- *Transfers* authority from the city administrative officer to the mayor to temporarily move city workers from one department to another.
- *Transfers* authority from the city administrative officer to the mayor to move money from one city account to another if the amount is less than a limit set by ordinance.
- *Adds* an Executive Budget Division in the mayor's office to assist the mayor in budget preparation and monitoring.

City Council

- *Retains* the present size of the council at fifteen members.
- *Retains* the process by which the council reviews commission decisions, but *changes* the process allowing council to approve or veto, but not modify, those decisions. Decisions of the Ethics Commission, Pension and retirement boards, and specified personnel decisions of other commissions would be exempt from this review.
- *Retains* the council and mayor roles in reorganizing city departments, but *adds* a provision requiring the council to approve or disapprove reorganization plans submitted by the mayor within forty-five days.
- *Retains* the council's authority to set city policy, but *adds* a provision requiring policy concerning proposed state and federal legislation to be set by the council by resolution, subject to veto by the mayor and override of the veto by the council.

Appointment and Removal of City Officers by Mayor and City Council

- *Retains* mayoral authority to appoint department heads, subject to confirmation by the city council.
- *Retains* provision authorizing the mayor to remove the city clerk or treasurer only with city council approval.
- *Changes* how most other department heads can be removed, authorizing the mayor to remove department heads without requiring council approval.
- *Authorizes* department heads to appeal the removal to the city council, and *authorizes* the city council, by two-thirds vote, to reinstate the department head.
- *Retains* process by which mayor appoints commissioners, subject to confirmation by the city council.
- *Authorizes* the mayor to remove city commissioners without requiring council approval.

Controller

- *Retains* the controller as an elected official, in charge of general accounting and auditing of the city's funds.
- *Adds* duty to monitor city debt.
- *Adds* duty to audit the performance of departments.

City Attorney

- *Retains* the city attorney as an elected official, in charge of civil litigation and criminal prosecution.
- *Retains* the city council's authority to settle most lawsuits, but adds a provision authorizing smaller claims to be settled by the mayor or a created claims board.
- *Adds* a provision authorizing the mayor and specified boards of commissioners to make decisions other than settlements in lawsuits involving matters over which they have authority.
- *Retains* the requirement for city council and city attorney agreement before outside counsel can be hired for most departments, but *adds* a provision allowing specified boards of commissioners to hire outside counsel with approval of the board and city attorney, but without requiring council approval.

FINANCE, BUDGET, AND CONTRACTS

(Article III)

Budget Process

- *Retains* the process by which the mayor proposes the budget to the council for adoption, but *adds* a provision requiring the mayor to publish his or her budget goals three months before submitting the budget to the council.
- *Retains* the duty of the city administrative officer (renamed the Office of Administrative and Research Services) to prepare revenue and cost estimates to assist both the mayor and council in budget preparation and adoption.

Office of Finance

- *Adds* a new Office of Finance to issue licenses and collect money owed the city, and to develop plans for the city's revenue policy. *Transfers* the current tax collection duties of the city clerk to this office.

Contracting

- *Retains* requirement of council approval of long-term contracts but limits review only to approval or veto.
- *Retains* the requirement for competitive bidding but *moves* many procedural details to ordinance.

Debt

- *Adds* a provision requiring preparation of a debt impact statement before new city debt is incurred.

Prevailing Wage

- *Retains* requirement that the city follow state regulations regarding paying prevailing wages on public works projects.

Living Wage

- *Adds* a requirement that those doing business with the city pay their workers a living wage, in an amount to be determined by ordinance.

ELECTIONS

(Article IV)

Elections

- *Retains* election rules concerning city and Board of Education elections, initiative, referendum, and recall.
- *Moves* many procedural details to the city election code, such as how polling place workers are selected, vote recounts are handled, and petitions are designed and signatures checked.
- *Retains* rules and restrictions on campaign financing, including oversight by the Ethics Commission.
- *Changes* signature rules allowing a voter to sign petitions for more than one candidate for the same office.

OTHER CITY OFFICES AND DEPARTMENTS

(Articles V through VIII)

Commissions

- *Retains* system in which citizen commissions manage or advise most city departments.

Office of Administrative and Research Services

- *Retains* the duties of the office with regard to budget preparation and administration.
- *Changes* the name of the office from City Administrative Officer to Office of Administrative and Research Services.

Ethics Commission

- *Retains* the Ethics Commission to enforce the rules concerning conflicts of interest, lobbying, campaign finance, and governmental ehtics.

Library

- *Retains* special set-aside of funds for libraries.

Planning

- *Retains* the City Planning Commission for general citywide planning issues and *increases* the size of the commission from five to nine.

- *Adds* at least five Area Planning Commissions to make determinations regarding land use permits. *Requires* members of each Area Planning Commission to live in the area served by the commission.
- *Transfers* the functions of the Board of Zoning Appeals to Area Planning Commissions.
- *Adds* a provision requiring the process for most land use permits to be established by ordinance, but *limits* the process to one level of appeal.
- *Retains* city council authority to review and modify decisions of the City Planning Commission, and *adds* authority to review and modify decisions of Area Planning Commissions.

Police Department

- *Retains* a citizen Police Commission to oversee the department.
- *Retains* term of office for chief of police and current system for hiring and firing the chief.
- *Retains* discipline system for police officers developed as a result of the recommendations of the Christopher Commission.
- *Retains* the position of police inspector general to oversee the department's handling of police misconduct.
- *Changes* the reporting duty of the inspector general, requiring the inspector general to report directly to the Police Commission instead of to the executive director of the Police Commission.
- *Adds* provisions authorizing the inspector general to initiate investigations without prior approval of the Police Commission, and giving the inspector general the same access to the Police Department information as the Police Commission.

Propriety Departments (Airports, Harbor, Water and Power)

- *Retains* authority of citizen commissions to manage the proprietary departments.
- *Adds* duties to the commissions to hire general managers, subject to approval of the mayor and city council, and to remove general managers subject to approval of the mayor and appeal to the city council.
- *Adds* two new members to the Airport Commission, and *adds* a requirement that at least one member of the commission live near the Los Angeles International Airport, and that at least one member of the commission live near the Van Nuys Airport.
- *Adds* a requirement that at least one member of the Harbor Commission live near the Harbor.

- *Adds* provisions requiring that the Airport Police remain under the independent control of the Department of Airports, and that the Harbor Police remain under the independent control of the Harbor Department.

Public Works

- *Retains* a full-time citizen commission to supervise the department which provides street lighting, street maintenance, trash collection, and design and construction services for public building and improvement.
- *Adds* the position of general manager for the department.
- *Retains* mayoral authority to appoint, subject to city council confirmation, the heads of the bureaus of Contract Administration, Engineering, Sanitation, Street Lighting, and Street Services.

Recreation and Parks

- *Retains* prohibition against using dedicated park land for other purposes.
- *Retains* special set-aside of funds for recreation and park use.

NEIGHBORHOOD COUNCILS

(Article IX)

Department of Neighborhood Empowerment

- *Adds* a department and a citizen commission to develop a plan for a citywide system of advisory neighborhood councils.
- *Requires* the plan to be adopted by the city council within a set period of time.
- *Requires* that all parts of the city have an opportunity to form neighborhood councils.
- *Requires* that neighborhood councils be informed before decisions are made by the city council, council committees or boards and commissions, in order for decision makers to receive input from neighborhood councils.
- *Authorizes* neighborhood councils to give input to city officials regarding budget priorities, the delivery of city services, and other issues affecting the neighborhoods.

CIVIL SERVICE, PENSIONS AND RETIREMENT

(Articles X and XI)

Civil Service

- *Retains* civil service system for city employees.
- *Increases* the number of non–civil service positions in top management of departments.
- *Authorizes* the mayor and council to increase the number of non–civil service positions up to a maximum of 1 percent of the city workforce.
- *Adds* a provision prohibiting discrimination in city employee benefits between employees with spouses and employees with domestic partners.

Pensions and Retirement

- *Retains* pension and retirement protections for city workers in the charter, but *moves* details to ordinance.
- *Increases* authority of the boards of the pension and retirement systems to make investment decisions.
- *Adds* authority for the boards of the pension and retirement systems to appoint and remove their general managers.
- *Adds* a retiree representative or *increases* the number of retiree representatives on the boards of all pension and retirement systems.

Source: City Clerk, City of Los Angeles, Sample Ballot. Prepared by Ronald Deaton, Chief Legislative Analyst, 1999.

Using Ecological Inference Model
to Verify Results

The analysis of City of Los Angeles elections in this book was based on vote counts in different groups of precincts and on regression models. Mark Drayse and I tabulated vote counts for all precincts as well as four groups of precincts with high concentrations of Jewish, white Republican, black, and Latino voters, respectively. The regression analysis modeled the association between ethnicity, education, income, and Valley residence and voting. The results suggested important connections between demographic variables and voting patterns. For example, while 60 percent of all voters approved charter reform, 82 percent of voters in Jewish precincts supported it, compared to 35 percent of voters in black precincts. The regression results showed a strong positive association between the percentage Jewish and the percentage voting for charter reform, and a strong negative association between the percentage black and the vote for charter reform.

While these results confirmed our expectations about support for charter reform among ethnic groups, we need to be concerned with the problem of ecological fallacy: making assumptions about individual behavior based on aggregate data. The political methodologist Gary King (1997) has developed a robust method for making ecological inferences. The model uses available aggregate information, such as ethnicity and voting across precincts, to estimate, for example, the percentage of voters representing a particular ethnic group who voted for a candidate. The model takes advantage of information from all precincts in order to estimate the results in any one precinct. For example, if a candidate was strongly supported by blacks, then precincts with a high percentage of blacks will show strong support for the candidate. This information is used to estimate the black vote in precincts with lower percentages of blacks, where the precinct vote might obscure the underlying black support for the candidate.

King's model, with software available on http://gking.harvard.edu/stats.shtml, was used to estimate support among Latino, black, white Republican, Jewish, and foreign-born voters for charter reform and a larger council (1999), Antonio Villaraigosa in the mayoral election (2001), and San Fernando Valley secession (2002).

The results for the charter reform vote are consistent with the conclusions reached using the vote table and regression model, which suggested strong Jewish support and black opposition to charter reform. The Latino vote was more difficult to interpret. In our model of Latino precincts, 59 percent supported charter reform. However, in the regression model, the percentage Latino was not a significant predictor of the vote for charter reform. King's model suggests that only 41 percent of Latinos supported charter reform.

The measure to increase the size of the city council to twenty-one members (Measure 3) was supported by 37 percent of voters. Our voting tables showed stronger support in Jewish and Latino precincts, and weaker support in black and Republican precincts. In the regression model, the percentage Jewish, Latino, and foreign-born were positively associated with the vote for a larger council, while the percentage black was negatively associated with the vote for a larger council. King's model suggests very strong Jewish support for a larger council and below average support from blacks and Republicans. The Latino and foreign-born vote was close to the thirty-seven percent overall support for a larger council.

In the 2001 mayoral election, we know from exit polling results that Latinos overwhelming favored Antonio Villaraigosa over James Hahn, while blacks favored Hahn. King's model confirms this.

In the 2002 election, 33 percent of voters supported San Fernando Valley secession. We know from polls and anecdotal evidence that support for secession was strongest among white conservatives in the Valley. Our vote table shows 53 percent of voters in white Republican precincts in favor of secession, compared to 31 percent in Jewish precincts, 23 percent in Latino precincts, and 11 percent in black precincts. The regression model shows that the percentage Jewish, Latino, black, and foreign-born were all negatively associated with support for Valley secession, while the percentage white was a positive predictor of Valley secession. King's model confirms strong opposition to secession among blacks and Latinos, and strong support among Republicans. However, his model estimates that

A2.1
Estimated Percentage Voting for Measure or Candidate in King's Model

Vote	Latinos	Foreign-Born	Blacks	Jews	Republicans
Charter Reform	41	47	15	87	84
Larger Council (Measure 3)	33	38	17	72	26
Villaraigosa	95	84	8	34	13
Valley Secession	16	17	1	65	75

65 percent of Jews supported secession, despite other evidence to the contrary, including pre-election polls conducted by the *Los Angeles Times*. We cannot explain this conflict, except to speculate that the low percentage of Jews in even "Jewish precincts" skewed the ecological analysis.

King's ecological analysis model provides a way to more carefully assess the results of the regression and geographical analyses in the book. Utilized in combination, the various methods of assessing votes where direct polling is not available help address some of the weaknesses of ecological analysis. They also allow the preservation of the value of geographical analysis in a political situation in which the politics of place were extremely important.

Bibliography

Abrahams, Marvin. 1967. Functioning of Boards and Commissions in the Los Angeles City Government. Ph.D. thesis, University of California, Los Angeles.

Abu-Lughod, Janet L. 1999. *New York, Chicago, Los Angeles: America's Global Cities*. Minneapolis: University of Minnesota Press.

Adrian, Charles R. 1959. A Typology for Nonpartisan Elections. *Western Political Quarterly* 12:449–58.

Ainsworth, Ed. 1966. *Maverick Mayor: A Biography of Sam Yorty of Los Angeles*. Garden City, NY: Doubleday.

Allen, Benjamin. 2000. ¿Amigo Sam? Mayor Sam Yorty and the Latino Community of Los Angeles. B.A. thesis, Harvard University.

Alozie, Nicholas O. 2000. The Promise of Urban Democracy: Big-City Black Mayoral Service in the Early 1990s. *Urban Affairs Review* 35, no. 3 (January): 422–34.

Amnå, Erik, and Stig Montin. 2000. *Towards a New Concept of Local Self-Government?* Bergen: Fagbokforlager Vigmostad and Bjorke AS.

Appointed Los Angeles Charter Reform Commission. 1997a. *Consistent Themes in Charter Reform*. Records Management Division, City of Los Angeles, September 4.

———. 1997b. *Road to Decision*. Records Management Division, City of Los Angeles.

———. 1998a. Transcript of meeting, March 25.

———. 1998b. Transcript of meeting, April 22.

———. 1998c. Transcript of meeting, October 7.

———. 1998d. *Report on Public Outreach*. Records Management Division, City of Los Angeles, November 4.

———. 1998e. Transcript of meeting, November 4.

———. 1998f. *Governing Body*. Staff Report to the Joint Conference Committee Records Management Division, City of Los Angeles, November 20.

Baldassare, Mark, ed. 1994. *The Los Angeles Riots: Lessons for the Urban Future*. Boulder, CO: Westview.

Banfield, Edward C., and James Q. Wilson. 1963. *City Politics*. Cambridge: Harvard University Press.

Benjamin, Gerald A., and Frank J. Mauro. 1989. The Reemergence of Municipal Reform. In Frank J. Mauro and Gerald A. Benjamin, eds., *Restructuring the New York City Government: The Reemergence of Municipal Reform*, 1–15. New York: Academy of Political Science.

Benjamin, Gerald A., and Richard P. Nathan. 2001. *Regionalism and Realism: A Study of Government in the New York Metropolitan Area*. Washington, DC: Brookings Institution.

Berry, Jeffrey M., Kent E. Portnoy, and Ken Thomson. 1993. *The Rebirth of Urban Democracy*. Washington, DC: Brookings Institution.

Bickhart, Jim. 1998. Taking It to the Streets: The Debate over Neighborhood Governance in Los Angeles. Center for Government and Public Policy Analysis, Occasional Paper no. 002, August.

Bissinger, Buzz. 1997. *A Prayer for the City*. New York: Random House.

Bollens, John. 1963. *A Study of the Los Angeles City Charter*. Los Angeles: Town Hall.

Bond, J. Max. 1936. The Negro in Los Angeles. Ph.D. diss., University of Southern California. Reprint. San Francisco: R and E Press, 1972.

Boudreau, Julie-Anne, and Roger Keil. 2001. Seceding from Responsibility? Secession Movements in Los Angeles. *Urban Studies* 38, no. 10: 1701–31.

Bowler, Shaun, Todd Donovan, and Jeffrey A. Karp. 2002. When Might Institutions Change? Elite Support for Direct Democracy in Three Nations. *Political Research Quarterly* 55, no. 4 (December): 731–54.

Bradley, Tom. Interview with the author.

Bridges, Amy. 1997. *Morning Glories: Municipal Reform in the Southwest*. Princeton: Princeton University Press.

Bridges, Amy, and Richard Kronick. 1999. Writing the Rules to Win the Game: The Middle–Class Regimes of Municipal Reformers. *Urban Affairs Review* 34 (May): 691-706.

Briffault, Richard. 1992. Voting Rights, Home Rule, and Metropolitan Governance—The Secession of Staten Island as a Case Study in the Dilemmas of Local Self-Determination. *Columbia Law Review* 92:775–850.

Browning, Rufus, Dale Rogers Marshall, and David Tabb. 1984. *Protest Is Not Enough: The Struggle of Blacks and Hispanics for Equality in City Politics*. Berkeley and Los Angeles: University of California Press.

Brownstein, Ronald. 1988. On the Move with Richard Riordan. *Los Angeles Times Magazine*. August 21, 12.

Butcher, Julie. General Manager, SEIU Local 347. Interview with the author.

Campanile, Carl, and Craig Schneider. 1996. Secession Foes Agree: It's Time for Action. *Staten Island Advance*, November 24.

Cannon, Lou. 1997. *Official Negligence: How Rodney King and the Riots Changed Los Angeles and the LAPD*. New York: Times Books.

Carmichael, Stokely, and Charles V. Hamilton. *Black Power: The Politics of Liberation in America*. New York: Random House.

Carney, Francis M. 1964. The Decentralized Politics of Los Angeles. *Annals of the American Academy of Political and Social Science* 353:107–21.

Carrick, Bill. Campaign Consultant. Interview with the author.

Chemerinsky, Erwin. Chair, Elected Charter Reform Commission. Interview with the author.

———. 2001. Riordan Ran Rings around the City Charter. *Los Angeles Times,* Op-Ed section, September 6.

Cheng, Lucie, and Philip Q. Yang. 1996. Asians: The "Model Minority" Deconstructed. In Roger Waldinger, and Mehdi Bozorgmehr, eds., *Ethnic Los Angeles,* pp. 305–44. New York: Russell Sage Foundation.

City Clerk, City of Los Angeles. 1999. *Official Sample Ballot and Voter Information Pamphlet*.

City of Los Angeles. 1925. *Charter of the City of Los Angeles* (as amended through 1999).

———. 1999. *Charter of the City of Los Angeles.*

Clarke, Susan E., and Gary L. Gaile. 2000. *The Work of Cities.* Globalization and Community Series, vol. 1. Minneapolis: University of Minnesota Press.

Clayton, Janet. 1985. Ferraro Connects Campaign Loan to Appointment by Bradley. *Los Angeles Times,* March 11.

Commission to Draft Code of Ethics for Los Angeles City Government. 1990. Ethics Commission Call for Charter Reform. Los Angeles, CA.

Crouch, Winston, and Beatrice Dinerman. 1963. *Southern California Metropolis: A Study in Development of Government for a Metropolitan Area.* Berkeley and Los Angeles: University of California Press.

Davis, Mike. 1991. *City of Quartz: Excavating the Future in Los Angeles.* London: Haymarket Press.

Dear, Michael J., ed. 2001. *From Chicago to L.A.: Re-visioning Urban Theory.* Thousand Oaks, CA: Sage Publications.

Dear, Michael J., H. Eric Schockman, and Greg Hise, eds. 1996. *Rethinking Los Angeles.* Thousand Oaks, CA: Sage Publications.

DeGraaf, Lawrence. 1970. The City of Black Angels: The Emergence of the Los Angeles Ghetto, 1890–1930. *Pacific Historical Review* 39:323–52.

Driscoll, Jack. Former General Manager, Los Angeles Department of Personnel. Interview with the author.

Dykstra, Clarence A. 1925. Los Angeles Returns to the Ward System. *National Municipal Review* 14 (May): 210–12.

Edsall, Thomas B., and Mary D. Edsall. 1991. *Chain Reaction: The Impact of Race, Rights, and Taxes on American Politics.* New York: W. W. Norton.

Elkin, Stephen L. 1987. *City and Regime in the American Republic.* Chicago: University of Chicago Press.

Erie, Steven P. 1992. How the Urban West Was Won: The Local State and Economic Growth, 1880–1932. *Urban Affairs Quarterly* 27 (June): 519–54.

Erie, Steven P., and James W. Ingram III. 1998. History of Los Angeles Charter Reform. In Kevin McCarthy, Steven P. Erie, and Robert Reichardt. *Meeting the Challenge of Charter Reform,* 58–83. Santa Monica, CA: Rand Corporation.

Ethington, Philip J. 2000. Los Angeles and the Problem of Urban Historical Knowledge. *American Historical Review* 105, no. 5 (December). Online essay, http://Historycooperative.org/journals/ahr/105.5/

Ferman, Barbara. 1997. *Challenging the Growth Machine: Neighborhood Politics in Chicago and Pittsburgh.* Lawrence: University Press of Kansas.

Ferraro, John. 1997. Letter to Mayor Richard Riordan, August 29.

———. 1998. Letter to Elected Charter Reform Commissioners, December 4.

Feuer, Michael. Los Angeles City Councilmember. Interview with the author.

Field Poll. 2000. The Expanding Latino Electorate. Release no. 1960, May 1.

Finegold, Kenneth. 1995a. Traditional Reform, Municipal Populism, and Progressivism: Challenges to Machine Politics in Early-Twentieth-Century New York City. *Urban Affairs Review* 31 (September): 20–42.

———. 1995b. *Experts and Politicians: Reform Challenges to Machine Politics in New York, Cleveland, and Chicago.* Princeton: Princeton University Press.

Finnegan, Michael. 1995. Senate Votes to Let S.I. Go. *New York Daily News,* April 13.

Fiore, Faye, and Frank Clifford. 1993. Mystery Mayor. *Los Angeles Times Magazine*, July 11.

Fogelson, Robert. 1967. *The Fragmented Metropolis: Los Angeles, 1850–1930.* Cambridge: Harvard University Press.

Fulton, William. 1997. *The Reluctant Metropolis: The Politics of Urban Growth in Los Angeles.* Point Arena, CA: Solano Press Books.

Fulton, William, and Paul Shigley. 2000. Putting Los Angeles Together. *Governing Magazine* (June).

Gelfand, Mitchell B. 1981. Chutzpah in El Dorado: Social Mobility of Jews in Los Angeles, 1900–1920. Ph.D. dissertation, Carnegie-Mellon University.

Gittell, Marilyn. 1994. School Reform in New York and Chicago: Revisiting the Ecology of Local Games. *Urban Affairs Quarterly* 30 (September): 136–51.

Gosnell, Harold. 1937. *Machine Politics, Chicago Model.* Chicago: University of Chicago Press.

Governor's Commission on the Los Angeles Riots (McCone Commission). 1965. *Violence in the City—An End or a Beginning?* Los Angeles.

Greene, Robert. 1998a. New Rights—New Fights. Civic Center NEWSource, March 30.

———. 1998b. The Powerlessness of the Mayor. *Civic Center NEWSource,* July 27.

———. 1998c. Charter Commissioners Trim CAO in Favor of Mayor, City Controller. *Metropolitan News-Enterprise,* August 31.

———. 1998d. Elected Charter Reform Commission. *Civic Center NEWSource,* November 9.

———. 1999a. Panel Refers City Charter Reform to Joint Committee for Another Try. *Civic Center NEWSource,* January 18.

———. 1999b. Spotlight on . . . City of Los Angeles Charter Reform Commission. *Civic Center NEWSource,* February 1.

———. 1999c. No title. *Civic Center NEWSource,* February 8.

———. 1999d. Charter Players Swing from the Heels. *Civic Center NEWSource* February 22.

———. 1999e. Joint Charter Drafting Panel, Commissions Approve Compromise Charter Plan. *Metropolitan News-Enterprise,* February 25.

———. 1999f. Key Valley Activists Sign Ballot Arguments in Favor of Charter Reform. *Civic Center NEWSource,* March 22.

———. 1999g. Spotlight on . . . Geoffrey Garfield. *Civic Center NEWSource,* March 22.

Haefele, Mark. 1998. Shaw's Ghost. *LA Weekly,* December 25–31.

———. 1999a. On Charter Reform, Mayor Makes Good Case against Himself. *Los Angeles Times,* Op-ed, January 10.

———. 1999b. The Final Frazzle. *LA Weekly,* February 5–11.

———. 2002. News From Up North: What the City of Smog Can Learn from the City of Light. *LA Weekly,* August 10.

Hahn, Harlan, and Timothy Almy. 1971. Ethnic Politics and Racial Issues: Voting in Los Angeles. *Western Political Quarterly* 24:719–30.

Hahn, Harlan, David Klingman, and Harry Pachon. 1976. Cleavages, Coalitions and the Black Candidate: The Los Angeles Mayoralty Elections of 1969 and 1973. *Western Political Quarterly* 29:521–30.

Halle, David, and Kevin Rafter. 2003. Riots in New York and Los Angeles, 1935–2002. In David Halle, ed., *New York and Los Angeles: Politics, Society, and Culture. A Comparative View,* 341–66. Chicago: University of Chicago Press.

Halley, Robert M. 1974. An Analysis of Ethnic Voting Patterns in the 1973 Los Angeles Municipal Elections. M.A. thesis, University of Southern California.

Halley, Robert M., Alan C. Acock, and Thomas Greene. 1976. Ethnicity and Social Class: Voting in the Los Angeles Municipal Elections. *Western Political Quarterly* 29:507–20.

Henig, Jeffrey R., Richard C. Hula, Marion Orr, and Desiree S. Pedescleaux. 1999. *The Color of School Reform: Race, Politics, and the Challenge of Urban Education.* Princeton: Princeton University Press.

Herbert, Adam W. 1971. The Los Angeles Charter: Lessons of Defeat. *National Civic Review* 60, no. 11 (December): 603–7, 636.

Hinckley, Barbara. 1981. *Coalitions and Politics.* New York: Harcourt Brace Jovanovich.

Hogen-Esch, Thomas. 2001. Urban Secession and the Politics of Growth: The Case of Los Angeles. *Urban Affairs Review* 36, no. 6 (July): 783–809.

Hogen-Esch, Thomas, and Martin Saiz. 2003. An Anatomy of Defeat: Why San Fernando Valley Failed to Secede from Los Angeles. In Ali Modarres, and Evelyn Aleman, eds., *Building a Civil Society: Separate Geographies, Shared Destinies.* California Policy Issues Annual, vol. 4. Joint publication of the Pat Brown Institute of Public Affairs and the Center for California Studies, 39–66.

Hunter, Burton. 1933. *The Evolution of Municipal Organization and Administrative Practice in the City of Los Angeles.* Los Angeles: Parker, Stone and Baird Co.

Isin, Engin F., ed. 2000. *Democracy, Citizenship, and the Global City.* London: Routledge.

Jeffe, Jerry. Former political adviser, Los Angeles Chamber of Commerce. Interview with the author.

Jeffries, Vincent, and H. E. Ransford. 1972. Ideology, Social Structure, and the Yorty-Bradley Mayoral Election. *Social Problems* 19 (Winter): 358–72.

Jones, Bryan, Tracy Sulkin, and Heather A. Larsen. 2003. Policy Punctuations in American Political Institutions. *American Political Science Review* 97 no. 1, (February): 151–70.

Jones-Correa, Michael. 2001. Structural Shifts and Institutional Capacity: Possibilities for Ethnic Cooperation and Conflict in Urban Settings. In Michael Jones-Correa, ed., *Governing American Cities: Inter-Ethnic Coalitions, Competition, and Conflict,* 183–209. New York: Russell Sage Foundation.

Joyce, Patrick. 2003. *No Fire Next Time: Black-Korean Conflicts and the Future of America's Cities.* Ithaca: Cornell University Press.

Katches, Mark. 1993a. Business Deals Made Riordan Rich, Now Draw Political Heat. *Los Angeles Daily News,* May 23.

———. 1993b. Riordan Clout Linked to Philanthropy. *Los Angeles Daily News,* August 9.

Kaufmann, Karen M. 1998. Racial Conflict and Political Choice: A Study of Mayoral Voting Behavior in Los Angeles and New York. *Urban Affairs Review* 32, no. 3 (January): 291–318.

Kayden, Xandra. 2003. Senior Fellow, School of Public Policy and Social Research, University of California, Los Angeles. Interview with the author.

KCRW Radio. 1999a. Transcript, *Which Way LA?* Warren Olney, interviewer, April 15.

KCRW Radio. 1999b. Transcript, *Which Way LA?* Warren Olney, interviewer, June 2.

Keil, Roger. 1998. *Los Angeles.* Chicester, UK: John Wiley and Sons.

Kieffer, George. Chair, Appointed Charter Reform Commission. Interview with the author.

———. 1988. *The Strategy of Meetings.* New York: Simon and Schuster.

———. 1998. A Stronger Mayor, but Not a CEO. *Los Angeles Times,* Op-Ed column, November 18.

King, Gary. 1997. *A Solution to the Ecological Inference Problem: Reconstructing Individual Behavior from Aggregate Data.* Princeton, NJ: Princeton University Press.

KNX Radio. 1999a. Final Charter. Editorial, January 5.

KNX Radio. 1999b. News Report, February 2.

Kotkin, Joel. 2002. The Roots of Secession's Stall: Identity. *Los Angeles Times,* Op-Ed column, February 3.

Kotkin, Joel, and Fred Siegel. 2002. The Best Way to Bust Up L.A. *Los Angeles Times,* Op-Ed column, June 9.

Kroessler, Jeffrey. 2001. The Race for Staten Island Borough President. *Gotham Gazette,* May 10. http://www.gothamgazette.com/searchlight2001/straniere.html

Kurtz, Howard. 1988. A Low-Profile Borough's High-Stakes Case for Secession. *Washington Post,* February 9.

Lait, Matt. 1998. Police Panel's Leader Admits to Anonymous Mailings. *Los Angeles Times,* December 4.

Levine, Peter. 2000. *The New Progressive Era: Toward a Fair and Deliberative Democracy.* Lanham, MD.: Rowman and Littlefield Publishers.

Li, Wei. 1998. Los Angeles' Chinese Ethnoburb: From Ethnic Service Center to Global Economy Outpost. *Urban Geography* 19:502–17.

Logan, John, and Harvey Molotch. 1987. *Urban Fortunes.* Berkeley and Los Angeles: University of California Press.

Long, Norton. 1958. The Local Community as an Ecology of Games. *American Journal of Sociology* 64 (November): 251–61.

Los Angeles City Charter Commission. 1969. *City Government for the Future: Report of the Los Angeles City Charter Commission.*

———. 1970. Los Angeles: Work Still to Be Done, Final Report, December.

Los Angeles Daily News. 1997. Policing the LAPD: Commissioners Must Withhold Judgment Until the Facts Are In. Editorial, October 31.

———. 1998a. Guard the Gates. Editorial, February 10.

———. 1998b. Lost Angeles. Editorial, May 25.

———. 1999a. Sinking Ship. Editorial, January 5.

———. 1999b. Uncompromising Position. Editorial, January 7.

———. 1999c. Rollover Reform. Editorial, January 22.

Los Angeles Times. 1998a. Don't Expand Bureaucracy. Editorial, May 18.

———. 1998b. Secession Group Submits 200,000 Signatures. December 10.

———. 1999a. Has Riordan Seen the Light? Editorial, January 10.

———. 1999b. Don't Let Date Snag Charter. Editorial, February 20.

———. 1999c. Charter: Fight Isn't Over. Editorial, March 3.

Los Angeles Times Poll. 1992. LA Six Months after the Unrest. Poll no. 300 (October).

———. 1993. The LA City General Election Exit Poll. Poll no. 316 (June 8).

———. 1996. City of Los Angeles Survey. Poll no. 376 (June).

———. 1997. City of Los Angeles Survey: Mayoral Race, City Issues. Poll no. 393 (March).

———. 2001. Exit Poll, Los Angeles City General Election. Poll no. 460 (June).

———. 2002. City of Los Angeles: Secession. Poll no. 472 (June).

Maccoby, Wendell. 1950. Report of Subcommittee to Assembly Interim Committee on State and Local Taxation: The Borough System of Government for Metropolitan Areas. State of California.

March, James G., and Johan P. Olsen. 1984. The New Institutionalism: Organizational Factors in Political Life. *American Political Science Review* 78, no. 3 (September): 734–49.

Martin, Hugo. 1997. Feuer Targets Mayor's Influence on Ethics Panel. *Los Angeles Times,* October 26.

Martin, Kelly. Deputy Mayor. Interview with the author.

Maullin, Richard. 1971. Los Angeles Liberalism. *Trans-Action* 8:40–50.

Mauro, Frank J., and Gerald Benjamin, eds. 1989. *Restructuring the New York City Government: The Reemergence of Municipal Reform.* New York: Academy of Political Science.

Mayo, Charles G. 1964. The 1961 Mayoralty Election in Los Angeles: The Political Party in a Nonpartisan Election. *Western Political Quarterly* 17:325–37.

Mayor's Task Force on Staten Island Secession. 1993. *Staten Island Secession: The Impact on City Workers* (April). City of New York.

McCarthy, Kevin, Steven P. Erie, and Robert E. Reichardt. 1998. *Meeting the Challenge of Charter Reform.* Santa Monica, CA: Rand Corporation.

McGreevy, Patrick. 1992a. L.A. Council Panel Calls for Limiting Terms of Mayor. *Los Angeles Daily News,* July 10.

———. 1992b. Bradley's Plan Spurs Speculation: Opinions Varied on Re-election Bid. *Los Angeles Daily News,* July 18.

———. 1997a. City Council OK's Charter Ballot Summary Despite Lawsuit Threat. *Los Angeles Daily News,* February 8.

———. 1997b. Charter Reform Suit Settled: City Council Agrees to Strike Two Ballot Statements. *Los Angeles Daily News,* February 15.

———. 1998a. Parks Wants More Power to Remove, Hire Aides. *Los Angeles Daily News,* February 7.

———. 1998b. Labor Leaders Key on Mayor's Role. *Los Angeles Daily News,* July 28.

———. 2003. Mayor to Dedicate 6 Neighborhood City Halls. *Los Angeles Times,* June 21.

McHenry, Dean. 2002. The State's Role in Urban Secessions. Paper presented at the Governance Conference of the John Randolph Haynes and Dora Haynes Foundation, University of Southern California, September.

McPhail, I. R. 1971. The Vote for Mayor in Los Angeles in 1969. *Annals of the Association of American Geographers* 6 (December): 744–58.

Merton, Robert K. 1968. *Social Theory and Social Structure.* New York: Free Press.

Meyerson, Harold. 1999. Powerlines: The Mayor Plays Hardball. *L.A. Weekly,* January 8–14.

———. 2001. A House Divided. *LA Weekly,* June 15–21.

———. 2002a. Boroughs under the City. *LA Weekly,* June 28–July 4.

———. 2002b. The Election Where Nobody Came. *LA Weekly,* November 15–21.

Mollenkopf, John. 1992. *A Phoenix in the Ashes: The Rise and Fall of the Koch Coalition in New York City Politics.* Princeton: Princeton University Press.

———. 1994. *A Phoenix in the Ashes: The Rise and Fall of the Koch Coalition in New York City Politics.* Princeton: Princeton University Press. Paperback edition with additional chapter on 1993 mayoral election.

Mollenkopf, John, David Olson, and Timothy Ross. 2001. Immigrant Political Participation in New York and Los Angeles. In Michael Jones-Correa, ed., *Governing American Cities: Inter-Ethnic Coalitions, Competition, and Conflict,* 17–70. New York: Russell Sage Foundation.

Muzzio, Douglas, and Tim Tompkins. 1989. On the Size of the City Council: Finding the Mean. In Frank J. Mauro and Gerald Benjamin, eds., *Restructuring the New York City Government: The Reemergence of Municipal Reform,* 83–96. New York: Academy of Political Science.

National Civic League. 1991. Guide for Charter Commissions, 5th Ed.

Neiman, Max. 2000. *Defending Government: Why Big Government Works.* Upper Saddle River, NJ: Prentice-Hall.

NewsSource. 1999. City Council Moves Forward on Advisory Councils Prior to Charter. March 29.

New York State Senate. 1990. *A Study of the Feasibility of an Independent Staten Island* (August).

New York State Senate Finance Committee. 1983. *Remedies of a Proud Outcast: The Legal Probability and Implications of Restructuring the Government and Boundaries of the City of New York.* Staff Report (July).

Newton, Jim. 1998a. Guiding a Fractured City into a New Century. *Los Angeles Times,* July 13.

———. 1998b. Labor Attacks Charter Reforms. *Los Angeles Times,* July 28.

———. 1998c. Top City Official Declares War on Charter Reforms. *Los Angeles Times,* September 11.

———. 1998d. A Flip-Flop on Mayor's Firing Power. *Los Angeles Times,* October 8.

———. 1998e. Mayor Won't Block "Living Wage" at LAX. *Los Angeles Times,* December 2.

———. 1998f. Charter Panel OK's Compromise on Key Power for Mayor. *Los Angeles Times,* December 11.

———. 1999a. Charter Panel Rejects Plan to Compromise. *Los Angeles Times,* January 6.

———. 1999b. Appointed Panel OK's Compromise Charter Plan. *Los Angeles Times,* January 7.

———. 1999c. Riordan Seeks City Charter Compromise. *Los Angeles Times*, January 9.

———. 1999d. Charter Groups Compromise. *Los Angeles Times*, January 21.

———. 1999e. Elected Charter Panel OK's Unified Plan Amid Dissent. *Los Angeles Times*, January 26.

———. 1999f. Glitches Found in Compromise Charter Draft. *Los Angeles Times*, January 30.

———. 1999g. Both Charter Panels Adopt Compromise. *Los Angeles Times*, February 2.

———. 1999h. Charter Draws Many Objections from Council. *Los Angeles Times*, February 12.

———. 1999i. City Charter Panel Seeks to Accelerate Reform Plan. *Los Angeles Times*, February 18.

———. 1999j. Joint City Charter Committee Approves Compromise Pact. *Los Angeles Times*, February 25.

———. 1999k. Council Sends Proposed New Charter to Voters. *Los Angeles Times*, March 3.

Oakerson, Ronald J. 1999. *Governing Local Political Economies: Creating the Civic Metropolis*. Oakland, CA: Institute for Contemporary Studies.

O'Laughlin, John, and Dale E. Berg. 1977. The Election of Black Mayors, 1969 and 1973. *Annals of the Association of American Geographers* 67 (June): 223–38.

Oliver, Melvin L., and James H. Johnson, Jr. 1984. Inter-ethnic Conflict in an Urban Ghetto: The Case of Blacks and Latinos in Los Angeles. In *Research in Social Movements, Conflict, and Change* 6:57–94. Greenwich, CT: JAI Press.

Orlov, Rick. 1992a. Riordan Plans Initiative to Limit City Officials' Terms. *Los Angeles Daily News*, May 19.

———. 1992b. Term-Limits Measure Approved for Ballot. *Los Angeles Daily News*, December 24.

———. 1998a. Charter Panel Votes to Include Living Wage. *Los Angeles Daily News*, December 9.

———. 1998b. Civic Group Joins Charter Fray. *Los Angeles Daily News*, December 23.

———. 1999a. New Plan Mandates Council Growth. *Los Angeles Daily News*, January 21.

———. 1999b. Valley Group Opposed to Consensus Plan. *Los Angeles Daily News*, January 23.

———. 1999c. City Charter Proposal Elicits Worries in Valley. *Los Angeles Daily News*, January 29.

———. 1999d. Panels Renew Aim for Unity. *Los Angeles Daily News*, February 2.

———. 1999e. Charter Panelists Remain Divided, *Los Angeles Daily News*, February 16.

———. 1999f. Mayor, labor unions get together. *Los Angeles Daily News*, March 8.

———. 1999g. Unlikely Allies Battle Reform. *Los Angeles Daily News*, March 15.

———. 2002. Tipoff: Police Commission Deliberates Parks' Future This Week. *Los Angeles Daily News*, April 8.

Pastor, Manuel, Peter Dreier, J. Eugene Grigsby III, and Marta López-Garza. 2000. *Regions That Work: How Cities and Suburbs Can Grow Together.* Minneapolis: University of Minnesota Press.

Pecorella, Robert F. 1989. Community Governance: A Decade of Experience. In Frank J. Mauro and Gerald Benjamin, eds., *Restructuring the New York City Government: The Reemergence of Municipal Reform.* 83–96. New York: Academy of Political Science.

Peterson, Paul E. 1981. *City Limits.* Chicago: University of Chicago Press.

Picus, Joy. Former Los Angeles City Councilmember. Interview with the author.

Pierson, Paul. 2000. The Limits of Design: Explaining Institutional Origins and Change. *Governance: An International Journal of Policy and Administration* 13 (October): 475–99.

Pimlott, Ben, and Nitmala Rao. 2002. *Governing London.* Oxford: Oxford University Press.

Piper, C. Erwin. 1979. *Review of Fundamental Powers and Duties of City Government.* Presented to Councilmember Robert Farrell, City of Los Angeles, June 21.

Planning Report. 2002. Seigel Supports Boroughs: More Suited to L.A. than NYC. Vol. 40, June.

Portz, John, Lana Stein, and Robin R. Jones. 1999. *City Schools and City Politics: Institutions and Leadership in Pittsburgh, Boston, and St. Louis.* Lawrence: University of Kansas Press.

Poulson, Norris. 1966. *Who Would Have Ever Dreamed?* Oral History Program of the University of California, Los Angeles.

Presberg, Steven. 1999. Memorandum to Elected Commissioners. January 29.

Purcell, Mark. 1997. Ruling Los Angeles: Neighborhood Movements, Urban Regimes, and the Production of Space in Southern California. *Urban Geography* 18, no. 8: 684–704.

———. 2001. Metropolitan Political Reorganization and the Political Economy of Urban Growth: The Case of San Fernando Valley Secession. *Political Geography* 20, no. 5: 101–21.

———. 2002. Politics in Global Cities: Los Angeles Charter Reform and the New Social Movements. *Environment and Planning A* 34, no. 1: 23–42.

Regalado, James. 1991. Organized Labor and Los Angeles City Politics: An Assessment in the Bradley Years. *Urban Affairs Quarterly* 27 (September): 87–108.

Reisner, Marc. 1986. *Cadillac Desert: The American West and Its Disappearing Water.* New York: Viking Penguin.

Rigby, George. 1974. Los Angeles City Administrative Officer: The Leask Years, 1951–1961. Los Angeles Records Management Division, September. Typescript.

Riker, William H. 1962. *The Theory of Political Coalitions.* New Haven: Yale University Press.

Riordan, William L. 1963. *Plunkitt of Tammany Hall: A Series of Plain Talks on Very Practical Politics.* New York: E. P. Dutton.

Rocco, Raymond. 1996. Latino Los Angeles: Reframing Boundaries/Borders. In Allen Scott, and Edward Soja, eds., *The City: Los Angeles and Urban Theory at the End of the Twentieth Century,* 365–89. Berkeley and Los Angeles: University of California Press.

Roderick, Kevin. 2001a. Valley of the Pols. *Los Angeles* (September): 62–66.

———. 2001b. *The San Fernando Valley: America's Suburb*. Los Angeles: *Los Angeles Times*.

Rohrlich, Ted. 1997. Riordan Plan Would Add to Mayor's Clout. *Los Angeles Times*, October 15.

———. 1998a. Charter Panel Compares Big Orange to Big Apple. *Los Angeles Times*, April 2.

———. 1998b. Support for Neighborhood Councils Plan May Be on the Wane. *Los Angeles Times*, May 24.

———. 1998c. Panel Endorses Neighborhood Council System. *Los Angeles Times*, 31 May.

———. 1998d. Coalition Forms Strategy to Get More Latinos Elected. *Los Angeles Times*, December 24.

Ross, Bernard H., Myron A. Levine, and Murray S. Stedman. 1991. *Urban Politics: Power in Metropolitan America*. 4th ed. Itasca, IL: Peacock.

Rusk, David. 1993. *Cities without Suburbs*. Washington, DC: Woodrow Wilson School Press.

Saguaro Seminar. 2001. *Social Capital Community Benchmark Survey*.

Salisbury, Robert H. 1961. The Dynamics of Reform: Charter Politics in St. Louis. *Midwest Journal of Political Science* 5 (August): 260–75.

Saltzstein, Alan, Raphe Sonenshein, and Irving Ostrow. 1986. Toward a More Centralized Local Political System: Federal Aid and the City of Los Angeles. In Terry Clark, ed., *Research in Urban Policy*, 2:55–76. Greenwich, CT: JAI Press.

Sassen, Saskia. 2000. The Global City: Strategic Site/New Frontier. In Engin F. Isin, ed., *Democracy, Citizenship, and the Global City*, 48-61. London and New York: Routledge.

Savitch, H. V. 1994. Reorganization in Three Cities: Explaining the Disparity between Intended Actions and Unanticipated Consequences. *Urban Affairs Quarterly* 29 (June): 565–95.

Sayre, Wallace S., and Herbert Kaufman. 1960. *Governing New York City: Politics in the Metropolis*. New York: Russell Sage Foundation.

Schockman, H. Eric. 1998. Is Los Angeles Governable? Revisiting the City Charter. In Michael J. Dear, H. Eric Schockman, and Greg Hise, eds., *Rethinking Los Angeles*, 57–75. Thousand Oaks, CA: Sage Publications.

Schwartz, Frederick A. O., and Eric Lane. 1998. The Policy and Politics of Charter Making: The Story of New York City's 1989 Charter. *New York Law School Law Review* 42 nos. 3 & 4): 729–1015.

Scott, Allen J., and Edward W. Soja, eds. 1996. *The City: Los Angeles and Urban Theory at the End of the Twentieth Century*. Berkeley and Los Angeles: University of California Press.

Scott, Allen J. 1998. *Regions and the World Economy: The Coming Shape of Global Production, Competition, and Political Order*. Oxford and New York: Oxford University Press.

Scott, Allen J., John Agnew, Edward Soja, and Michael Storper. 2001. Global City-Regions, in Allen J. Scott, ed., *Global City-Regions: Trends, Theory, Policy*, 11–32. Oxford and New York: Oxford University Press.

Sears, David O., and Donald R. Kinder. 1971. Racial Tensions and Voting in Los Angeles. In Werner Z. Hirsch, ed. *Los Angeles: Viability and Prospects for Metropolitan Leadership*, 51–88. New York: Praeger.

Sears, David O., and John B. McConahay. 1973. *The Politics of Violence: The New Urban Blacks and the Watts Riot.* Boston: Houghton Mifflin.

Service Employees International Union. 1998. Mayor's Authority to Fire General Managers: Los Angeles City "High Propensity" Voters. Poll conducted by Fairbank, Maslin, and Maullin. December.

Shefter, Martin. 1983. Regional Receptivity to Reform. *Political Science Quarterly* 98 (Fall): 459–84.

Sheppard, Harrison. 2002. Secession Leader May Try to Block L.A. Votes. *Los Angeles Daily News,* July 12.

Shuster, Beth, and Patrick McGreevy. 1999. Council Concerned over LAPD Issues. *Los Angeles Times,* January 27.

Siegel, Fred. 1997. *The Future Once Happened Here: New York, D.C., L.A., and the Fate of America's Big Cities.* New York: Free Press.

Siegel, Mark. SEIU Local 347 political adviser. Interview with the author.

———. 1999. Appointed Commission Okays Latest Compromise. *Charter Watch,* January 25.

Singleton, Gregory H. 1979. *Religion in the City of the Angels: American Protestant Culture and Urbanization, Los Angeles, 1850–1930.* Ann Arbor, MI: UMI Research Press.

Sitton, Tom. 1999. *The Haynes Foundation and Urban Reform Philanthropy in Los Angeles: A History of the John Randolph Haynes and Dora Haynes Foundation.* Los Angeles: Historical Society of Southern California.

Sleeper, Jim. 1993. The End of the Rainbow? The Changing Politics of America's Cities. *New Republic,* November 1: 20–25.

Soja, Edward. 2000. *Postmetropolis: Critical Studies of Cities and Regions.* Malden, MA: Blackwell.

Sonenshein, Raphael J. 1971. Mayor Kenneth Gibson's Newark. B.A. thesis, Princeton University, Princeton, NJ.

———. 1993. *Politics in Black and White: Race and Power in Los Angeles.* Princeton: Princeton University Press.

———. 2001. When Ideologies Agree and Interests Collide, What's a Leader to Do? The Prospects for Latino-Jewish Coalition in Los Angeles. In Michael Jones-Correa, ed., *Governing American Cities: Inter-ethnic Coalitions, Competition, and Conflict,* 210–29. New York: Russell Sage Foundation.

———. 2003. Gotham on Our Minds: New York City in the Los Angeles Charter Reform of 1997–1999. In David Halle, ed., *New York and Los Angeles: Politics, Society and Culture, A Comparative View,* 291–313. Chicago: University of Chicago Press.

Sonenshein, Raphael J., and Mark H. Drayse. 2003. The New Institutionalism Meets the New Diversity: Charter Reform and Secession in Los Angeles. Paper presented at the annual meeting of the Western Political Science Association, Denver, CO.

Sonenshein, Raphael J., and Thomas Hogen-Esch. Global Cities under the Gun: Facing Secession in New York and Los Angeles. Paper presented at the annual meeting of the American Political Science Association, Philadelphia.

Sonenshein, Raphael J., H. Eric Schockman, and Richard DeLeon. 1996. Urban Conservatism in an Age of Diversity: A Comparative Analysis of the Mayoralties of San Francisco's Frank Jordan and Los Angeles's Richard Riordan. Paper presented at the annual meeting of the Western Political Science Association.

Sonenshein, Raphael J., and Mary Strobel. 1999. Analysis of Charter Draft. Appointed Charter Reform Commission.

Sonenshein, Raphael J., and Nicholas Valentino. 2000. The Distinctiveness of Jewish Voting: A Thing of the Past? *Urban Affairs Review* 95 (January): 358–89.

Southern California Studies Center. 2001. *Sprawl Hits the Wall: Confronting the Realities of Metropolitan Los Angeles.* Los Angeles: University of Southern California.

Spencer, Gary. 1996. Staten Island Secession Ruled a Legislative Matter. *New York Law Journal.* February 23.

State of New York Charter Commission for Staten Island. 1993. *Report to the Governor and the Legislature* (February).

Steinacker, Annette. 2001. Prospects for Regional Governance: Lessons from the Miami Abolition Vote. *Urban Affairs Review* 37, no. 1 (September): 100–118.

Steinberg, Arnold. Pollster. Interview with the author.

Stern, Norton B. 1981. Los Angeles Jewish Voters during Grant's First Presidential Race. *Western States Jewish Historical Quarterly* 13 (January): 179–85.

Stone, Clarence. 1989. *Regime Politics: Governing Atlanta, 1946–1988.* Lawrence: University of Kansas Press.

———, ed. 1998. *Changing Urban Education.* Lawrence: University of Kansas Press.

Stone, Clarence N., Jeffrey R. Henig, Bryan D. Jones, and Carol Pierannunzi. 2001. *Building Civic Capacity: The Politics of Reforming Urban Schools.* Lawrence: University of Kansas Press.

Sullivan, Deborah. 1998. "It's a Study!" Cityhood Advocates Celebrate. *Los Angeles Daily News,* December 7.

Svorny, Shirley, and Leah Marcal. 2000. Support for Municipal Detachment: Evidence from a Recent Survey of Los Angeles Voters. *Urban Affairs Review* 36, no. 1 (September): 93–103.

Swanson, Bert E. 2000. Quandaries of Pragmatic Reform: A Reassessment of the Jacksonville Experience. *State and Local Government Review* 32, no. 3 (Fall): 227–38.

Viteritti, Joseph P. 1989. The Tradition of Municipal Reform: Charter Revision in Historical Context. In Frank Mauro and Gerald Benjamin, eds., *Restructuring the New York City Government: The Reemergence of Municipal Reform,* 16–30. New York: Academy of Political Science.

Vorspan, Max, and Lloyd P. Gartner. 1970. *History of the Jews of Los Angeles.* San Marino, CA: Huntington Library.

Waldinger, Roger, and Bozorgmehr, Mehdi. 1996. The Making of a Multicultural Metropolis, in Roger Waldinger and Mehdi Bozorgmehr, eds., *Ethnic Los Angeles,* 3–37. New York: Russell Sage Foundation.

Waldinger, Roger, and Michael Lichter. 1996. Anglos: Beyond Ethnicity. In Roger Waldinger and Mehdi Bozorgmehr, eds., *Ethnic Los Angeles,* 413–45. New York: Russell Sage Foundation.

Wardlaw, William. Political strategist. Interview with the author.

Welch, Susan, and Timothy Bledsoe. 1998. *Urban Reform and Its Consequences: A Study in Representation.* Chicago: University of Chicago Press.

Widom, Chet. 1999. Reply to a KNX Editorial, January 7.

Wilgoren, Jodi. 1996. Key Riordan Aide's Firing Demanded. *Los Angeles Times,* April 20.

Wilson, James Q. 1962. *The Amateur Democrat: Club Politics in Three Cities.* Chicago: University of Chicago Press.

Woo, Elaine. 1987. He Gets with the Program: Lawyer Gives Computers, Staff to Teach Students at Inner-City Schools. *Los Angeles Times,* July 3.

Woods, Joseph. 1973. The Progressives and the Police: Urban Reform and the Professionalization of the Los Angeles Police. Ph.d. dissertation, University of California, Los Angeles.

Index

Abu-Lughod, Janet, 22
Addonizio, Hugh, 11. *See also* Newark, New Jersey
administrative decentralization, 242. *See also* Hahn, James R.; LaBonge, Tom
Adrian, Charles R., 44
African Americans: and Tom Bradley, 215–216; and charter measure, opposition to, 194; and coalitions, xvi, 9; in competition with other minorities, 12; in conflict with James Hahn over Bernard Parks, 229; and council size, 133, 143, 145–146, 159, 198, 201–204; and ecological inference, 275–277; exclusion of, in Los Angeles, 30; and James Hahn, attitude toward, 215, 217, 220–226, 227; and Jews, 17; and Latinos, 223; and Bernard Parks, 228; and Proposition BB, 97; and Proposition F, 124; and Proposition 187, 216; and reform, 227; and Richard Riordan, 68–69, 215–216; and the San Fernando Valley, 73; and secession, 232–237, 249; and Sam Yorty, 228
African American–Jewish Leadership Conference, 186
Airport Police: in final charter proposal, 273; Bernard Parks's position on, 129
Alarcon, Richard: and possible Valley mayoral candidacy, 231; and State Senate race, 79
Alatorre, Richard: charter measure opposed by, 194; and labor meeting on charter, 187; Richard Riordan endorsed by, 63
American Political Science Review, 4
Angelenos for Better Classrooms, 97
appointed charter reform commission, xviii; Barriers to Access report by, 134; beginning work of, 84–85, 87–88; and chairs' recommendations, 156–160; and city council, 182; and city hall officials, 178; and council size, 146; draft charter by, 161, 173–175; early decisions by, 114; and elected commission, alliance with during campaign, 185; and final draft of unified charter, 175–176; and neighbor-

hood councils, 134–135, 152–153, 179; and New York City community boards, 131; and participation, decisions by, 135–136; and pensions, decisions by, 152–153; and police reform, 128; and reform process, 252; and residual powers, decision by, 18; style and approach of, 104–106; and unified charter, 164–167; and unilateral firing authority, decision by, 119–120
appointment and removal of general managers and commissioners, 269. *See also* unilateral firing authority
Archie-Hudson, Marguerite: as candidate for elected commission, 100; and neighborhood councils, 137; and resignation from commissions, 102
area planning commissions: in charter proposal, 272; genesis of, 142–143; implementation of, 214; in joint conference committee, 157; and new charter, 20, 241; and VICA objections, 172
Asian Americans: and African Americans, relationship with, 12; on council size, 143; population of, in Los Angeles, 47–48; and reform, 254
at-large elections, 4

Banfield, Edward, 35
Beccerra, Xavier, 217–218
behavioral movement, 4
Bell, Sam, 138–139. *See also* Los Angeles Business Advisers (LABA)
Benjamin, Gerald: on New York City boroughs, 242–243; on reform, 6
Benson, Julie, 164
Berlin, 242
Bernson, Hal: and CIVICC, 74; and neighborhood councils, 131–132, 146, 176; and opposition to unified charter, 182–183
Berry, Jeffrey M., 5
Beverly Hills, California, 23, 32
Beverlywood, California, 23
Bickhardt, Jim, 140